HOUSE OUT OF ORDER

HOUSE OUT OF ORDER

by *Richard Bolling*

Representative from Missouri

NEW YORK: E. P. DUTTON & CO., INC.

1965

Grateful acknowledgment is made to the following for
permission to quote from copyright material: *American
Presidency: An Interpretation* by Harold J. Laski, copy-
right 1940 by Harold J. Laski (Harper & Row, Publishers,
Inc.); *Confessions of a Congressman* by Jerry Voorhis,
copyright 1947 by Jerry Voorhis (Doubleday & Company,
Inc.); *Congress Makes a Law* by Stephen K. Bailey, copy-
right 1950 by Stephen K. Bailey (Columbia University
Press); *Member of the House: Letters of a Congressman*
by Clem Miller, copyright 1962 by Clem Miller (Charles
Scribner's Sons); *The Legislative Process in Congress* by
George B. Galloway, copyright 1953 by Thomas Y.
Crowell Company (Thomas Y. Crowell Company); "Mr.
Speaker" by David L. Cohn, copyright 1942 Atlantic
Monthly.

A portion of Chapter Eleven was adapted for an article in
The New Republic (November 21, 1964)

This book is dedicated to my Colleagues in the United States House of Representatives

Contents

Acknowledgments   9

Preface   11

The United States House of Representatives   17

The Members of the House   42

The Leaders of the House of Representatives
    The Speaker   62

The Leaders of the House of Representatives
    The Committee Chairmen   79

The Executive, Judicial and Legislative Branches   116

The Lobbies   131

The Politician and the Press   145

The Landrum-Griffin Labor Bill   156

Civil Rights—1956 and 1957   174

The Committee on Rules   195

The Road to Reform   221

Index   245

Acknowledgments

I wish to acknowledge my debt to former President Harry S Truman, to Tom L. Evans, to my loyal staff, and to my friends in the Fifth District of Missouri. These men and women gave me the opportunity to serve in the House of Representatives for more than fifteen years. My debt to the late Sam Rayburn, the Speaker of the House for longer than any person in history, is equally great, for he gave me, when I was a junior Member of the House, a unique opportunity to see the House at work from the inside. I am indebted, also, to so many others in the House—officers, employees, and colleagues—that it is impossible to list them by name.

The opportunity to write this book in ideal surroundings was given me by the Center for Advanced Studies at Wesleyan University, Middletown, Connecticut. I am particularly grateful to Victor Butterfield, President of Wesleyan, and to the distinguished novelist and historian Paul Horgan, who as the Director of the Center during the two years I was, intermittently, a fellow there, gave me much help and encouragement. I am also conscious of a debt to all those at Wesleyan and the Center with whom I talked and worked, faculty, staff, fellows, and students.

Finally, a word about my collaborator, Wes Barthelmes. In the fall and winter of 1962 and 1963, I wrote in longhand two complete drafts of the book. They were unsatisfactory because of my lack of skill as a writer. When it became clear that my duties in the House would prevent me rewriting the book myself, I was fortunate to find Wes, a former newspaperman and presently the Administrative Assistant of the Honorable Edith Green, United States Representative from Portland, Oregon. Our combined knowledge of the House and his skill as a writer resulted in this book. For the proposed reform and my recollection of the facts and the events discussed in the book I assume full responsibility, but without Wes there probably would be no book.

Preface

This book has been written at a time when informed commentators on politics, and indeed politicians themselves, are expressing the belief that national representative assemblies have deteriorated in power and effectiveness in recent years.

Certainly the middle decades of the twentieth century have been challenging to national legislatures. In some countries the popular assembly has become so weak that it has been reduced to nothing more than an automatic registrar of the acts and views of a chief executive who purports to represent the "national will."

Happily, no such lamentable change has occurred in the United States. But there are justifiable misgivings concerning the political health of our Congress. In the age that dawned so terrifyingly at Hiroshima nineteen years ago, too many members of the House continue to function in an atmosphere of self-satisfaction; and the ruling clique of the Senate still holds the illusion that it is the most exclusive club in the world. To the contrary, that special status has moved beyond the national scene, and now is held by the nuclear-arms club composed of the United States, Great Britain, France, the Soviet Union, and Red China.

Fortunately, in the 435-Member House and the 100-Member Senate there are signs that the glow of self-esteem is dimming. Members of diverse political positions are becoming openly critical, and from outside Congress disapproving voices have been raised, particularly against the House.

The rising critical temper has led, for example, to the publication of a collection of floor speeches made by Senators during three days of February 1963, under the title *The Senate Establishment*. Senator Joseph S. Clark of Pennsylvania finds the Senate deficient in the same respects as is the House. Its positions of power are generally occupied by men with nineteenth century minds. Structural and procedural reform are needed. Procedural fairness is essential to justice in legislation. Apparently the Senate does not have it; and from my experience as a Member, neither does the House. Wherever legislative conflicts of interest exist—ethical violations— they are largely the result of structural and procedural deformities.

During Sam Rayburn's eight terms as Speaker of the House, the need for reform was obscured by his personal strength and persuasive power. But since his death, the state of the House has been revealed—it is a shambles. The Speakership as an institution has become atrophied. Power is dissipated among senior Democratic committee chairmen whose views do not accord with those of the party majority. The Democratic leadership does not have the allegiance of all its party members. Instead of ensuring their loyalty by distributing positions of power equitably among them, it relies on the stratagem of giving key posts to extreme conservatives in the hope of tempering their opposition to much-needed legislation.

The leadership of the minority party, the Republicans, is unashamedly conservative, and appoints conservatives to key committees. It insists on party loyalty, and punishes deviators in unpublicized ways. Acting wholly and cohesively and understandably on its convictions, the Republican House leadership retains control of its members.

I believe the Democratic party should exercise a similar control over its members by the same means. I came to this conclusion shortly after becoming a Member of the House in 1949, having been elected to represent Kansas City, Missouri, by a political accident that involved a bitter factional fight in the party. After having received my revelatory education as a Member from Speaker Rayburn, whom I served for many years as lieutenant and legman, I am even more convinced that the Democratic party should initiate the reform of the House by beginning within its own ranks.

Reform of the House has been too long delayed. When the states were the locus of power and the federal government was less active, fewer demands were made on the efficiency of Congress, and some degree of slackness was tolerable. But now, with the problems of international tensions, widespread poverty and chronic unemployment, new complexities in labor-management relations, and a more assertive executive branch in government, it is necessary for Congress to function effectively and responsibly.

Moreover, Congress must play a vital role in the free world's struggle against Communist tyranny. The ideology of Communism holds parliamentary institutions in contempt; representative assemblies are regarded as an apparatus that reflects the oppressive forces of capitalism. The Communists seek to persuade us and the new nations of the world that parliamentary institutions are a sham, masking greed and exploitation.

We are trying to encourage representative government in developing countries and in nations threatened by the domination of the Soviet Union and the Chinese Communists. It is imperative that our Congress be an example to the world; tyranny cannot flourish where there are responsible and effective parliaments.

Today the work of a Congressman is vastly more demanding than ever before. In addition to his legislative functions, he must carry an overwhelming load of administrative duties to fulfill his obligations to his constituents. Only a smoothly operating and genuinely representative legislative structure will enable him to discharge all his responsibilities.

Reform must come in areas where, now, power is vested in the hands of a few unrepresentative groups, especially in key committees. The concept of seniority in respect to committee assignments and chairmanships should be modified. Members must regard committee positions not as personal perquisites but as opportunities to administer and legislate for the public good. Responsibility must be made identifiable instead of being concealed behind committee and subcommittee doors.

Congressional reform involves such a drastic redistribution of power that some of its advocates are skeptical that it can be accomplished. The historian C. Vann Woodward suggests that acceptance of reforms by the incumbent holders of key positions would require the "greatest wholesale forswearing of privilege and prerogative since the Tennis Court Oath during the French Revolution."

I am more sanguine; I believe it is possible to restore representative government to the people of the United States.

That is why I decided to write this book, although after some hesitation. There are already many valuable critical books on the subject, written with insight and scholarly care. A new one may be used by those who have an interest in perpetuating the low esteem in which the House is held by a segment of public opinion. Some critics, notably Woodrow Wilson, have always been hostile to the climate of accommodation and makeshift decisions that is necessarily inherent in even the most effective legislative systems. Moreover, I am congenitally disinclined to run with the hounds. My colleagues may be quick to point out that faultfinding is easier than praise, and produces a more marketable commodity. A critical book is often an imperfect portrait, though I have not tried to paint an irremediably negative picture of the House. Finally, there is the hazard of politics, in which one runs the risk of having one's motives analyzed at the expense of the end results.

But now the book is written. Eight terms in the House, including ten years on the Committee on Rules, with its crisis politics, have not been a completely disenchanting experience. The proved responsibility and dedication of scores of Republican and Democratic House Members reinforces my belief that the faulty organization and procedures of the House can be corrected and that, instead of being a block to the achievement of an effective national policy, the House may substantially help us to that goal. The present disorder is not entirely a consequence of the irreparable failure of the House as an institution, or of a lack of ability or integrity on the part of its Members. It is rather the result of outside events whose effects are beginning to be perceived—our assumption of world leadership in international affairs, and our transformation from a rural society into an intensely industrialized one.

I have drawn numerous generalizations that may, in some cases, illuminate the spirit of an event but distort actual details. I have relied heavily on memory, for example, in the chapters on the civil rights and Landrum-Griffith legislative battles, and memory is always an improvement on the facts. Memory tells a story with a moral. And if in the heat of argument there are exaggerations, I trust they will be regarded as "truths that have lost their tempers."

HOUSE OUT OF ORDER

Chapter 1

The United States House of Representatives

"There is one thing better than good government and that is government in which all the people have a part . . ."

—WALTER HINES PAGE

The constituent, after showing the blue-suited doorkeeper his pass, seats himself a few moments before twelve noon in a visitors' gallery overlooking the floor of the chamber of the House of Representatives.

He asks himself what issue of great moment will be discussed this afternoon on the floor of the vaulted chamber. Perhaps his imagination is fed by recollection of the heroic painting of the Haynes-Webster debate reproduced in his eighth-grade history text.

An elderly man ascends the dais flanked by flags, and raps the gavel. His opening remark is the customary "The House will be in order." The chaplain of the House gives the customary opening prayer. Something called the "Journal" is ordered read and approved.

The constituent, briefed beforehand by his Congressman, recognizes the man with the gavel as the Speaker of the House. To the Speaker's right is a silver-encrusted black staff called the Mace. Seated below the Speaker at a semicircular desk are employees of the House writing industriously in ledgers. Others, the tally clerk and bill clerk and their assistants, sit looking solemn and wise awaiting their work. Official reporters stand with their stenographic notebooks. Around the Chamber fresh-faced page boys move, carrying messages and running errands for the men and women Members of the House.

The constituent leans forward in expectation of the first act of this day's legislative drama as several Members rise and seek recognition from the Speaker.

"The Gentleman from Tennessee," the Speaker intones. The recognized Member says a few inaudible sentences.

"Without objection, so ordered," the Speaker says.

Now one of the Members leaves his seat and walks to a chest-high lectern equipped with a microphone.

"Ah," says the citizen-constituent to himself.

The Member at the microphone coughs, rebuttons his suit coat, and, after glancing solemnly at the sparsely filled galleries, begins to address his colleagues on the topic of preservation of marine life along the Florida shores.

The constituent, after a few minutes' concentration, shifts inattentively in his upholstered seat. Perhaps the major discussion of the day comes later on, he thinks, as the Member talks on about the breeding and feeding of infant shrimp. None of the Members seem to be listening either.

Aren't there supposed to be 435 Members of the House in attendance, he asks himself, instead of the 50 Members now present? And those 50 are reading newspapers, talking to one another, or moving, indeed, milling about seemingly with no apparent purpose. One Member, hands folded across his stomach, appears to be dozing.

The Member from Florida begins to gesture at the microphone and warns that the supply of bait shrimp will certainly diminish, with consequent disaster to the economy of his "Sunshine State." One, perhaps, two, Members in the back row, laugh.

His admonitions gravely pronounced—and duly recorded for publication in the Congressional Record for the Florida shrimp lobby to read—the Member leaves the lectern and walks off the floor through a swinging door into the lobby outside.

Another Member rises and, addressing the Speaker, "suggests" the "absence of a quorum." Another Member rises and says, "Mr. Speaker, I move a call of the House." The Speaker instructs the attendance clerk to call the roll of Members, which will take about twenty-five minutes. Three bells are sounded. These ring throughout the House wing of the Capitol, and in each Member's office located in one of two House Office Buildings a block away.

The summoned Members answer to their names either the first or second time the roll is called. As each Member answers "Here," or "Ho" or "Ayeh," the clerk says, "Present."

The constituent's hopes are rallied. Upon completion of the roll, the clerk hands the Speaker a slip of paper. The Speaker announces, "Three hundred and sixty-seven Members having answered to their names, a quorum is present."

Incredible. There are still only about fifty Members on the floor. The constituent now realizes he has been watching the most august kind of revolving-door game. Most Members simply walked in, answered to their names, and walked out again.

The visitor's hopes flare briefly when a Member arises from behind a large rectangular table at the Speaker's right and says, "Mr. Speaker, I move that the House resolve itself into the Committee of the Whole House on the State of the Union for the consideration a bill, H.R. 250."

The Speaker puts the motion. There is scant response. Nevertheless, the Speaker states that "the Ayes have it. . . . The Gentleman from Texas, Mr. Brooks, will kindly take the Chair."

The Gentleman from Texas replaces the Speaker in the Chair. The Speaker steps down and disappears into the adjoining lobby. The Mace, symbol of his authority, is removed from its stand to a lower place. The gavel is rapped, discussion begins, and the bill, it is apparent, seems to parallel the shrimp speech in the degree of interest shown by the Members.

The constituent rises and leaves the gallery to seek greener legislative pastures—a scheduled visit with his Representative in the House. Walking down the corridors, decorated in the style of the Gilded Age, he wonders how the national legislature functions if the Members of the House conduct themselves as they did during the disappointing hour just passed. Who is minding the store?

Following directions, he reaches his Congressman's office on the fifth floor of the "old" House Office Building. The outer office is cluttered with desks. Secretaries busily type away. One pleasantly greets him, takes his name, and by intercom notifies the Member in the adjoining room, the Member's inner, private office, that his scheduled visitor has arrived. The ringing of two telephones distracts the constituent's gaze from the four walls adorned with a framed, autographed photograph of the President and photographs of the Member during notable events in his legislative life. Framed and hung on the wall are commemorative special pens used by the President to sign bills successfully sponsored by the Member.

A buzzer rung by the Member sounds twice, and the receptionist rises and escorts the constituent into the Member's private office. A handshake and, after a minute of conversational small change, the constituent cannot resist blurting out his confusion, laced with indignation, about the House floor proceedings.

The Congressman, having heard a variant of this much-told tale many times, seeks to bank the fires. He recites his own confusion upon his arrival as a freshman Member of the House from a Midwest district. He tells the constituent that prolonged exposure to the House helps understanding. Still not reassured, the constituent shakes his head and repeats his tale of an empty House chamber, mumbling Members, and speeches on inconsequential matters. The constituent persists. Why wasn't the Member on the floor for that H.R. 250 bill? he asks. The Member draws aim and replies that the bill is a completely uncontroversial measure unanimously supported by Democrats and Republicans on the committee that held hearings on it. Furthermore, a sounding of the leadership indicated no amendments would be offered and no roll call made. "So," says the Member hopefully, "I stayed here in my office to see two other visiting constituents, redraft a speech I give next week at a college, meet with two lobbyists for the residual oil interests, keep an appointment with a State Department chap who wants to discuss tactics and strategy on the forthcoming foreign-aid bill, and dictate replies to some of the forty-seven letters received so far today."

Finally, after a few anecdotal pleasantries, the constituent rises, shakes hands, and leaves for home to rejoin the Member's 450,000 other constituents. As far as his visit with the Member is concerned, he has seen the smiling aspects of politics. But the Member, left alone in his office, must continue to cope as best he can amid the unrelenting and infinitely complicated struggle for power, recognition, advancement, spoils, and alliances that underlie his efforts to serve honorably his constituents and his Nation.

The Member reflects that he might have told the constituent that legislative "combat" on the House floor is generally a sham. Usually, the disposition of a bill has been decided by the presence or absence of an influential Member, or a feud or favor remembered by the committee chairman. Or someone in the leadership may have pulled an accessible power lever that propelled the bill to the floor.

If the visitor had been present at the opening session of a new Congress, he would have seen the Speaker "elected." The roll would have been called solemnly, the victor installed, and the public, through press, radio, and television, informed that, for example, on January 9, 1963, Representative John McCormack of Massachusetts, successor to Rayburn, was re-elected Speaker of the House of Representatives. All this, in fact, is ceremonial. McCormack was assured of election on the previous day, January 8, when the caucus of Democratic House Members, representing a majority of seats in the House, renominated him without opposition as their candidate for Speaker. The ceremonial election is held to comply with Article I, Section 2, of the Constitution, which states:

"The House of Representatives shall choose their Speaker and other officers . . ."

"There shall be elected by the House, at the commencement of each Congress, the following standing Committees: . . ." according to Rule X, Section 1, of the Rules of the House. But, again, the actual election results are ordained in advance. The composition of the committees, in fact, is determined by the unwritten but iron rule of seniority and the earlier decisions of the Committee on Committees of the Republican and Democratic parties.

Our Member knows this, and he knows that the Speaker and the other leaders of the House attempt to govern in a chamber where at present power is divided among a few autocrats and unrepresentative groups. He knows that key committee posts have prestige and authority that enable them to obstruct legislation, make behind-the-scenes deals, reward political favors without regard to the public good, defy their party leadership and the House majority and the will of the voters at large. The tactics of power groups result in cumbersome procedures as well.

Such are some of the anomalies in the House that the visiting constituent does not fathom but that the Member of the House must deal with daily. If he is sponsoring or supporting a bill, he must spend a large part of his time politicking behind the scenes; he must know what the power groups are, by what channels to approach them, how to win their support or head off their opposition; he must constantly devise stratagems against them, find loopholes in procedure to advance his cause.

A knowledgeable observer, Stephen K. Bailey, in his book *Congress Makes a Law*, compared the proceedings of Congress to a theatrical production on which the curtain never rises: "It is much as though the citizenry were seated in a huge auditorium, allowed printed programs, but kept in total ignorance of what was happening on the stage. To the handful of citizens who have watched the show from the wings, this separation of players from audience is a dual tragedy; a tragedy for the players who might profit from audience reaction, and tragedy for the members of the audience who miss both entertainment and vitally needed education."

Thus the House today sometimes seems to resemble the French Chamber of Deputies when Gambetta described it as a "broken mirror in which the Nation cannot recognize its own image." There are breakdowns and irregularities of procedure and machinery; predictable institutional responsibility is lacking; the useless din of oratory and forays against the executive branch's duly delegated powers alternates with periods of careless yielding to the executive branch's legislative prerogatives.

In a sense, the disordered condition of the House is the result of a self-fulfilling prophecy. Just as a youngster may be delinquent partly because his elders have predicted that he would be, so the House sometimes seems to be living up to the apprehensions the early statesmen of America felt for it. James Madison and Alexander Hamilton, among others, were skeptical; the people were a "great beast." Fisher Ames spoke of the "mobocracy." The House, it was feared, would pass "emotional" legislation, and George

Washington is said to have remarked that "We pour House legislation into the Senatorial saucer to cool it." The Constitution itself,
with its system of excessive checks and balances, reflects the eighteenth century fear of arbitrary power and the traditional American
bias in favor of weak central government.

The House of the First Congress, assembling in New York on
March 4, 1789, seemed respectable enough. Fifty-five Members
were Federalists and ten were anti-Federalists. Half of the Members came from the South, with its more restricted suffrage, and
one-quarter each came from New England and the Middle Atlantic
states. Fifty-two of the sixty-five Members, whose average age
was forty-four, had past experience in the state assemblies, the
Continental Congress, or the Constitutional Convention. Nineteen
Members were college graduates and twenty-four were attorneys.
The composition hardly seemed that of a Jacobin mob. Yet a patri-
cian bias was evident in the writings of Thomas Jefferson, third
President of the United States, who complained of the "stock
jobbers and king jobbers" in the House.

In Philadelphia, John Adams, who presided over the Senate,
known as the "upper body" possibly because it met in a chamber
on the second floor above the House, insisted on dignity and de-
corum, and would permit no whispering while a Senator held the
floor; but downstairs, Representatives, with their hats on, read
newspapers or whispered during speeches. In the early 1800's
House Members caned each other, had fist fights, and issued chal-
lenges to duels. In 1880 Lord Bryce remarked in *The American
Commonwealth* that "no high qualities of statesmanship are expected from a Congressman."

Nevertheless, the First Congress passed about sixty major measures, many of which helped to shape the federal Union as we know
it today.

When Frederick A. C. Muhlenberg of Pennsylvania, the first
Speaker of the House, was able to call the popularly elected as-
sembly to order on April 1, 1789, it marked the end of a month's
delay in getting down to business. Only thirteen of the sixty-five
House seats were represented by Members in attendance when the
First Congress convened in New York City on March 4. It was

April before there were sufficient Members present to enable the House to begin its duties as the "grand depository of democratic principles."

Unlike the disappearing quorums, which our imaginary constituent observed, the Members who came in 1789 remained to enact a prodigious amount of work. This included approval of the first ten amendments to the Constitution, the so-called "Bill of Rights." Its members argued and decided issues that were crucial for American federalism, consisting as it does today of more than 100,000 governmental units operating at the national, state, and local levels. At one point, Elbridge Gerry of Massachusetts argued, although unsuccessfully, that the states should collect customs duties. A change of two votes would have authorized county officials to collect excise taxes. Samuel Livermore of New Hampshire argued against creation of lower federal courts. In short, the basis of the national government's administrative structure was formed by substantive debate.

In providing for the membership of the House, the framers of the Constitution allotted the sixty-five seats to congressional districts in the thirteen states, laid out on the basis of population. Congress was to make future apportionments based on a decennial census, with three-fifths of the slaves counted in allocating seats in each state; untaxed Indians were not to be counted. At that time each Congressman [as Representatives are usually referred to] represented thirty thousand persons. Questions of voter qualifications and the geographical boundaries of congressional districts were to be determined by the individual states.

The Constitution provides that each Representative shall be a resident of the state in which he is elected, although there is no requirement that he be a resident of his electoral district. In practice, however, a Representative does maintain a residence in his district and is expected to place its interests above all other considerations.

It is this electoral basis of representation that some critics have seized upon as a fundamental flaw in the structure of the House. The seniority system and the rule of perverse elderly congressional barons in important committee positions are more symptoms than

root causes, they argue. The basic fault is in the congressional
district, whose Member promotes local interest and self-advance-
ment, thereby creating an unstable political climate that boils with
each Supreme Court decision, or any House action on domestic or
foreign matters that its residents disagree with. Thus the House,
in its parochialism, is the principal seat of opposition to national
power; while the Senate, whose Members have been elected state-
wide by popular suffrage (since the ratification of the Seventeenth
Amendment in 1913) represents broader concerns than the local
preoccupations of the House. The Supreme Court, too, its members
chosen by the President and confirmed by the Senate, has a broader
perspective on the country as a whole than the House.

Lord Bryce in 1880 questioned the wisdom of the electoral basis
of the House:

"Fierce as is the light of criticism which beats upon every part
of that [political] system, this point, which at once strikes the
European as specially weak, remains uncensured, because assumed to be part of the order of nature."

And he quotes approvingly the Speech of Edmund Burke, who
in 1774 told his electors of Bristol, England:

"Parliament is not a congress of ambassadors from different
and hostile interests; which interests each must maintain, as an
agent, and advocate, against the agents and advocates; but Parliament is a deliberative assembly of one nation, with one interest,
that of the whole; where, not local purposes, not local prejudices,
ought to guide, but the general good, resulting from the general
reason of the whole. You choose a member indeed; but when you
have chosen him, he is not a member of Bristol, but he is a member
of Parliament."

The House of Representatives today is still to a large degree a
"congress of ambassadors from different and hostile interests." In
addition, the electoral basis established by the Constitution has led
to unequal representation. Of the present 435 congressional districts,

about 250, geographically laid out by the state legislatures, are predominantly rural, at a time when, according to the 1960 census, approximately two-thirds per cent of Americans live in urban areas. Another 125 House seats represent central city areas, and 60 others are suburban in character. A study by *Congressional Quarterly*, a reliable and informed privately operated weekly, estimated in 1962 that the suburbs are entitled to 15 to 20 more seats in the House. The study also estimated that it takes about 350,000 votes to elect nearly 100 House Members from rural districts in the South, while it takes more than 500,000 votes on an average to elect approximately 25 Members from urban districts and perhaps 600,000 votes to elect a Member from some suburban congressional districts. It is easy to see that this disproportionate representation gives senior Members from the rural districts undue power in the House committees and that urban concerns are frequently neglected or suppressed.

Such is the electoral basis of the House at present. After the Supreme Court decision in *Brown* v. *Tennessee* in 1962, twenty states set about redrawing the boundaries of their districts; and a decision of the Supreme Court in *Baker* v. *Carr* in June 1964 requires, in effect, that all states reapportion their congressional districts so as to reflect population equitably. In the near future, the House will, on a population basis at least, more fairly represent the voters.

The Constitution made a few specific requirements for eligibility for election to the House: a Member had to be at least twenty-five years of age and to have been a citizen of the United States for at least seven years. The only other stipulation was that all Senators and Representatives were prohibited from holding another government post simultaneously. Today it has become an issue, with the House Membership having risen to 435, whether or not a Member of Congress may constitutionally hold a reserve commission in the military services.

The Constitution, in addition, gave the House the power to make its own rules of procedure and to judge the qualifications and proper election of its Members. The House has the power to choose a President, if a candidate fails to receive a majority of votes in the electoral college. The House also is provided with the grave and sole power to impeach (indict, that is) a President. And the House has the power to initiate all revenue bills. The House and Senate in recent times have engaged in unseemly rows over whether this grant of constitutional authority applies as well to originating appropriation bills.

In the early years of the Republic, parties in the modern sense did not exist, nor was their creation encouraged.

"Among the numerous advantages promised by a well constructed Union," wrote James Madison in Number 10 of *The Federalist* papers, "none deserves to be more accurately developed than its tendency to break and control the violence of faction [party]. The friend of popular governments, never finds himself so much alarmed for their character and fate, as when he contemplates their propensity to this dangerous vice." And coupled with the admonishment is George Washington's warning about the "baneful effects" of political parties.

Nor, with all but ten of the sixty-five House seats in 1789 occupied by Members with Federalist inclinations, was partisanship a noteworthy problem. Alexander Hamilton, as Secretary of the Treasury, was the first and last occupant of that Cabinet post to dominate the Congress. He and fellow Federalists ruled the roost. The first Ways and Means Committee, in fact, turned over most of its duties to Hamilton. There was some grumbling among Members to the effect that with Hamilton running affairs, Members of Congress might just as well break camp and return home. Hamilton showed skill in holding organized meetings to obtain support among the legislators for his measures. These gatherings were somewhat similar to the later party caucus.

The House, indeed, in those early decades was not a body of Members all equally discussing and passing judgment upon legislation, but rather the organ of ratification of the decisions presented to it by those Members representing the dominant political tendency, who, in fact, sat as agents of the President and his advisers.

In the Administration of President Jefferson, the executive branch virtually dominated the Congress. The Speaker of the House served as the "President's man," and the President tolerated no defections. This congressional docility toward the executive branch has been sporadic. Henry Clay, whose years as Speaker, beginning in 1811, set a precedent for outstanding leadership by future Speakers, was anything but docile toward President Madison.

Lord Bryce, possibly having in mind the Administrations of Grant through McKinley, noted that in times when the House was firmly directed by its Speaker "the President's wishes conveyed in a message have not necessarily any more effect on Congress than an article in a prominent party newspaper." This applied to the Senate as well. Historians have noted that legislation sent to the Congress alone by anyone but the President has sometimes been returned to the sender without action. George Galloway, in his book *The Legislative Process in Congress*, observed that on occasion "many committees, in fact, refuse to consider legislation that has not been cleared by the Bureau of the Budget," an arm of the White House apparatus. He cites a specific example that occurred in 1908 when the Secretary of the Interior sent to the Senate a draft of a proposed bill. Upon the urging of Senator Henry Cabot Lodge, the measure was turned aside on the grounds that such a communication should not be accepted unless the President himself sends it to Capitol Hill.

The early years of President Franklin D. Roosevelt's Administration, on the other hand, saw a resurgence, under the goad of deep economic distress, of the leadership of the executive branch. But Congress grew restive and increasingly assertive as a consequence of the President's maneuvers, which were primarily legislative in character. Among them were the proposal to increase the number of Justices of the Supreme Court and efforts to defeat such elder Administration foes as Senator Walter George and Representative John O'Connor of New York, chairman of the powerful and much criticized House Rules Committee.

World War II and the ensuing dominance of foreign affairs resulted in uneasy cooperative arrangements in the area of foreign policy. As for domestic legislation, President Truman, for example, proposed and the Congress disposed—in the wastebasket. During the Eisenhower years the Congress manifested its nay-saying disposition even more broadly. Sufficient time has not yet passed to permit a valid generalization on the relationship between the Congress and the executive branch during the thirty-five month Presidency of John Kennedy, despite the Administration's verbal adherence to a policy of strong executive power and responsibility. Again, the unrepresentative House proved unresponsive to needed domestic legislation proposed by President Kennedy, while remaining fairly receptive to his foreign-policy measures. But even this receptivity began to wane, when the House gave strong support in August 1963 to a move to return the foreign-aid-authorization bill to committee, and when that failed, to reduce the authorization by about $900 million. This crankiness continued into December when the largest cut ever made in the foreign-aid program resulted in the recommendation of a $2.8 billion authorization. President Johnson, during the months following the assassination of John Kennedy, enjoyed a more productive relationship that may not have been entirely due to his years as Senate majority leader.

The character of the Congress and its relation to the Executive was analyzed by the late Harold J. Laski, chief political theorist of the British Labor party, and more sympathetic to American political problems than he has been given credit for. In *The American Presidency* he pointed out that the House is not an American variant of the British Commons. While the Commons is a legislative assembly, its "real business is to act as the cabinet's organ of registration." Then he calls into question the whole concept of the American Congress:

"It was the principle, long ago adumbrated by John Stuart Mill, that the formulation of legislative proposals is not a task for which a legislature is fitted. A legislature can criticize; it can ventilate grievance; its power to investigate through committees is invaluable; and, not least, as it fulfills these tasks it provides a process of public education which is pivotal to democratic government. But a legislature like Congress is at once too big and too incoherent of itself to devise an organic and unified approach to the problems of the time. It is not effectively organized to take a continuous initiative. Its members are not compelled to think by their position in terms of the problems of the whole Nation. Each house of Congress has a separate prestige; their common prestige is by their nature, inherently anti-presidential in character. To be something Congress is forced to take a stand against the

President; it cannot be anything if it merely follows his lead.

"And the weakness of the system is magnified by the fact that though it can seek its own elevation only by discrediting him, it cannot destroy him. He is there, whether it will or no, for his term; and his power to appeal against its decisions is but interstitial in character. The result of this system, normally, is therefore to dissipate strength rather than to integrate it. The President is usually less than he might be, because the stature of Congress is diminished the more fully he has his way; and Congress is never all that it might become, because it is so organized as to prevent the acceptance of clear sailing directions."

Thus Congress, and particularly the House, labors under the disadvantages of being unrepresentative, parochial in its outlook on national policy, and inherently in conflict with the Executive. Compounding these faults is the unwieldy procedure by which it handles legislation. The system has evolved with the development of a party system not envisaged by the First Congress, by the proliferation of committees and subcommittees, the establishment of the seniority privileges that determine their membership, and the fluctuations in the authority of the Speaker.

In the First Congress, the House decided to permit the Speaker to establish the committee needed to handle various categories of legislation—taxes, tariffs, public improvements, and so on. The Speaker also appointed Members to committees of three or fewer persons. Members of committees of more than three were elected to the committees by ballot of the whole House. Almost immediately this was changed to give the Speaker exclusive power to name Members to all committees. Generally, the House committees in the early Congresses were established to handle a particular bill. When work on the legislation was completed, the committee to which it had been assigned was dissolved. Then as the work load increased, standing or permanent committees were established. Standing committees varied in number up to 9, from one Congress to another until 1810. As years passed, legislative business in the House increased, and by 1891 when the Fifty-second Congress convened there were 52 standing committees, and in 1913, a total of 61. After that, the number dwindled slightly. Under the La

Follette-Monroney Legislative Reorganization Act of 1946, the number of House standing committees was reduced from 48 to 19. Since then, the standing Committee on Aeronautics and Space has been added, bringing the total at present to 20.

The jurisdictions of the standing committees have continued and grown through the years, by accretions of rule, custom, and expediency. Originally the Speaker referred bills to the proper committee. In actual practice, the referring of bills to committee is handled by the House Parliamentarian, a non-Member appointed by the Speaker, whose functions will be discussed in detail later. The Parliamentarian is guided by a body of rules and precedents on which he is the authority. The result of the procedure is to disperse jurisdiction among the various committees with, often, bizarre consequences.

For example, a study, entitled *The Federal Government and Education* and supervised by Representative Edith Green of Oregon, notes that, while the school lunch and school milk programs are administered by the Department of Agriculture, in the House, school lunch legislation is referred to the Education and Labor Committee, while school milk legislation is referred to the Agriculture Committee. Legislation to provide assistance for construction of college classrooms, when introduced as an amendment to the College Housing Act, was referred in a recent Congress to House Banking and Currency Committee. Yet similar legislation introduced separately was referred to the House Education and Labor Committee. A tabulation of education bills introduced in the House during the Eighty-fifth, Eighty-sixth, and Eighty-seventh Congresses, according to the study, showed that approximately 753, or 42 per cent, of 1,778 education bills were referred to the Education and Labor Committee. The remaining were distributed among eighteen other committees.

Indeed, from 1885 to 1920, authority to report appropriation bills to the floor was divided among nine committees of the House. Now the Appropriations Committee has exclusive jurisdiction over all general appropriations bills.

As the committee system crystallized, critics pointed out that Congress had abrogated its intended function as a lawmaking body by assigning its work to committees, since a rule of the House stipulates that all proposed legislation should be referred to them. The real lawmaking power became, not the House as a whole, but the Speaker, with his absolute control over the membership of committees.

During the tenure of Henry Clay the Speakership was shaped so ably that Clay became the most important officeholder in the United States, and its Number One power. Under Clay, and for many years thereafter, the House prospered as an institution in direct proportion to the authority and the willingness of its Speaker to control it.

With the establishment of standing committees came their continuing jurisdiction over various categories of legislation. The standing committees were creatures of the caucus, which, as drilling ground for discipline, issues, and leadership, played such a prominent role during Clay's Speakership—hence the nickname "King Caucus." The caucus of the majority party chose the Speaker, the caucus in this case being private meetings of Representatives to decide party programs, policies, and political measures in the House. The Speaker selected the members of the committees. The result was, compared to the present situation, a disciplined legislative apparatus that produced a legislative program dovetailed in all major respects.

Thus the system worked effectively; moreover, it did not diffuse or blur responsibility and power. It provided power reins for those who held responsible positions, and it identified their leader—the Speaker.

The system had its critics during its development. John Quincy Adams, writing from his experience in the House, complained in his memoirs of "the old and beaten track, the error of which consists, first, in parcelling out all the business of the House among the standing committees; secondly, in authorizing the Speaker to appoint them all and to designate the chairman, and, thirdly, in that domination of party spirit which rules over the House, the Speaker and the committees—the ineradicable infirmity of human nature."

The party discipline that sustained the system deteriorated as regional passions rose in the years before the Civil War. President Lincoln's political skill contained the bitter contest between the executive office and the aggressiveness in the House as personified by Thaddeus Stevens of Pennsylvania, but after Lincoln's death the legislative "radicals" became dominant. They came within one vote of impeaching President Andrew Johnson, and they put across a policy of reconstructing the rebellious states, the excesses of which engendered lasting bitterness and hostility among many white Southerners.

Within the House, the years after the Civil War were marked by struggles between the leadership and the rank-and-file Members, who were sometimes organized into a formal or informal minority opposition. The Speaker, leader of the majority, held a potent weapon by which he could favor or obstruct legislation—the power of recognizing a Member who wished to speak. Through it the Speaker and party leaders could predetermine what measures would come before the House, by whom they would be introduced, by whom opposed. On one occasion "Uncle Joe" Cannon, who became Speaker in 1903, was asked by a Member of the opposition, a Democrat, if a certain bill would be passed. Cannon is said to have replied: "Oh, this house could pass an elephant if the gentleman in charge of it could catch the Speaker's eye." This was of course a teasing reply, not to be taken literally; in practice the Speaker had a list of Members who had asked beforehand to be recognized and had stated their intentions; a Member had to ask in advance.

That power has been diluted by the adoption of so-called calendars, each a grouping of bills prepared for floor action, which establish an order of preference for introducing measures. Today the Speaker's power of recognition is hemmed in by practices and rules. One requires that the chairmen of Ways and Means and the Appropriations committees be recognized when they seek to bring bills out of their committees to the House floor. As for other than revenue and appropriation bills, the members of a committee in charge of a bill before the House now control the general debate time. Bills, too, may be brought up at certain times under suspension of customary House rules. Bills from the District of Columbia Committee may be called up on the second and fourth Mondays of each month. In addition, there are bills on the consent calendar that have a right of way under certain conditions. There is also a difficult

Calendar Wednesday procedure, which will be described in a later chapter, that is designed to enable bills that have been blocked in the Rules Committee to be brought to the floor for a decision.

The procedure of suspending the rules, like Calendar Wednesday, was adopted in 1909. It may be used two days each month—usually on Mondays. Bills may be called up out of order for floor action on these days, whether or not the Rules Committee consents. However, to suspend the rules of the House is difficult because it requires a two-thirds vote of approval.

The calendars represent a trend toward parceling out the Speaker's control over the order of business. The private calendar, established in 1839, lists bills dealing with specific individuals, corporations, and institutions as distinct from public bills, which deal with classes of legislation. On the first Tuesday of each month, the Speaker directs a call of the private calendar. If two or more Members object to a private bill being called up in this fashion, the bill is automatically recommitted to the committee from which it came. On the third Tuesday of each month, the private calendar is also called, with priority assigned to the bills objected to on earlier calendar calls.

Other means have been used to thwart the Speaker either by individual Members or by a group of them. One was quite simple—that of the nonvoting quorum. The presence of a majority of House Members is required to transact business, and up until 1890, Members who were present could prevent the House from taking any action simply by not answering roll call.

Then in December, 1889, Thomas Brackett Reed, Republican of Maine, who for years had been minority leader, became Speaker. Expert parliamentarian, skilled debater, mordant wit, Reed, having himself practiced obstructionist tactics as a minority Member, came to the Speakership with a conviction that no minority should have unabridged power to obstruct the majority. In January, 1890, a contested election case was before the House. On the vote to determine if the disputed election would be considered, the vote was Yeas, 161; Nays, 2; and not voting, 165. This was three votes short of a quorum. When the objection of "no quorum" was raised, Reed directed that the names of Members present but refusing to vote be recorded as part of the quorum. Thereby, a quorum was easily achieved.

The furor raised by this decision was tremendous. Reed then made a further ruling that he would disregard all motions and appeals that he considered designed to delay proper transaction of the business of the House—in short, the dilatory motion and the dilatory appeal. However, despite the cries of "czar" and "tyrant," the House actually adopted these rulings into its body of formal rules. Added to these two was a major rule providing that a simple majority rather than a two-thirds vote could adopt a special order prescribing the order of business on the floor and the manner and length of debate on a particular bill.

In Reed's time, the Speaker held extraordinary powers. He appointed the standing committees of the House, selected the chairman of each, served as chairman of the Committee on Rules, which controls the flow of legislative business to be considered by the House; he had the unlimited power to recognize Members for debate and could determine, in effect, what would be discussed on the floor.

Until 1896 the Speaker hand-picked his majority floor leader, who was often the chairman of the Appropriations Committee, and thereafter usually the chairman of Ways and Means when it became a separate committee. Today the floor leader is chosen, in the case of Democrats, by a party caucus on the eve of the opening of a Congress. This practice began in 1911 when the Speaker was Champ Clark of Missouri, chosen after the House had successfully revolted against the inordinate power wielded by the Republican Speaker Joseph Cannon of Illinois.

Cannon, last in the line of institutional-minded Speakers that included Clay and Reed, developed and used the powers of his position with such ruthlessness that dissatisfaction spread beyond the House to the country; the revolt against him was a decisive blow to the prestige of the office, and a serious impairment of the Speaker's—and his party's—ability to control House procedures.

Two preliminary setbacks to the Speaker's power heralded the revolt. In the first, the House narrowly adopted a resolution giving the House, not the Speaker, the right to name five Members to a joint select congressional committee to investigate possible misuse of coal and timber land leases in Alaska. Second, the House voted to overrule Cannon, who had stated that it was not improper to take up a census bill out of order on the grounds that a constitutional provision (such as the census provision of Article I, Section 2, of the Constitution) was entitled to precedence over the general rules of the House.

George Norris of Nebraska, a progressive Republican insurgent, seized on the implication of Cannon's ruling: other constitutional provisions had precedence over House rules. Therefore, Norris reasoned, a constitutional provision that gave the House the right to make its own rules was similarly privileged. In March 1910 he offered a resolution that was to prove "the unhorsing of Speaker Cannon." He proposed to strip the Speakership of the power to appoint committees and to sit on and chair the Rules Committee.

At that time the Rules Committee, which Reed had made a major power center, consisted of five members—"three very distinguished Republicans and two ornamental Democrats," as one member said. Another Democrat observed that sending a resolution to Rules was as fruitful as referring it to the sleepers in the catacombs.

Cannon ruled that Norris's resolution did not have precedence over House rules, but Norris did not let the matter drop; he pressed forward his resolution to enlarge the Rules Committee from five to fifteen members, eight from the majority party, seven from the minority. The country was to be divided into eight geographic districts for the majority, seven for the minority party. From each of these districts, Members of the respective parties would choose one of their number to sit on the Rules Committee. In addition the reconstituted committee, not the Speaker, would have the power to name Members to all other standing committees of the House.

However, Norris needed Democratic votes, and the Democrats balked. Reluctantly Norris altered his resolution to provide that the House as a whole would elect the Rules Committee, of six majority and four minority Members. After a bitter debate lasting twenty-nine hours, the resolution as amended was adopted, 191 to 156. The power of the Republican Speaker had been curbed, although his party had a forty-four-vote margin over the Democrats.

GOP insurgents represented about 15 per cent of the party's over-all strength.

When the Democrats won control of the House in November 1910, the procedures of the amended Norris resolution were incorporated into the House rules, along with a rule providing that the standing committees of the House be "elected by the House, at the commencement of each Congress."

For the next six years the Democratic Speaker Champ Clark shared power with Oscar Underwood, the majority leader, who was also chairman of the Committee on Ways and Means. Under Democratic party congressional procedure, the Democrats on Ways and Means made the appointments—from their own party Members—to the standing committees, including Rules. Thus the Speaker's once absolute power over committees was divided.

As the Speaker's power dwindled after the 1910–1911 revolt, that of committee chairmen increased. All legislation must be referred to committees, and the power of the chairman is broad. He arranges committee agendas, appoints subcommittee chairmen, decides what bills will be referred to subcommittees. He determines when committee meetings shall be called, appoints committee staff members, approves lists of witnesses for hearings (with the implied veto power over advocates of views of which he disapproves). In addition he sets the tone and shapes the work of the committee's professional staff, placing off limits those areas of public policy he chooses to leave unexplored.

Thus even legislation with broad popular support may be strangled by the chairman of a committee, who is a legislative baron with supreme power over his fief. A recent example is the 1964 foreign-aid-appropriations bill, which the House cut by $900 million; the bill was prepared in a subcommittee whose chairman is hostile to the concept of economic aid to other countries. Today the committee barons are usually Southerners from rurally oriented districts whose constituents have been sending them back to the House every two years since the days of the crystal-set radio. Many, indeed, have not been opposed in a primary or general election, or both, for decades. Of the twenty standing committees of the House in 1964, fourteen have chairmen from rural areas, ten of these from the South. Of the senior Republicans on each of these twenty committees, sixteen of them, who would presumably become chairmen if the Republicans gain control in the 1964 fall election, are also from rural areas. In the 1960 election, there were only sixteen contested elections out of twenty-two congressional district races in Texas, and contests in only three of ten districts in Georgia. Until reapportionment gives broader representation to urban and suburban areas, the situation is likely to remain unchanged. The Democratic big-city machines have also in some cases returned rubber-stamp timeservers to the House again and again. There has been a long and fruitful association between these two types of Democrats in opposing progressive legislation.

The privileges of seniority, of course, account for the committee chairman's long tenure in his position of power. Yet, it is a relatively recent development. In 1869 only 98 out of 243 House Members, or 40 per cent, had served in previous Congresses. Bryce observed in 1880 that nearly half of each successive House consisted of new men. But by January 1964 the House had only 71 first-term Members. Perhaps in the early 1800's the electorate felt that the emoluments and status of office should be passed around, and more candidates competed. Then too, Members found traveling to, and living conditions in, Washington uncongenial. But the increasing complexity of the legislative process and the growth of urban political machines helped to change the trend.

Usually, once a Member is assigned to a committee he remains there, unless the assignment is undesirable, as in the case of the District of Columbia Committee, regarded as a minor and unsatisfactory committee post, to be turned over to newly elected and unsuspecting freshman House Members as soon as possible. Two kinds of Members remain on it: those with a compassion for the District of Columbia, and Southern Democrats who, in deference to their segregationist background, stay there to keep the District in the social and economic status of a nineteenth century middle-border community.

The longer a Member remains in the House, the greater his seniority. The defeat, retirement, or death of fellow committee members helps him up the ladder to the apex of power. Senior members of committees become chairmen of subcommittees, some of which are equal in power and prestige to the committees of which they are a part. The few Members who reach the ultimate goal, chairmanship of a full standing committee, do so by virtue of sheer endurance, and by being re-elected and re-elected by their constituents.

The heady rank of full chairmanship can heighten a Member's self-esteem to the point of insolence. Representative Charles Campbell, chairman of the Rules Committee from 1919 to 1923, told his colleagues: "You can go to hell; it makes no difference what a majority of you decide; if it meets with my disapproval it shall not be done; I am the committee; in me reposes absolute obstructive power."

Those who defend the seniority rule claim that it places the most experienced men in important positions; that it is a system of promotion based upon length of service; that it satisfies those whom it favors, and of all workable systems least endangers the morale of the rest.

In any case, it is firmly entrenched and—generally—accepted by many who closely follow the Congress. A respected television and radio commentator, Joseph F. McCaffrey, observed in 1963: "The fact is that Congress has, is now and will continue to operate on the basis that the longer you serve as a Member the better your chances are of being a Congressional mother hen. Until the day comes when there is a better way to pick Congressional mother hens, the present system of picking them on the basis of seniority will stay in force."

In retrospect, the revolt against Speaker Cannon and the ensuing "reform" can be regarded only as a disappointment. It is true that the much-abused powers of the Speakership were curtailed. Yet the reins of power are still in the hands of a very few men who, so far as the public is concerned, remain anonymous and are not called to account for their highhandedness. The result has been increasing irresponsibility. The Committee on Rules is no longer the Speaker's instrument of domination, but the change has brought about no signal benefits. The manner in which Members are named to standing committees is no more representative than before. The Republicans established a "Committee on Committees" chosen by party conference to assign party Members to other committees, while the Democrats gave the task to their fellow Democrats on the Ways and Means Committee. But it has brought about no significant diminution of the concentrations of power.

The committee system based on seniority has deterred Congress from exercising its full responsibility of laying down broad policies in domestic and foreign affairs and providing legislation that would enable the executive branch to function effectively as the surrogate for many millions of Americans of diverse opinions, problems, and interests.

In the past thirty years the legislative load that Congress must bear has become increasingly heavy—owing to our rapid growth in population, our involvement in world affairs, and to the scientific and technological developments of the age. There has also been a quickening of the humanitarian impulse that is part of our national tradition; we have a disturbed conscience about social, political, and economic injustice, and the means of alleviating distress is through legislative measure.

In addition the federal government has assumed heavier responsibilities that result in a complex skein of relationships with state and local governments. In fiscal 1962, for example, the federal government granted $10.4 billion to state and local and individual jurisdictions to help finance 110 different programs, such as highways, health facilities, education and welfare, and research and conservation projects.

In the last quarter-century federal government programs such as these, and the social security system, have drawn to the central government the attention of millions of Americans who hitherto had had no more than a casual encounter with the postman or the income-tax return.

Yet the electorate does not know enough about the institution to which it gives a mandate to make laws in its name. Lacking sufficient information, as well as a familiarity with its larger design, the people at once demand too much in their ignorance, and not enough in their wisdom.

House Members, too, know too little of the body in which they serve—not from stupidity or incompetence or lack of the desire to learn, but because they do not have the time and training to study and analyze it; they have all they can do to keep up with their own legislative work, their constituents, and their overcrowded political life. Hence they are timid about taking legislative measures to reform it.

Gertrude Stein once observed that the United States is in fact the oldest country in the world because it was the first to enter the twentieth century. But we have entered it encumbered by attitudes and institutions formed in a simpler age. Congress clings to politically shopworn issues, such as "statism" and "states' rights," and neglects the exciting work of discovering necessary new ways of solving our perplexing problems.

Chapter 2

The Members of the House

> ". . . single men in barricks don't grow into plaster saints."
>
> —RUDYARD KIPLING

If a Member of the House closes his eyes and reaches out to touch the first colleague who passes by on the House floor, it is predictable on the basis of statistics that the colleague will be a man in his fifties, Protestant, native-born, reared in a middle-class family in a smallish community. He will likely hold a college degree, and if so, most probably will have graduated from law school. He will usually be a veteran and possibly hold a reserve commission in the Armed Forces.

When the Eighty-eighth Congress opened on January 3, 1963, the average age of the 435 House Members was 51.7 years; the average age of freshman Members was 43 years. The youngest was Ed Foreman of Texas, 29; the oldest, Thomas J. O'Brien of Illinois, 84. The most frequently cited work background was "politics and civil service"—406 Members. But many listed more than one occupation. Fifty-seven per cent, or 249 Members, listed themselves as lawyers; 134 listed banking and business backgrounds. Only one Member listed himself as a union official. The most numerous church denomination given was Roman Catholicism, 88 Members. Second most numerous was Methodist, 79. Protestant denominations accounted for 75 per cent of the Membership. Two hundred and ninety-one Members listed themselves as war veterans. There were eleven women in the House.

The typical Member will be either a Republican or a Democrat, but his party label will not provide conclusive evidence of his political coloration.

The new Member will learn to recognize among his colleagues certain types of individual who are the shadow symbols of particular attitudes among the American electorate.

One type is the old-timer for whom politics is a simple affair of the heart. He waves Old Glory occasionally and votes for appropriations for his own district. Back home he is a public figure; in the House he is a backbencher, translating a complex problem for the intellect into a simplistic moral affair of the heart. Another familiar figure is the fence straddler who rhetorically favors brotherly love, government solvency, pensions for everybody, and the greatest good for the greatest number. A third type is the anxious and indecisive Member who cannot make up his mind on any issue. He is a loner; distrustful, disillusioned, and doubting, he lives in fear of the next election, at which time he is unlikely to be returned to his seat.

Another is the arch-intellectual who dreams, in T. S. Eliot's phrase, "of systems so perfect that no one needs to be good." His approach to legislative problems tends to be totalitarian; he will settle only for the perfect, not for the possible. His career is usually short and ineffectual.

All these types become chained to the back benches; they are timid, and their fears play into the hands of the mandarins of the House power structure.

Another type comes to the House, inevitably—the smooth dealer, newly arrived from the state legislature or the board room of the local Chamber of Commerce. To him politics is largely the art of exchanging favors. He waits patiently on the House barons in the expectation that he will eventually be granted access to the levers of power. One of his early assignments may be to help staff the back door through which the House is robbed—the hidden channels by which special favors are dispensed to special interests. This helps him develop and refine a keen scent for the attitudes of individual Members or groups on the eve of great legislative battles. Usually an attorney, the hidden persuader displays a public posture of evenhandedness and fairness in his approach to major issues.

Through these surface traits he may frequently develop sufficient national renown to become a frequent guest on those Sunday television and radio discussion panels. However, when the committee room doors shut for an executive session, he fights skillfully and relentlessly and single-mindedly for the private economic interest to which, by exposure or by financial remuneration, he has become attached.

He must be alert, wary, and knowing. He has, of course, a retentive memory, attention to detail, mastery of techniques—parliamentary and personal—and an acute ability to sense collective and individual moods of Members. These are the necessary baggage of skilled professionals of whatever political affiliation. He "keeps book," as does the baseball manager, on his colleagues, opponents, and potential opponents. He catalogues their weaknesses, their reactions in the "clutch," their interests and hobbies, their extracurricular activities. As he gathers the components of these profiles he comes to realize whether carrot or stick, or combination thereof, is most persuasive with a Member whose support he needs. He knows, of course, how to disagree without being disagreeable. He seeks to ingratiate himself with the most vigorous opponents of his interest because he knows that no matter how much a man may disagree with him, he is not likely to be as determined in his opposition if he has a personal liking for him.

Our hidden persuader also cultivates the policy-making civil servants in the Departments of the executive branch, who remain in their decisive positions, regardless of who is the Department head. He knows that certain agencies and bureaus within Departments are run by their chiefs almost without a deferential nod to the Department heads upstairs. These agencies are "inbred" and semiautonomous in operations. The Forest Service, within the Agriculture Department, and the Bureau of Land Management and the National Park Service within the Department of Interior, are examples. The Federal Bureau of Investigation and the Immigration and Naturalization Service, in the Justice Department, are others. He knows that it is almost impossible to obtain funds for an important river or harbor project in his district from the House Committee on Appropriations if the supervising agency, the Army

Corps of Engineers, is opposed; and, if he represents a congressional district in a western state, he will proceed on this knowledge accordingly. If he is from an urban area, he will know about the personnel shuttle that goes on between urban-renewal developers and the Housing and Home Finance Agency.

He must be alert and wary and knowing. In time he will, in Oscar Wilde's phrase, know the price of everything and the value of nothing. And his value will not always lie in obtaining passage of legislation. Often, the greatest service he renders will be to have deleted or modified an objectionable provision in a bill, or perhaps to have a hearing on an objectionable bill prolonged until it is too late in the congressional session for favorable action. If he is a high-ranking committee member, which he may become in time, he can simply and unilaterally decide not to have a hearing at all on a bill distasteful to his "clients."

Our hidden persuader subverts the processes of representative government. His constituents are deprived of representation, for he does not represent the kaleidoscope of their interests; rather he represents a single interest, which, indeed, may not even be located in his congressional district. He undermines the confidence of voters and those around him in the democratic process. He is likely to disturb the new and responsible Member. Those who catch a glimpse of his workings generalize his image into an image of all politicians. He is powerful out of all proportion to his numbers. He is corrupt, but he has been corrupted by forces that are equally culpable. Our hidden persuader represents a problem of democracy, particularly in its legislative aspect, which must be exposed and made to wither away, regardless of whether he is a conservative, a liberal, Democrat or Republican. In the last chapters of this book suggestions will be proposed, which, if adopted, would make it more difficult for the hidden persuader to exist.

Happily for the new Member's peace of mind, there are also in the House men and women of quite a different type. They live lives of quiet desperation, clutching splinters of hope amid wretched conditions, as they strive to fulfill their obligation as legislators.

This is not a simple obligation and it is not discharged by the Members who merely vote for an appropriation for their district.

A legislator's responsibility was defined by Edmund Burke, speaking to constituents at Bristol who had elected him to Parliament in 1774:

> "Certainly, gentlemen, it ought to be the happiness and glory of a representative to live in strictest union, the closest correspondence and the most unreserved communication with his constituents. Their wishes ought to have great weight with him; their opinions, high respect; their business, unremitting attention. It is his duty to sacrifice his repose, his pleasure, his satisfactions, to theirs—above all, ever, and in all cases, to prefer their interest to his own.
>
> "But his unbiased opinion, his mature judgment, his˜enlightened conscience, he ought not to sacrifice to you, to any man, or to any set of men living. These he does not derive from your pleasure, no, nor from the law and the Constitution. They are a trust from Providence, for the abuse of which he is deeply answerable. Your representative owes you not his industry only, but his judgment; and he betrays, instead of serving you, if he sacrifices it to your opinion."

Members who exemplify Burke's attitude do exist and function in the House, and they are apt to appear in unexpected places. The doctrinaire northern liberal would be surprised to find them among southern Democrats during a civil-rights struggle. During the legislative battle preceding the Civil Rights Law of 1957, those Members from the South and Southwest who did not denounce the bill in typical wool-hat fashion were politically brave enough. But even braver were a handful of Southerners who by private word or public deed helped to achieve enactment of the legislation. Eventually, some—such as Representative Brooks Hays of Arkansas—suffered undeserved political defeat; others survived to serve in the House without recognition for their efforts, and continued to be lumped with their conservative and reactionary colleagues. There is probably more political courage per man in this group than in any other regional group in the House.

Another example is the small band of Members on the Education and Labor Committee, each of whom came from a district where organized labor was strong if not dominant, and was elected because of labor support. In 1958 and 1959 opinion was strong inside Congress and outside for a labor reform bill. The five Members—Frank Thompson of New Jersey, Stewart Udall, subsequently Secretary of the Interior; Mrs. Edith Green of Oregon, James O'Hara of Michigan, and Carl Elliott of Alabama—foresaw that a bill would have to be reported from the Education and Labor Committee on which they sat. In the face of vitriolic threats and pressure from organized labor, which wanted no reform bill, they took the position that a bill with more plus than minus provisions should be reported, so that a fair and equitable law could be passed instead of the really vicious labor bill favored by some segments of the House. They had the courage to take this stand in opposition to a large number of their constituents.

In the fall of 1963, a young Member from Idaho, Ralph Harding, rose on the House floor to reprimand the leaders of his church, the Church of Latter-day Saints, for permitting fellow Mormons, such as Ezra Taft Benson, father and son, to associate their extreme right-wing views, notably support for the John Birch Society, with the Mormon Church. In the district Harding represents, Mormons are numerous, and his political strength was imperiled by his speech.

During the period when Joseph McCarthy was terrorizing his congressional colleagues, many Members publicly denounced him, and such denunciations were all to the good. If the Member came from a district that was anti-McCarthy, he was in the happy position of speaking his conscience and making political hay. On the other hand, a Member whose district had a heavy numerical concentration of modern political Know-Nothings risked his political career by taking an anti-McCarthy position. This Member's courage gave comfort and support to his more timorous colleagues. In a small way he was supplying leadership where the nominal party leaders had failed.

Such acts of courage are significant because they induce further acts of courage; and the men and women who perform them bring to Congress not only energy and ability but inspiration. Conscientious new Members can take heart from their example.

Equally, when acts of cowardice and venality and unforgivable silence in the face of injustice are exposed and condemned, they are less likely to multiply.

The new Member will need all the encouragement he can find against the countervailing forces that offset the superb individual assets of many Members—clumsy legislative machinery, staffed by the committee barons and their smooth-dealing lackeys, Members affiliated with his own party who thwart the will of the majority, and the disheartening human tendency to accept the situation, bad as it is, rather than incur the displeasure of the party elders by seeking to alter it. He will shortly observe that his party in the House does not follow the principles of his party on the national scene.

If the new Member is a Democrat he will soon come to recognize the two faces of the Democratic party. The national party, without power inside the legislative branch, makes promises in the form of a party platform adopted every four years at the party's presidential nominating convention. And the Democratic party in the House breaks the promises—or more exactly, does not act effectively to translate promises into legislative accomplishment. This situation exists because a minority of the House Democratic party in its privileged sanctuaries of power does not believe in its party platform in the first place. A debilitating stalemate results when an attempt is made to implement the party's platform by enacting laws.

However, any prolonged scrutiny of the philosophical implications of this is fatal. The Member, backbencher or pewrenter, must develop an agile sense of survival. To some extent, in the words of the late Speaker, Sam Rayburn, "To get along you have to go along."

He may be disconcerted to find that on a major issue, a majority vote in party caucus, if such is ever held, does not bind all Members. There are loopholes in the form of standing reservations providing that a Member is not obliged to vote against his conscience, a prior pledge to constituents, or a belief that caucus position is unconstitutional. The new Member will find that once his party claims its committee assignments, if it is in the majority, this may be the first and only evidence of party discipline during the two years of this particular Congress. He finds that the party legislative program or the legislative program of the President is treated with disdain. He finds himself dependent upon a handful of powerfully placed House Members, the committee and subcommittee chairmen particularly, for assistance in obtaining favorable action on vital bills his district, his state, his region, and his Nation want and need. And the Member will find that his influential colleagues wield in varying proportions both personal power, based on personality and favors granted, and power stemming from the position of influence itself—such as a chairmanship.

The new, responsible Member will also take care to do no more than cross his fingers when a favored appropriation bill is nipped at on the floor by self-styled economy-minded Members with their minds of the first crank. Later, he will become simply bored at the windy grandstand posturing of such peevish Members, who consume time but seldom achieve results.

Thus surrounded by varied types of legislator, from the smooth dealer to the effective idealist, hedged by rules, precedents, maneuvers, and shabby deceptions, the new Member will find himself burdened with the manifold duties of the Congressman: he is a maker and co-signer of national policy; he is a statesman-politician attempting to judge the merit and the implications of measures that come to his attention on the floor or in committee; he may be the sponsor and pilot of a bill he introduces, and hopes to guide to safe passage through undreamed-of hazards; he is the advocate for pleading constituents seeking favors or escape from some bureaucratic crossfire. He will be fortunate indeed if he has time to contemplate the larger responsibilities of his task and discern the ethical boundaries beyond which he may not conscientiously move.

In addition his motives will be relentlessly scrutinized by colleagues and constituents and observers, and his objectives will be trimmed, limited, and perhaps thwarted accordingly; and he will in turn examine his colleagues' motives with equal acuity. His plight is made more difficult by the fact that in Calvinist America, the elect consider the politician as among the damned—although he is expected to practice his black arts for their benefit.

The new Member in the House will generally become aligned regularly in one of two categories of Representatives that cut across party lines. Until recently Members could be catalogued by the party label under which they were elected. But their legislative inclinations do not conform to the label. Some members vote against proposals that are in line with the national party platform. Democrats from the North and West come closest in their voting patterns to following the national party platform in legislative action. This platform, however, is balked by the conservative alliance between Democrats from the South and midwestern Republicans. In terms of party affiliations at the opening of the Eighty-eighth Congress, there were 258 House Members who were elected as Democrats, 176 who were elected as Republicans, and one vacancy. *Ergo*, the House had a Democratic majority and was "controlled" by the Democrats. It was not so, of course. In view of defections, mostly among their southern party fellows, the Democrats fell short by several votes of controlling the House.

Another somewhat loose classification in the popular mind is "liberal" and "conservative." This makes some sense only if the terms are construed to mean that a conservative favors a reduction or restriction of the role of the federal government in national affairs, while the liberal favors an expanded role.

Roughly, there were about 175 House liberals in the 1963–1964 Congress—including about 15 Republicans, such as Representative John V. Lindsay of New York City, Charles McC. Mathias, Jr., of Maryland, and Bradford Morse of Massachusetts; a dozen southern Democrats, such as the skilled, courageous, and able Carl Elliott of Alabama, who was successfully ambushed by Wallace-led racists in the 1964 state primary; and the bulk, about 145 Democrats from the urban areas of the East, Midwest, and West.

Confronting this group are about 185 hard-core conservatives, mostly Republicans, but including perhaps 45 Democrats from southern states. This accounts for about 360 Members. The remaining 75 vote in such a way as to preclude a definite assignment to one of the two groups.

Depending on the issue, liberals can muster the votes of 210 to 230 Members—218 being a majority. This comes about with the support of a dozen to 15 Republicans, mostly from suburban and urban districts, and perhaps as many as 55 border-state southern Democrats.

The coalition of Republicans and Dixiecrat Democrats, reflecting a reactionary or conservative hue, depending on the issue, can put together 200 to 220 votes.

The lines blur more on some issues. For example, conservative Pacific Northwest Republicans will join liberals in support of a public hydroelectric power issue, while liberal Democrats representing districts with strong United Mine Workers strength will break ranks to join pro-public-power conservatives in opposing such legislation. But generally speaking, the Member remains with his group, which is not synonymous with his party label.

However, these are only broad classifications, and there are many deviations among individual Members. For example, Representative Fred Schwengel of Iowa votes on orthodox Republican lines on most economic issues. However, on issues such as disarmament, civil rights, and local self-government for the District of Columbia, Schwengel takes leave of his orthodox Republican colleagues. Similarly, the late Representative Francis Walter of Pennsylvania, regarded as anathema to the liberal establishment, cast liberal votes on social legislation.

A legislator with a heavy proportion of Roman Catholics in his urban district will vote a straight New Dealish line and then break away to vote for the most outlandish anti-Communist proposals that, if enacted, would do all but repeal constitutional safeguards for individual freedoms. And the blue-ribbon liberal is not above casting a "Chamber of Commerce" vote by opposing, for example, the creation of a Department of Urban Affairs proposed by President Kennedy in 1962. The proposal was evidently foredoomed to defeat in any case, which meant that the Democratic leadership did not insist upon liberal party Members holding firm in favor of the proposal.

There is, nevertheless, some justification for describing in general terms the principles, attitudes, and behavior of House "liberals" and "conservatives."

THE LIBERALS

Anthony Trollope, an astute observer of English political life, once observed, "A man in the right relies easily on his rectitude and, therefore, goes about unarmed."

This applies to the House liberal of both parties. He is regarded as "not quite true blue" by the leadership of his party, be it Republican or Democrat. One Republican liberal on the House Education and Labor Committee is cuttingly called by his orthodox party fellows "our ADA member."

The liberal in the House has certain characteristics in common with his fellows. One is a fabulous faith in the power of ideas. He tends to be issues-oriented. Unlike his Progressive forebears, he is usually an internationalist. He accepts, if he does not promote, federal intervention in private sectors of our economy, and he supports a generally increasing role for the federal government in other aspects of our national life. He is dissatisfied with the condition of the world. He is receptive to all sorts of palliatives. This may be a disadvantage to him occasionally, but it develops in him, at best, a spirit of inquiry and intellectual curiosity, and at worst, a tendency to tinker.

His staff assistants, who come to work early and stay late, are often a step or two ahead of him in programs to advocate or situations to deplore. And like the Frenchmen of the anecdote, three liberals in a room will produce four violently advanced viewpoints.

The liberal also exhibits a characteristic vulnerability in several ways. One species of House liberal is totalitarian in temperament and occasionally seized with fits of voodooism. He sees the liberal program as a holy tablet to which liberals all must give complete unswerving allegiance—or else risk being read out of the liberal ranks. The liberal is always spreading himself too thin. One just cause tends to have equal significance and merit with another. He will dissipate his energies preparing to do battle against a bill to provide federal funds to hire legal counsel for the indigent in criminal trials because the provisions of the bill are not to his complete satisfaction, when in fact the bill in question ought to be supported, so that future Congresses can improve it.

He tends to indulge himself in verbal support of bills, utter cries of frustration, but shy away from the necessary confrontation of power needed to put legislation across. He distrusts power; indeed, he treats it as some sort of dirty weapon. Indeed, some liberals give evidence of possessing a legislative "will-to-lose," a sort of death-wish. If more than a dozen votes show up for a bill he favors, he begins to wonder, like the fastidious literary critic confronted with sudden popularity of a hitherto obscure novel, that perhaps there is something "wrong" with the bill. He is beset by apocalyptic and utopian visions.

Someone has said bluntly that "liberals are lousy legislators—they have never learned to count." More tactfully, the liberal, in contrast to the conservative, exhibits neither the aptitude nor the appetite to learn, master, and apply legislative technique. This same liberal reveres George Norris, the great Nebraska Congressman. But if he read his dog-eared copy of Norris's autobiography he would realize that Norris recognized the value of compromise and vote-counting and parliamentary techniques. As Norris tells it, he was able successfully to offer a resolution that led to the mutiny against Speaker Cannon in March 1910 because he observed the precise time a chief lieutenant of Cannon's left the House floor each day to go to lunch. I remember being horrified when in my ninth year in Congress, a leading liberal, many years my senior in service, asked me, "How do you go about getting a Rule for that bill of mine?"

The liberal assigns Franklin Delano Roosevelt first rank in his Hall of Fame. But he becomes a bit uneasy as he reads the biographies of Harry Hopkins and Harold Ickes that illustrate the Rooseveltian power plays.

And therefore the liberal is ordinarily not so effective a legislator as is the conservative. In part this is true because many liberals do not have "safe" districts that guarantee re-election. Representative Robert Kastenmeier of Wisconsin, whose district includes conservative rural communities surrounding the liberal University of Wisconsin at Madison, wins by the slimmest of margins term after term. Representative John Brademas of South Bend, Indiana, is in an analogous position. Former Representative Frank Burke won two of his races by 50.1 and 50.2 per cent of the votes cast in the swing district of Louisville, Kentucky, and finally, in 1962, lost to a right-wing Republican.

On the other hand, many conservatives, particularly from the South, are assured of long tenure by the courthouse gang. In addition, more conservatives seem to be willing and able to make a career of being a Member of the House. Many of the ablest House liberals, Representatives Eugene McCarthy of Minnesota, Lee Metcalf of Montana, and George McGovern of South Dakota, have moved to the Senate. This leaves the conservatives to preempt the intricate field of legislative politics.

The "good ideas" in the field of domestic welfare and in foreign policy remain just that as long as the liberals refuse to take the time and the infinite pains necessary to transform them into legislation.

A certain slackness in the organization and methods of liberal forces have caused them, through ignorance or negligence, to miss opportunities to pass legislation they wanted. The more experienced senior conservatives are seldom guilty of oversight or carelessness in supporting or opposing legislation. The tactical successes of the senior conservatives led the House Democratic liberals to form the Democratic Study Group (DSG)—so named to avoid giving the impression that it was established to infringe on the regular party leadership.

The DSG applies one of the important lessons learned from conservative tactics—the dovetailing of a common strategic plan so that each supporting Member has an assigned role, whether it be to lead the floor discussion, participate in debate at selected crucial points, or merely to be on hand to vote when important amendments are offered.

These steps, so obvious that it is surprising that they were not taken years earlier, were originally adopted under the leadership of an unusually talented Member from Minnesota, Representative, now Senator, Eugene McCarthy, who in the late summer of 1964 emerged as a vice-presidential possibility.

In 1956 the Southern Manifesto, a denunciation of civil-rights proposals, was signed by nearly all the Southern Democratic conservatives in the House. McCarthy countered this with a broad statement—going well beyond the civil-rights issue—which turned out to represent a platform of objectives and methods of the liberal Democrats in the House. At that time the DSG was loosely formed; it came into focus organizationally only as critical issues came before the House.

One of the concrete techniques it adopted was the DSG "whip system" apart from the traditional whip system operated by each party in the House. This consists of a whip, perhaps a deputy chief whip and several assistants, each coming from a different geographical area. In the case of the Democrats, the whips' task is to sound out party Members in advance on their views on legislation that is coming to the floor, and to prod Members by telephone and personal contact into being present for important votes. To be effective, whips have to be just that on occasion.

The traditional whip system contains an anomaly—certain regional whips are responsible for getting out the vote for bills, such as civil rights and welfare measures, that they themselves are opposed to. The DSG whip system was established to correct this incongruous situation. It is not employed on every bill but only in those situations where the traditional party whip system will be predictably faulty. The DSG whips proved effective during the 1956 and 1957 civil rights struggles and astoundingly so during the 1964 civil rights legislative struggle.

However, the establishment of the DSG whip system led to newspapers promoting a rift between DSG leadership and the party leadership under Speaker Rayburn and Majority Leader, now Speaker, John McCormack of Massachusetts.

There was, of course, no such rift. The DSG leaders made it clear to Rayburn that, while they wished to maintain an independent influence on his decisions, they also were loyal to his leadership. Rayburn accepted this. And his trust was maintained by the liaison I kept, as a trusted lieutenant of his between Rayburn and the DSG, whose leadership, unlike some of the Members, regarded me sympathetically. The occasion to exercise the role of middleman soon presented itself.

Some days in advance of its issuance, I became aware of the existence of Eugene McCarthy's statement on the Southern Manifesto. I suggested to a DSG leader that it would be wise to show the draft to Rayburn before it was made public. It seemed to me that this would provide assurance to Rayburn that this fledgling organization was not trying to go behind his back or undercut him. Furthermore, it would enable the Speaker to become familiar with its contents so as to avoid placing him in the position of being surprised when newspapermen asked him for comment on a document, issued by a wing of his party, that he had not seen.

It was agreed Rayburn should be shown a draft on the understanding that it was not done to give him a chance to modify it. Rayburn, after reading it, commented, "There is nothing in here I disagree with."

I returned the draft to the same DSG leader, swearing him to secrecy as to Rayburn's comment, which meant an endorsement of civil rights legislation, particularly in the area of voting rights. The pledge was demanded because if Rayburn's views were discussed prematurely it might cause him political embarrassment in his east Texas constituency and with opposing Southerners. It might even force him to oppose the legislation, which meant its certain defeat. Within hours a telephone call came from a legman of Drew Pearson, the political columnist who specializes in "behind the scenes" stories of public issues. He knew about Rayburn's comment. I called Pearson and pointed out the consequences if Rayburn's comment were published, and Pearson did not print the item.

As the DSG developed, it became in large measure research-oriented. William Phillips, a capable former assistant to Representative George Rhodes of Pennsylvania, directs the staff operation. He produced top-notch research background papers on issues and bills during the Eisenhower Administration when Democrats were denied more than nominal information from the executive branch departments. Under a Democratic Administration, stronger emphasis is being placed on long-range policy, cohesion, and campaign financing.

DSG has served to pull together liberal Democrats, who incline to independence and even irascibility, into a semblance of a cooperative group that grasps the importance of legislative technique, the "how" of legislative endeavors. Tangible victories to date have been small, but there is an appreciable advance in the development of a pragmatic sense among many House liberals. They now realize that, without losing their ideals or their passion for ideas, they can be more realistic in their assessment of what can actually be accomplished under given circumstances. They have come to know the difference between what "should" or "ought to be" and what "is" and "may be."

There are fewer dismaying defeats due to negligence and lack of information, and Members have learned the value of the endless tiresome chores to be done—phone-call lobbying, gathering information on when which Members will be in town, consulting the calendar to make sure that a favored piece of legislation requiring urban votes is not scheduled on Yom Kippur.

The DSG has also helped to make changes in the composition of committees that, hopefully, will be significant in years to come. Adopting a tactic learned from the conservatives, they work to persuade the party leadership to fill committee posts with liberals from time to time.

Notable success has been achieved in changing the complexion of the Education and Labor Committee from deep conservative to liberal. This is only a minor gain, because this committee is not essentially one that deals with direct bread-and-butter legislation, and has not the legislative muscle of the Rules, Ways and Means, and the Commerce committees. It can seldom pull rank on a competing committee. For example, the President in 1963 gave his blessing to a medical- and dental-school construction bill held by Interstate and Foreign Commerce, rather than a broader bill held by Education and Labor. The reason may have been that the former committee held a number of bills on which the Administration wanted specific action, whereas Education and Labor had no such bargaining power. Nevertheless, liberal domination of the committee, coming after years of reactionary leadership under Representative Graham Barden of North Carolina at least serves to prevent malicious union-busting legislation. At present, its Negro chairman, Representative Adam Clayton Powell of New York, is able, eloquent, and courageous, but unfortunately erratic in the application of his skill, and given to bizarre travels abroad and long absences from committee work.

The leadership and members of the DSG have been diminished by defeat, retirement, and election to the Senate. Of the original cadre, only Frank Thompson of New Jersey remains. McCarthy and Metcalf now sit in the Senate, and Stewart Udall is Secretary of the

Interior. The present DSG chairman, John Blatnik of Minnesota, is a man of capability and energy, and the continuing effectiveness of the group is a hopeful portent for congressional reform.

It is not the only hopeful sign. Men and women on both sides of the aisle express their dismay at the unrepresentative character of Congress and its outworn procedures, burdened with the accumulation of seniority, spoils, and senility.

THE CONSERVATIVES

The world of the conservative, as summed up by the homilies of Ben Franklin, Horatio Alger, and Calvin Coolidge, has profoundly changed. Two world wars and the depression of the 1930's have pulled the shorings from under it—not to speak of the consequences of Einstein, Darwin, Marx, and Freud.

The past three decades have been an unhappy time for the conservative. Among his numbers are many responsible and public-spirited men—Clarence Brown of Ohio and Thomas B. Curtis of Missouri, for example—but unfortunately others—the vulgar political primitives with their demonology and warped historical sense—have partially succeeded in becoming identified as conservatives. So for the responsible conservatives the terrain is bleak whether they look to the right or the left. Their political victories, the election of the first Republican Congress in sixteen years in 1946 and the election of a President in 1952, at best stemmed the trend to the "welfare state."

Whatever his public morality, the conservative is highly responsible on a personal level—more so perhaps than his liberal counterpart. But the tide of world affairs has engulfed him. In foreign affairs the House conservative has made common cause with his opponents on major bills and programs—the Marshall Plan, the Truman Doctrine in Greece and Turkey, the North Atlantic Treaty Organization, and the United Nations (but less so with its specialized agencies such as UNESCO). This support among conservatives shows signs of weakening, as in the case of the heavy vote to recommit and then cut the 1964 fiscal year foreign-aid authorization bill in late August 1963. Another example of the distemper of the House occurred in October 1963, when conservatives pushed across an amendment to the National Aeronautics and Space Administration appropriation bill prohibiting use of any such funds for any joint space exploration project carried on in cooperation with the Soviet Union. This is a typical case of provincial David Harums venting their churlish tempers.

In spite of the lackluster House Committee on Foreign Affairs, the House conservatives' record on foreign policy at moments of crisis has been reasonably satisfactory.

Their positions and votes on domestic legislation have been another kettle of fish.

The Senate had its Robert Taft, a conservative who learned from observable facts. This led him to become a co-sponsor of the Taft-Ellender-Wagner housing bill. The House was not so fortunate. The bill's future lay in the hands of Representative Jesse Wolcott of Michigan, chairman of the Banking and Currency Committee, and Representative Clarence Brown, also a Republican and conservative anchor man on the Rules Committee. The story is told that Taft called his dear friend and admirer, Brown, a fellow Ohioan, to assist in pushing the housing bill through the House. Brown declined, expressing the view the legislation would lead to nationalization of the housing industry, Socialism, or worse.

Such was the story in the Republican-controlled House during the 1947–1948 years of the Eightieth Congress—blindly consistent conservatives digging the very pit into which Whistle Stop–Give 'Em Hell Harry consigned them on election Tuesday in November 1948. Thomas Dewey, Truman's Republican opponent, was stuck with the record of the Eightieth Congress, particularly in domestic affairs, and Truman won a presidential term of his own. A major housing Act, including the basic urban renewal statute, was passed in 1949; social security coverage was extended, and some benefits increased. Health, civil rights, and farm legislation continued to meet bad fortune.

At the 1952 election, the twenty-year exile of the Republican party from the White House ended. The Republicans also won control of the House.

The sweet taste of partisan pleasure in seeing a President wearing the Republican label turned sour at the proposals of the new Chief Executive—excise-tax extension, federal aid to higher education, and continued foreign aid.

Two years later, the Republicans lost control of the Congress. The orthodox conservatives dolefully continued their basic self-assigned mission to ward off progressive domestic legislation. Their premise still is that the intervention of the federal government should be restricted to the collection of taxes, but not too many, maintenance of the military establishment, and operation of the courts.

Being outvoted in the country, however, did not leave them outvoted in the House. The conservatives of the Midwest, Republicans, and the conservatives of the South, Democrats, successfully continued their nay-saying roles.

Conservative chairmen, possessing unchecked power of appointment for committee staffing, still made all sorts of difficulties about time to hold hearings or arrange for witnesses for liberal legislation. If the hearing was held, the witnesses, in some cases, were selected to create a climate of adverse testimony. If sheer weight of numbers, or a particularly potent presidential appeal managed to dislodge a bill from the legislative committee, then the measure still had to run the gamut of the Rules Committee, that contemporary version of a French Bourbon soirée.

The conservative successes, largely negative, have been significant.

The achievement is remarkable because the Democratic party has held a majority in the House in fifteen of the seventeen Congresses elected since 1930. In sixteen of the seventeen, the majority of Democrats in the House maintained liberal to moderate voting records on domestic and social welfare legislation. But the seniority system and the method of appointing to standing committees, combined with the skill of conservatives and the ineptness of the liberals, have blunted this advantage.

In the Eighty-sixth Congress, for example, the Appropriations Committee was composed of fifty Members—thirty Democrats and twenty Republicans. But in terms of viewpoints of the Members there were thirty-two conservatives and eighteen liberal or moderate Members. This was the line-up on the purse-strings committee, during the most liberal House since 1938. Actually, the outlook of the committee, because of the custom of seniority, had been fixed years earlier. It is said that measures reported from conservative committees can be modified on the House floor to suit the majority views in the House. However, there is a strong habit of supporting committee recommendations that grows out of inertia, respect for the specialist, and fear of reprisal.

In 1964, an example was the deadlock on the King-Anderson hospital-benefits bill held in bondage by the Ways and Means Committee. It would provide hospital and nursing-home benefits for millions of Americans sixty-five years of age or more, to be financed by a slight increase in the social security tax. This is a perfectly sound, conservative method of financing. It is, in effect, a user's tax, as pointed out by Representative Hastings Keith of Massachusetts, an insurance man whose credentials as a traditional Republican conservative are unchallengeable.

A majority of Democrats in the House supported the measure when it was sent to Congress by President Kennedy in the 1961–1962, Eighty-seventh Congress. However, the bill never came to a vote because a majority of the Ways and Means Committee opposed it. The committee consists of fifteen Democrats and ten Republicans. On the basis of party label, this would seem to assure the bill a fair hearing and a pathway to the House floor. However, the seniority system with its conservative bias long ago assured that conservative Democrats outnumbered liberal Democrats, regardless of the liberal majority among the House Democrats. The ten Republicans, conservatives, needed only three of the fifteen Democrats to fashion a committee majority to keep the bill bottled up. The committee chairman, himself a southern Democrat, provided one of the three. The others were also easily rounded up. Again, the majority voice of the majority party was made ineffective.

Chapter 3

The Leaders of the House of Representatives
The Speaker

"Nobody can rule guiltlessly."
—Saint-Just

Americans have an ambivalent attitude toward leadership and power. Our social system is a comparatively open one. There are cliques and claques and caste, but we do not acknowledge class or hereditary powers. The privileges and immunities that pertain to historically evolved positions of authority are not automatically conferred upon the elected political leaders of the United States, as they are, for example, in Great Britain. When a public office attains what seems to us excessive institutional authority, its power is apt to be curtailed, and our titular leaders are not discredited if they are disobeyed from time to time. No writ or inviolable custom defines the limits of their power.

In the case of the Speakership of the House, the position is sanctioned by the Constitution. But the Constitution is silent as to the requirements of eligibility, the manner in which the Speaker shall be chosen, his role, and the limits of his authority.

At first the Speaker was chosen by a ballot of Members; in 1855 it took 136 ballots to elect the Speaker—a reflection of heightened national tensions preceding the Civil War. Now election is by roll call; but actually the caucus of the majority party selects its candidate on the eve of the opening of each new Congress; when the full House gathers to elect the Speaker, the majority party has sufficient votes. There is no clear line of succession to the Speakership; usually the majority leader becomes Speaker, but it has not always been so.

62

The Speakership is the product of American political inventive-ness. It bears no resemblance to the Speaker of the British House of Commons, who was once the king's agent; nor is there any require-ment that he be the spokesman of the executive branch.

From reading early commentaries on the Speaker, it is clear that his position in the United States was never intended to be that of a moderator. From the beginning, Speakers were expected to exer-cise political leadership. The first Speaker, Frederick A. Muhlen-burg of Pennsylvania, in 1795 cast a tie-breaking vote on an ap-propriation to carry out the provisions of the unpopular Jay Treaty; the treaty having already been ratified, the House had to provide funds.

Clay's landmark Speakership, extending over a period of twelve years, from the day he first entered the House as an elected Mem-ber, gave the position a strong institutional cast. He exercised both the judicial and the political functions of his office, and his three roles as Speaker—private Member of the House, titular leader of his party, and presiding officer. Clay stepped the fine line between being political and being partisan. Speakers then had the exclusive power to name Members to standing committees: politically this power is exercised by appointing a majority of committee members from the political party that controls the House. Being partisan is to appoint so many Members of the majority that the minority is swamped. Clay showed good temper and courtesy, was impartial on questions of order, and dealt with legislative business promptly. He used his powers boldly to put forward a legislative program including a system of internal improvements that we would call today a public works program; in foreign affairs, including the rush to war with Great Britain, he overshadowed President Madi-son. Unlike today's Congress, which is a conduit for legislation, the Congress of Clay's time was the originating body. Clay believed that the House is best ruled by the firmest Speaker, disturbing as it was, in the words of one observer, to the "beatific visions of men of largest liberty." He enhanced the prestige of the Speakership; he is said to have passed up a state dinner rather than be seated below the Attorney General.

The Speakership developed to the point where in the late 1840's a Member of the House wrote Horace Greeley that the Speaker "exerts more influence over the destinies of this Nation than any other member of the Government except the President."

A study of the great Speakers prompts the judgment that they all set out with a legislative policy of their own and also kept a firm hand on parliamentary procedures. They were also politically minded. Thomas Reed regarded himself as the Speaker-General of his party, and was a fighter for majority rule, "without which there is no hope of legislation."

He dealt firmly with obstructionism, as in the case of the disappearing quorum, and tolerated no motions or appeals whose purpose was to delay action.

In contrast, in 1949, after southern Democrats had consumed five hours by demanding quorum calls, and a Member suggested it was being done for purposes of delay, Rayburn said, "He [Rayburn] has yet to hold a motion dilatory and will not until it becomes obvious to everybody that dilatory tactics are being conducted."

This is only one small indication of the deterioration of the strength of the Speakership since the revolt against Cannon and the decline of the institutional authority enjoyed by the able Speakers of the nineteenth century. The progressives' action in 1910 against an autocratic Speaker all but abolished the authority of the office that had resulted from its historical development.

In consequence, the authorized apparatus of leadership has become secondary to personal power. This in turn often shapes legislation when it is wielded by the majority leader. As legitimate power becomes inadequate, personal or extralegal power may become excessive; or in some instances not effective enough to work the will of the majority.

Sam Rayburn, who enjoyed being described as the "baldest and levelest head in Washington," served fifty years in the House. For sixteen of these he was Speaker, the longest anyone has ever served in that position.

In November 1961, Sam Rayburn, still Speaker, died in Bonham, Texas. He gave a poignant description of his beloved town to David

L. Cohn in 1942: "When I go home to Bonham and see farmers' cars parked in the courthouse square, while the womenfolk walk around window shopping with their children or talking with their neighbors, I'm glad to see it even if they haven't got a dime in their pockets. Many a time when I was a child and lived 'way out in the country, I'd sit on the fence and wish to God that somebody would drive by in a buggy—just anything to relieve my loneliness. Loneliness consumes people. It kills 'em eventually. God help the Lonely. That's why I'm glad to see farmers have cars and use 'em."

There's a great deal of rural America wrapped up in that comment about an East Texas county-seat town in the black-soil cotton country. Rayburn's loneliness as a child, as it turned out, proved a reservoir of strength to the stubby figure who became one of the most powerful and renowned men in the history of the Congress. From behind his façade of imperturbability and aloofness, Rayburn watched and waited and won some of the great legislative battles of the day. Won some, not all. At the age of seventy-nine, dying, he left Washington to return to Bonham. Yet the House he left behind and revered so highly was then less representative of the American people than it had been when he arrived for his first day in service in March 1913.

A strong man during his tenure as Speaker, Rayburn surely was first among legislators. An avowed partisan, he presided, nevertheless, with fairness, and once was referred to as "the greatest compromiser since the Great Compromiser." During his service in the House he accumulated a capital budget of personal influence that drew interest. As a result he often commanded decisive support in the House on major issues. His power was so personal, so immense that it masked the institutional frailties of the House in general, and the Speakership in particular. Rayburn knew it. Yet he did not attempt to remedy this condition when the opportunity arose.

Rayburn, with all his personal influence, derived in part from innumerable kindnesses, favors, compliments, and courtesies afforded Members, their families, and their constituents, never once moved for fundamental reform of the House and the Speakership. He was ailing in 1961 when an opportunity presented itself to clip the powers of the acquisitive Rules Committee. Even with the incentive of a Democrat in the White House for the first time in eight years, he could not exercise his dominant personality in such a way as to enable the majority party, his party, to carry out its legislative program.

As one whom he had chosen to be a member of his political entourage, I have never really understood this inaction. I know he was thoroughly familiar with the history of the House. He knew that its great Speakers—Clay, Carlisle, Reed, Crisp, Cannon, and Longworth—had exercised not only great personal power but had enhanced the prestige of the Speakership itself. Moreover, Rayburn understood and disapproved of many of the consequences of the existing organization and methods of operation in the House. The 1946 Legislative Reorganization Act, once a hopeful enterprise, was a disappointment to him. The adoption of a pension plan for Members of Congress, a pay raise, and a few peripheral reforms were its only legacy. Although it had reduced the number of standing committees, that gain was vitiated to a large extent by the proliferation of subcommittees within full committees.

A proud and sensitive man, his sporadic outbursts of fury in his private office made it obvious that he did not relish having to submit the Speakership to the arrogant whiphand of such barons as Howard W. Smith of Virginia, the Rules Committee chairman, and Clarence Cannon of Missouri, Appropriations Committee chairman.

Nevertheless, Rayburn resisted use of the Democratic party caucus in the House as an instrument of leadership. My surmise is that this reluctance was based upon his fear that the papered-over splits in the Democratic party in respect to such legislation as civil rights would be further deepened if caucuses were held that inevitably would express the opinions of the party's northern wing.

We have dusted each other off after legislative slugging matches, on and off the floor. My admiration, as friend and student, for this man on the occasions of his bitter as well as his shining hours has overflowed. So it is with chagrin that I set down the observation that the Rayburn who stood on the floor on occasions to tell his colleagues, "I love this House," lived so long within the institution that it tempered his dissatisfactions. He distrusted reform, and counseled freshmen Members to accommodate themselves to the existing situation.

The circumstances of Rayburn's early life were not dissimilar to those of hundreds of other Americans, including present Members of Congress, who by grit, chance, and ability achieved standing in our national life.

Although Tennessee-born, he grew up in the cotton country of Texas. His father was a Civil War veteran, a Confederate. His childhood was marginally adequate in terms of material possessions, but his parents had ambitions for him. He went off to East Texas Normal College with the Rayburn family savings, $25. He taught school, but found it confining. He liked politics and—what does not always follow—he liked politicians. During his last two years of a six-year service in the Texas state legislature he served as the youngest Speaker of the House ever to serve up to that time. In 1913, when Woodrow Wilson, by temperament and training hostile to Congress, left New Jersey to enter the White House as our twenty-eighth President, Sam Rayburn left Texas for Washington to become the representative of the Fifth Texas congressional district in the House.

There is a story that Speaker Champ Clark of Missouri drew aside the new Member from Texas and suggested a reading list that Rayburn followed to the end and beyond. Rayburn was to make only one trip outside the continental United States during his congressional service. He visited Panama. But his imagination led him beyond the confines of his Bonham-Washington pathway, so that he became a strong and vigorous supporter of the foreign-aid program in later years.

In Washington, he usually drank bourbon and branch water. Sometimes, to the puzzlement of Texans, he drank Scotch. He kept convivial male company, but always disdained sex-with-a-snigger jokes. He wore his plain-cut clothes until he needed new ones, and he looked the world in the eye. He had a penchant for homespun homilies in the fashion of Elbert Hubbard. Once when I suggested that for a photograph I sit down while he stood, because I towered over him, his reply was, "Haven't you learned yet that the size of a man has nothing to do with his height?"

He faithfully served his constituents, "the folks," whether it was to get the Army son back to the farm for harvest time, to assist the ailing parents, or to straighten out innumerable social security and veterans' problems.

By 1931 he became chairman of the Committee on Interstate and Foreign Commerce, guardian over the financial well-being of the Texas oil and gas interests.

He zealously protected the $27\frac{1}{2}$ per cent depletion allowance for oil, a major focus of attack by the congressional liberals. The reasons, I would guess, were direct enough. He regarded the oilmen as the explorers who brought in the new wells and the new fields; he knew also that to be consistently re-elected a House Member from Texas he simply had no other course.

Once, over drinks with Rayburn, several Texas friends criticized a newspaper columnist for listing the steps Rayburn had taken to assure that the oil-depletion allowance would not be changed at the current session of Congress. After a few minutes of listening while sipping, he put his glass down and said puckishly: "But that fella is right. I did all those things he said."

Rayburn became majority leader in 1937. Three years later he was elected to the first of eight terms as Speaker. He achieved what he had set out to do when he was elected to the first of twenty-five consecutive terms as a Member of the House. He had carefully cultivated and hoarded his personal popularity with other Members. Small and large favors had been rendered. There was hardly a Member, however strong a political opponent, for whom he had not done a favor—securing a more desirable committee assignment, obtaining a federal project to help in a difficult re-election campaign, an appointment to a board or commission for prestige purposes, or the assignment of extra office space. Rayburn knew that the Speakership had been shorn of much of its substantive power. Therefore he built up, in place of it, a vast backlog of political "IOU's" with compound interest.

He seldom attempted to bind a Member to a position on a major political issue that meant political suicide. In turn, he had scorn for the Members who ran scared on every vote and were, in fact, afraid of their constituents. To such Members he described his toughest campaign, when he opposed the railroad operating brotherhoods after World War I. They wanted the government to continue to operate the railroads. "I won, and later a lot of people told me that that was the thing I'd done which convinced them I was going to try to do what I thought right regardless." Members are not glorified polling devices of the majority opinion of their constituents on each issue. Constituents are to be represented and led, not followed. In this connection, one of his favorite anecdotes was about the Frenchman who took one look at a howling mob that rushed by, and exclaimed: "Those are my people. I must follow them wherever they are going."

As Speaker, Rayburn used his strength sparingly. He subscribed to the belief that oftentimes withheld power is preferable to committed power that may not carry the day.

An example of this occurred during the Eisenhower Administration when the Democrats controlled the House. The Appropriations Committee had made an unusually drastic cut in the foreign-aid bill. Rayburn agreed with the Republican Administration that the cuts were harmful. He made checks of the feeling in the House. The result showed that it would be hopeless to attempt to put back the deleted funds. The effort was made, in spite of his advice. It failed.

On one occasion in 1955 he used his creditor status to support a proposed extension of the Reciprocal Trade Act. On a procedural action a majority vote was cast that seemed to modify the extension drastically and perhaps defeat it. Rayburn took the floor to speak in favor of extension. He held the floor long enough for a few of his lieutenants to carry the message to some of Rayburn's friends and debtors that this was one issue "the Speaker really wants you on." Enough votes were changed, and the extension bill passed.

Tough as a pine knot, he was decisive when the occasion arose. Several months before the Pearl Harbor disaster, legislation came to the House to extend the military draft for one year. Though isolationism and the "American First" group were strong, the House approved the extension by a vote of 203 to 202 on the first tally— perhaps the most notable issue decided by one vote in this century. Speaker Rayburn ordered a recapitulation by the tally clerk to determine the accuracy of the close vote. A Member may not change his recorded roll-call vote during this process. When the recheck showed the vote was accurately recorded, Rayburn with legal but unusual haste announced the tally, thus freezing the vote, immediately pronouncing the standard parliamentary phrase that locks in the result—"without objection a motion to reconsider is laid on the table." At this point Representative H. Carl Andersen of Minnesota questioned whether the parliamentary lock-phrase had been acted upon. Andersen asked a second time. Rayburn banged the gavel: "The chair does not intend to have his word questioned by the gentleman from Minnesota or anybody else." And then, moving on to the next order of business, Rayburn said, "The Gentleman from Kentucky has been recognized."

There were occasions less happy, as when a majority of the Texas delegation voted against him. He had nursed many of them personally and legislatively. He was kind to their wives and children. On one occasion he rounded up sufficient votes from liberal Democrats to save a project for the district of one of the most reactionary Members of the Texas delegation. He was thanked for this, but not by the Texas Members' votes.

Rayburn seldom allowed himself to show resentment, even privately. Similarly, he did not reveal his disappointments to anyone except members of his immediate entourage. He thought it was necessary to pass over any reverses in order to perpetuate the belief that he was a powerful Speaker. A modern Democratic Speaker is something like a feudal king—he is first in the land; he receives elaborate homage and respect; but he is dependent on the powerful lords, usually committee chairmen, who are basically hostile to the objectives of the national Democratic party and the Speaker. Republican Speakers have not been at such a disadvantage: Joseph W. Martin, Jr., of Massachusetts, during his Speakership in 1947–1948 and 1953–1954, shared much more common ground with Republican committee chairmen.

Rayburn was frequently at odds with the committee oligarchs, who rule their own committees with the assured arrogance of absolute monarchs.

With one of them, Clarence Cannon of Missouri, chairman of the

House Appropriations Committee late in the 1950's, he ran a collision course. Cannon was unfriendly to the foreign-assistance program. Representative Vaughan Gary of Virginia, chairman of the subcommittee handling budgets on foreign aid, was critical but not hostile. One day Cannon simply replaced Gary, selecting in his stead Otto Passman of Louisiana, a vociferous opponent of foreign-assistance programs. Rayburn could do nothing about it. All the subsequent reductions in foreign-aid budgets have been due to Cannon's appointment of Passman.

But the principal bane of Rayburn's later years was consistently the Committee on Rules. Its chairman was Representative Howard Smith of Virginia, a deceptively mild-appearing, skilled ultra-conservative known affectionately even by his political opponents as "Judge" Smith.

Smith ran, and still runs, an abattoir for liberal legislation. Once a bill is reported out of a standing legislative committee, such as Education and Labor, it comes before the Rules Committee, which is simply directed to determine how much time should be spent discussing the legislation on the floor and the scope of amendments that may be offered. Instead, it has taken to itself, without permission, the authority to judge the merits and demerits of the legislation itself. The committee was dominated by conservative Republicans and Democrats, even when the House as a whole had a liberal character.

On many occasions Rayburn virtually had to beg Smith to release important bills. Smith relented often enough so that Rayburn never quite reached an irreversible decision to break the power the committee had usurped. But in 1960, with more liberals in the House than it had had in twenty-two years, Smith and his supporting cast overstepped.

After John Kennedy was elected President, he recognized that the Rules Committee would have to be curbed somehow. Rayburn agreed, knowing that the primary burden in this undertaking would fall on him. He rejected the counsels of advisers who suggested that it be done by purging a Democratic Member who had refused to support the Kennedy-Johnson ticket, and eventually chose to try to enlarge the committee with Members who would dilute if not completely dissolve the conservative majority. The bruising battle by which this was accomplished will be recounted in detail in a later chapter. Rayburn won the fight by a narrow margin when the House voted to enlarge the committee in January 1961 from twelve to fifteen Members.

In November 1961, eleven months after the Rules battle, Rayburn was dead. Behind him he left his beloved House lurching on a ponderous, uncertain course.

John W. McCormack, majority leader, became Speaker. McCormack, now seventy-three, represents a generation of Boston Roman Catholic Irish who had fought their way out of the ghettos assigned them by the Boston Brahmins into the precincts of political power—first in Boston and subsequently in Massachusetts. With McCormack came the Curleys and Hurleys and Devers and Buckleys and Frankie Kellys, singing the ribald South Boston folk song, "Southie Is My Home-town."

McCormack himself is far from ribald. Childless, he and his wife, Harriet, live quietly at the Washington Hotel downtown when Congress is in session. Their devoted relationship has become a minor legend. It is said that they have never had dinner apart. He is as devoted to his brand of politics, developed in the fiery caldron of the Massachusetts General Court, as is his wife in the practice of her religious faith and good works. For years, McCormack's only recreation seemed to have been a weekly game of poker for stakes that were not low. Many of those who sat in believe him to have always been the best player. In recent years even that weekly diversion seems to have lost its interest for him.

Much has been ascribed to his devoutness. Beyond matters of faith and morals, however, his Church does not call the tune for him. As he is a Roman Catholic, so are many of his constituents. Therefore, on the matter of federal financial assistance to parochial schools, these constituents and he are of one mind, just as Rayburn reflected the possessive attitude of Texas oilmen toward the oil-depletion allowance.

With justification, he resents the contentions that he is dominated by the Roman Catholic hierarchy. One House wit has dubbed him the Archbishop—"Archie," for short. This has made life no easier for McCormack—or for the wit.

McCormack came to the House in the fall of 1928. He became a protégé of Rayburn and another Texan, John Nance Garner. Like Rayburn, he set out to accumulate credit status among his colleagues. One practice in the House is to assign Members with little service to sit in the Speaker's chair during the humdrum drone of discussion on minor matters. When this was McCormack's assignment, he would permit a Member, allocated five minutes, to speak not five but upward of ten or fifteen minutes. He was liked for this.

McCormack and Rayburn worked out a relationship within a few years. In 1936 Speaker Joseph W. Byrnes of Tennessee died, and Representative William B. Bankhead of Alabama became Speaker. A contest developed between Rayburn and Representative John O'Connor of New York for the position of majority leader. McCormack and O'Connor shared a common religious faith, racial descent, and urban background. But O'Connor, Rules Committee chairman, had become increasingly an opponent of President Roosevelt and the New Deal, which led to his defeat. McCormack backed Rayburn, and produced about ten votes in the New England delegation to help put Rayburn across. In September 1940, Rayburn became Speaker upon the death of William Bankhead of Alabama; McCormack succeeded him as majority leader.

In this position, McCormack developed a conspicuous style. He clearly considered his role as primarily that of a partisan leader. A quick mind combined with oratorical and debating ability sharpened his long political needle. In the heat of battle, he was often brusque and impatient, and went for the political jugular vein. On occasions when Democrats needed Republican votes to win, McCormack would pour forth a fire-branch speech that would drive potential Republican defectors back into the hands of their party whips. He showed signs of legislative myopia, but a single-minded industriousness compensated in many ways.

Between McCormack and Rayburn there was a marked contrast, temperamentally and physically: Rayburn—small, stocky, and controlled; McCormack—tall, thin, volatile and, unlike Rayburn, anxious to take immediate partisan advantage of legislative situations. However, they usually worked in harmony. McCormack tended increasingly to defer to Rayburn's judgment, but Rayburn was unstinting in his praise for McCormack's skill in respect to a matter always foremost in his mind—the potential irremediable split in the Democratic party. As the northern and southern wings of the party fought over civil rights, McCormack, as chairman of the platform committee at the Democratic National Convention, engineered compromises in 1944, 1952, and 1956 that prevented wide-open splits. It is significant that in 1948, when he was not in the position to shape a compromise, southern delegates bolted and supported a Dixiecrat ticket headed by Senator Strom Thurmond of South Carolina.

McCormack developed lines into the camp of the southern Democrats on the grounds that one worked with what one had. On this score, he and the "voodoo" liberals had a falling out. When Rayburn died, he was first in the line of succession. McCormack was unopposed in the Democratic caucus for Speaker. Elected to succeed him as majority leader was Carl Albert of Oklahoma, then the majority whip. In protest against the new leadership ticket, I had announced my candidacy against Albert. Sufficient votes did not materialize, however, and I withdrew. Despite my position, McCormack insisted I continue to work with him as Speaker just as I had with Rayburn.

Even though differences had arisen between Kennedy and McCormack, due in part to Kennedy's refusal, when a Member of the House, to sign a petition requesting President Truman to grant an executive pardon for James Michael Curley, Massachusetts' "Purple Shamrock," mayor of Boston four times and governor once, convicted of fraud, McCormack wholeheartedly, rumors to the contrary, tried to push President Kennedy's program through the House.

McCormack was unsuccessful in his relations with Cannon, the Appropriations Committee chairman. He was, for example, unable to prevent Cannon from causing months of unnecessary delay in the passage of major appropriations bills. Cannon simply refused to meet with his counterpart in the Senate, Carl Hayden of Arizona, unless Hayden met with him on the House side of the Capitol building. Cannon took this position on the grounds that under the Constitution the House was the originating body for revenue-raising measures. Hayden wanted to abide by the past practice of alternating meetings on the House and Senate sides. After weeks, the two men finally met—in the middle of the Capitol Building.

On October 13, 1962, the last day of the Eighty-seventh Congress, Cannon rose on the floor and excoriated McCormack and Albert and the Democratic whip, Representative Hale Boggs of Louisiana. In fairness, Cannon was evenhanded in his attitude toward the leaders of his party. Democrat Cannon even refused to meet with Democrat Kennedy, the President, to discuss the foreign-assistance bill.

Rayburn often said, "It doesn't make any difference how smart a man is, unless he has judgment." And a most revealing illustration of the present Speaker's judgment came when the Eighty-eighth Congress convened in January 1963. Unlike the Senate, at the opening of each Congress the House adopts anew its rules and procedures, sometimes with major changes, sometimes not.

Consequently the 1963 battle that enlarged the Rules Committee to fifteen members had to be fought. The voting alignment in the new House was somewhat similar to what it had been in January 1961 when the House first approved the enlargement of the committee. There were indications that the margin this time would be larger than the five votes that had previously carried the measure. Nevertheless the Speaker set out to make bargains that he did not have to make to assure the second victory, eventually won by a 39-vote margin, 235 to 196.

An analysis of the vote showed a significant shift within the Georgia delegation. In 1961, only two of the ten Georgians had voted for enlargement. In 1963, all ten did so. It lent credibility to the belief that McCormack had a "deal" with the dean of the Georgia delegation, Carl Vinson. In return for its support of Rules Committee enlargement, McCormack and, presumably, the other Democratic leaders would support Representative Phil Landrum of Georgia for one of two Democratic vacancies on the Committee on Ways and Means, which not only writes tax legislation but whose Democratic members serve as a Committee on Committees choosing Democratic members to sit on the other committees.

Indeed, soon after the successful vote to enlarge the Rules Committee, McCormack passed the word that Landrum was the candidate of the leadership for one of the seats on Ways and Means. Opposing Landrum, conservative co-author of the antilabor Landrum-Griffin bill, was Representative Pat Jennings of Virginia, who was something of a liberal. Jennings was elected in place of Landrum at the House Democratic caucus on January 14, 1963, by a vote of 161 to 126.

This vote showed that some members of the Georgia delegation could vote either way on the Rules Committee question without being hurt politically in their districts. A knowledge of the political inclinations of those who voted in the caucus showed that the vote was not based on issues. Otherwise, Jennings's margin would have been larger, corresponding with the liberal-conservative line-up in the House. It was smaller because the leadership prevailed upon some Democrats to vote for the more conservative Landrum as part of the "deal." But the deal did not carry.

Now, an institutionally strong Speakership would have precluded the legislative and political timidity that motivated the quest for the ill-fated "deal." Moreover, able House leadership possesses that extrasensory perception as to when to strike a political bargain and when to bring a bill to the floor or to withhold it because a hostile political wind is blowing. If the Speaker had correctly gauged the temper of the House, he would have known that it was unnecessary to strike any bargains.

Vinson himself had gone along with the Kennedy Administration during the first session of the Eighty-seventh Congress, probably as a result of Kennedy's having solicited his support early in the session.

Today the Speakership as an institution has atrophied. The personal influence the Speaker may wield by means of bartering favors does not compensate for adequate legitimate authority.

Since the deposing of Joseph Cannon, the Speaker has lost many of his major prerogatives. Until that time, he appointed all standing committees, selected their chairmen and the members of the Rules Committee; and from the late 1850's until 1910 served as chairman of Rules. Until the eve of the insurrection against Speaker Cannon, a Member had to obtain advance permission from the Speaker in order to be recognized on the floor. Thus his leadership, however autocratic it may seem, was at least visible and accountable.

Today a Committee on Committees appoints all committee members. The Speaker has no control over the several calendars by which bills of certain categories may be called up for action on the floor. The chairmen of Appropriations and Ways and Means need only to rise to move the consideration of their bills before the House. Committee members in charge of other types of legislation control the time allocated for debate on them.

The Speaker retains, aside from his prestige as Speaker and as titular head of his party in the House, two helpful powers. Although not a member of Rules, it is still his prerogative to have a major say in naming members of the Rules Committee.

The Speaker, of course, can delay announcement on a close vote going against him so as to give his lieutenants time to flush out absentee Members or to persuade Members to change their vote. One such delaying technique is to have a number of Members request the tally clerk, "How am I recorded?" even though they know how they voted.

The Speaker still appoints Members to select special committees that are usually established for investigations into particular problems, such as improprieties in the operation of certain government programs.

Stripping the Speakership of powers has not, as was intended, rescued the House from autocratic control. It has merely scattered the powers among the committee chairmen, none of whom are responsible for the over-all effectiveness of the House.

Today the fullest power lies in the personal influence of the occupant of the Speakership. It is relied upon for more than a legitimate share of authority. To maintain personal influence, the Speaker is forced to engage in a savage political scramble involving sectional interests, local claims, and personal advancements, all of which are more fondly regarded by the inner circle of the House than party loyalties or vital national issues.

All too often, wise and just legislation becomes a subordinate issue and frequently a total casualty. Consequently the House is not a training ground and a field of action for legislators, but a lobby for arrogant brokers of special privileges.

Chapter 4

The Leaders of the House of Representatives
The Committee Chairmen

"The worst cliques are those that consist of one man."
—GEORGE BERNARD SHAW

Howard Worth Smith is the leader of the archconservatives on the Rules Committee. By virtue of his position he directs the conservative fugue in the House chamber. On days when major legislation is being discussed on the floor, Smith can be seen sitting on a rear bench among a few like-minded conservatives and lieutenants who listen deferentially as he dispenses judgments from his storehouse of political wisdom.

His real power is wielded in the Rules Committee, of which he is chairman, on meeting mornings beginning at ten-thirty, except when the able Virginia gentleman refrains from calling a meeting in order to delay consideration of any legislation that strikes him as being liberal or ill suited to his desired world.

His stature as a bulwark of conservatism has perhaps received no greater homage than the deference paid him by a better-known entrenched conservative, Harry Flood Byrd, senior Senator from Virginia.

"I never ask Howard to come to my office," Byrd has said. "I always go to his." In view of the snobbery of the Senate toward the House and the fact that Byrd is also eighty-one, this is the ultimate compliment.

Smith has led the bipartisan conservative alignment that has generally always been able to command a clear majority since about 1937. Until that date the Rules Committee had operated more as a legislative "traffic cop" on behalf of the leaders of the majority party.

When Smith's position in committee is occasionally imperiled, he resorts to various devices to preserve it. He will let a backlog of needed domestic legislation he opposes accumulate. Then he will let supporters of the accumulated bills know directly or indirectly that they are going to have to choose two or three preferred bills from the backlog for clearance to the floor. Supporters also sense that Judge Smith would be pleased if the bills selected were those that would least damage his nineteenth century world. If the support for a major liberal bill is so great that Rules can't quite manage to keep it in the committee pigeonhole, Smith forces modification of it. Its desperate supporters are then grateful. They may win a skirmish and occasionally a battle, but the tide of the legislative war generally continues in favor of Smith and his doughty coalition. Stonewall Jackson would be pleased.

Leaders of the bipartisan conservative alignment, whose most visible Republican Member is Representative Charles A. Halleck of Indiana, minority leader, deny that any coalition exists. There is nothing as tangible or dramatic as a Halleck-Smith pact. There is nothing conspiratorial about it, as the "voodoo" liberals would make out. It simply is an understandable consequence of convictions common among southern Democrats and certain Republicans, mostly from the Midwest, in respect to domestic legislation involving civil rights, welfare, labor, education, and fiscal affairs. There is increasing evidence of disaffection among Southerners on foreign aid, which brings the coalition into play in foreign affairs. When a majority of each group votes together on an issue, win or lose, the coalition is in operation. Its basic assumption is that the most desirable state of affairs is the narrowest possible scope for action by the federal government in any matter, except defense and certain domestic subsidy programs for farmers, business, and industry.

At the outset of the Eighty-eighth Congress, there were 105 southern Democrats and 176 Republicans, making possible a total of 281 coalition members—a majority of the House with 63 votes to spare. In January 1963, when twelve more southern Democrats had voted for a Rules Committee of fifteen members than had voted for it in 1961, newspapers carried stories that the coalition was weakening. This was not actually the case. The extra southern votes probably stemmed from the fact that the Kennedy Administration had cultivated a pivotal figure, Carl Vinson of Georgia, perhaps offering a quid pro quo.

In June 1963, the coalition pushed across an amendment to the 1949 Reorganization Act, prohibiting the President from creating any new executive-branch department by powers granted him under the Act. Eisenhower had created the Department of Health, Education, and Welfare by these powers. The coalition's amendment, sponsored by Clarence J. Brown, Ohio Republican, was aimed at preventing establishment of a Department of Urban Affairs. Republicans in the coalition envisioned such a department as enlargement of the federal bureaucracy. Southerners supported the limitation because, when the Kennedy Administration first broached the proposal in 1962, the President said he would appoint Housing and Home Finance Agency Administrator Robert C. Weaver, a Negro, as Secretary of the Department.

In 1963 the coalition within the Rules Committee was also successfully blocking the urban mass transportation bill and the youth employment bill.

Judge Smith leads the coalition because, Rayburn excepted, he has been the ablest legislator in the House.

A lean and stooped figure with a long and mournful face, Smith considers himself a political descendant of Thomas Jefferson—the philosopher Jefferson who said that the government is best that governs least. Rayburn, too, regarded himself as a descendant of Jefferson—but of the "other" Jefferson, who, upon becoming the third President, was persuaded by the exigencies of affairs to a forceful exercise of presidential power, as in the case of the Louisiana Territory Purchase.

Smith, living as the squire of the Jeffersonian manor, exercises a sense of *noblesse oblige*. He meets every private and public responsibility, as he defines them, with paternal kindness, but he frowns on collective action by those who prefer fraternity to paternity. He opposes self-sufficiency as implied in the formation of trade unions. He opposes federal action on domestic problems involving the underprivileged. He holds to the view that if men were left to their own devices, the world would be a better-ordered place. He and his like-minded colleague, Senator Harry Byrd, hold their own state, Virginia, in thralldom to this blinkered viewpoint. Unlike Tammany Hall, upon which the rural moralists center their fire, Byrd's Commonwealth is seldom criticized. The Byrd organization has escaped general censure for encouraging, if not insisting, that a Virginia county, Prince Edward, shut down its public school system, depriving more than one thousand Negroes of schooling for five years, rather than operate it on a desegregated basis in keeping with the Supreme Court decision in May 1954.

In keeping with this view, Smith has introduced in Congress after Congress a bill he has managed to have assigned the same number—H.R. 3. The press gallery refers to it as the bill to repeal the federal government. The measure stipulates that state laws shall have precedence over federal laws in each subject area, unless Congress specifically says otherwise, or when federal and state law can not consistently stand together.

Smith became chairman of Rules in 1955. Until 1961, when the twelve-member committee was enlarged by three to dilute somewhat its conservative cast, Smith's hands, instead of Rayburn's, were at the legislative controls. Smith's sidemen in this masterful performance are William M. Colmer, Democrat of Mississippi, whose political position is perhaps slightly to the left of Ivan the Terrible, and Clarence Brown, able Taft-type Republican of Ohio.

Smith, Colmer, and Brown, whose ages total 223 years, affect a folksy, bland manner with legislators who come as supplicants before the committee to ask that a bill be granted the rule to bring it to the House floor. The hungrier the supplicant, the more the three men toy with him in the small rectangular-shaped committee room with its nineteenth century décor and stopped clocks.

If it is an education bill, Brown will wonder aloud whether the "Treasury will go broke" during the life of the program. If he is in particularly reminiscent mood, Brown might recall the American myth—part Lincoln, part Horatio Alger—of the boy walking miles through the snow to the one-room schoolhouse in search of an education. And Brown will wonder why all those fancy school buildings with "all those auditoriums and things are being built." A tough, shrewd, and able Republican wheelhorse, Brown sometimes shows a sharp tongue when the nostalgia for the days of *McGuffey's Reader* becomes acute. A Roosevelt landslide cost him the Ohio governorship in the 1930's; Halleck defeated him for the majority leadership in 1946; and his beloved Robert Taft was bested by Ike in 1952.

If a woman Member of Congress is seated in the witness chair at one end of the long, narrow table, then Smith, Colmer, and Brown will utter a long series of compliments on the birth, breeding, and ability of "the distinguished gentlewoman." Once, Representative Edith Green of Oregon, when she could stand it no longer, good-humoredly broke in to remark, "Ah, the novocaine before the needle, gentlemen."

With Representative Adam Clayton Powell of New York, a Negro and chairman of the Education and Labor Committee, the Southerners on the committee will be just as folksy. But somewhere a reference will be dropped to Powell's much-publicized travels while Congress is in session. Once Brown said he was pleased to see Powell, as "we don't get a chance very often to ask you questions."

Behind the misleading pleasantries and bland words, however, there is iron control. Most bills must be run through the Rules Committee before going to the floor for a vote. The Rules Committee has jurisdiction of the order of business in the House. It has the power to prescribe the length and manner of debate on a bill. This is called giving a bill a "rule." The committee, likewise, has power not to give a rule and thereby prevent the measure from going to the floor where the full membership of the House can discuss and amend and ultimately vote whether to pass, alter, or kill the measure.

The conservatives ruled the roost even when New Dealer Adolph Sabath of Illinois was chairman. On one occasion Sabath was trying to make himself heard at a meeting of his own committee. Finally, Leo Allen of Illinois, who was later chairman during the 1953–1954 Republican-controlled Congress, said grandly: "Adolph has a right to be heard. Let him speak for two or three minutes."

When the committee consisted of twelve members, Smith controlled at least six votes. Under House rules, a tie vote meant defeat of any motion to give a bill a rule.

On occasions Smith acknowledges criticism of the committee's power. He simply but speciously argues that if a majority of House Members really want a particular bill brought to the floor, all they have to do is to obtain 218 signatures of Members—half plus one of the total Membership of the House—on a discharge petition. Such an endeavor, hemmed in by restrictive procedures and congressional attitudes, is seldom successful in discharging Rules from custody of a bill.

On "Meet the Press," a network television Sunday program, in January 1964, Smith was asked:

"Judge, it appears that the role of the Rules Committee has changed, evolved over the years. It used to be concerned with an orderly flow of bills, and now it seems to judge bills on their merits. Why has this change come about?"

The Judge replied in this way:

"It would take a little long answer for that, but remember there are about 15,000 bills that are introduced in the House every Congress. The weeding process begins with the legislative committees, and they weed out, and then the Rules Committee weeds out, and after we get through weeding out sometimes the Speaker weeds out and won't call up a bill that we have introduced. So there is a lot of weeding out that is done, and I think that the Rules Committee only does a fair share of it. When the chips are down, we refuse rules on very, very few bills."

In fairness, it should be said that the Rules Committee and some powerful Members do have a cozy arrangement. Sometimes bills are favorably reported from their legislative committees. They may be improper bills, such as general veterans' pension legislation, for which there is pressure that the legislative committee is unable or unwilling to resist. Or the bills may be legitimate ones on which the chairman of the legislative committee was outvoted. The opponents of such bills ask Rules to sidetrack them. The Member then can tell the veterans' posts in his district or state that he favors the pension bill, but that awful Rules Committee won't let it come to the floor.

When pressure to move a blocked bill becomes irresistible, Smith will adjust. This occurred in mid-December 1963, with a comprehensive civil rights bill that Smith was sitting on. Faced with tremendous pressure generated by some of his own committee members and a discharge petition with about 160 signatures, Smith agreed to hold hearings on the bill. On December 19 the *Washington Post* quoted him as saying, "I know something about the facts of life around here."

When progressive legislation, such as civil rights, is propelled to the floor by brute force, Smith deploys his troops in the large arena of the House chamber. With conservative control of Rules somewhat diminished since the 1961 enlargement, Smith carries on his campaigns today mostly from the floor. Halleck, as Republican leader, contributes the larger number of votes as well as the fiery histrionics. Smith acts as legislative analyst and strategist. If a bill does pass, and the Senate passes a different version, then under existing general rules of the House the committee can manage to prevent the bill from going to a conference of selected House and Senate Members where a compromise could be worked out.

Smith is not a tricky or devious opponent. He keeps clear of the twilight zone between fair and foul. To my knowledge his maneuvers could be said to have barely approached this murky area on only two occasions. Both involved civil rights legislation that has caused him not only to lose his customary impeccable control and impassive demeanor but has also plunged him into an uncharacteristic gambling mood.

However, Smith has been known to take legislative French leave to stall action on a bill distasteful to him. In the summer of 1957, for example, he left Washington, and the committee had no effective power to call itself into meeting. Members were led to understand that Smith was back on his Virginia farm where he was inspecting a "burned barn."

"I knew Howard Smith would do most anything to block a civil rights bill, but I never suspected he would resort to arson," Rayburn remarked.

Nevertheless, not all powerful House Members fight so consistently on fair territory as does Smith.

On one occasion when I was a new Member I notified the chairman of an important committee, according to courtesy and custom, that I planned to offer an amendment to a bill he was sponsoring. The bill came to the floor. Just as the reading clerk was to start on the particular section of the bill that I was to try to amend, I suddenly found myself surrounded by noisy committee members who distracted me and permitted the reading clerk to get through the section before I could be recognized by the chair to offer the amendment.

On another occasion, a three-member subcommittee, consisting of a Virginia Democrat, myself, and one Republican, worked out compromise language on a difficult provision of a bill. We shook hands all around, so to speak, agreeing to support our revised version, which actually was more to the Democrats' liking. My Democratic colleague on the subcommittee was elated, but I had suffered enough lumps and disappointments by now to be wary. Finally, I sensed what would happen, and told my colleague in advance. He did not believe me. When the bill came to the floor, the Republican on the subcommittee honored his commitment; but, as I feared, another Republican offered an amendment that gutted the compromise provision.

These are not Smith's ways. His pledge means not only that he will abide by it but that his colleagues will also.

I have seen Smith caught off guard only once. It occurred during an amending stage of one of those perennially unsuccessful federal-aid-to-public-schools bills.

During the Eisenhower Administration the Democratic-controlled Education and Labor Committee brought out a bill that did not conform to the recommendations of the President. The Republicans in floor debate supported their President's viewpoint. Therefore they said they could not even consider the committee's version of the bill. Once the Republicans had taken this position, Democrats managing the bill staged a prearranged retreat. They announced they would accept the President's version down to the last semi-colon. This embarrassed Republicans who, privately opposed to any such education bill, hitherto had felt safe in giving it verbal support.

Smith and Halleck got the point of this Democratic maneuver. They hastily conferred on the floor—in the open. Moments later, Smith offered a privileged motion that stopped debate. The motion, if adopted, would have struck out all the provisions after the open-ing enacting clause. The motion carried by five votes, thereby killing the bill before the Republicans' embarrassment could be recorded in the form of a roll call on the ungutted bill. Smith had won again. A little later, I passed Smith on the floor. I mentioned that the Democratic maneuver had almost worked. Smith said nothing but made a gesture of wiping his brow.

The South, with its surfeit of one-party congressional districts, has sent other Members like Smith to the House. Not so patient, not quite so able, they nevertheless provide the captains and skirmishers whom Smith commands as he exercises his role as the greatest negative force in Congress.

Another effective conservative regular is Carl Vinson of Georgia, chairman of the Armed Services Committee, who announced he would retire at the end of the 1964 session. During his fifty years of service in the House, longer than that of any other Member, Vinson has acquired several indicative nicknames—"Uncle" Carl to his friendly admirers; "the Admiral," a carry-over from the period when he was chairman of the Naval Affairs Committee; and the "Swamp Fox," a tribute to his triumphs and survival amid the perils of the long knives in the legislative halls and committee rooms. Carl Vinson became chairman of the committee by going the sure route—living long and getting re-elected regularly—since he first won a seat in November 1914. Because of his longevity and that of Richard B. Russell, chairman of the Senate Armed Services Com-mittee, their home state, Georgia, has profited. If the state had one more military installation, it would sink.

Vinson must have looked over his shoulder at least once. When he did he saw behind him as Number Two ranking Democrat, Overton Brooks of Louisiana, whom he apparently regarded as an unacceptable successor. When the Committee on Science and Astronautics was established in 1958, Brooks was assigned to it and became chairman.

"The Admiral" runs a tight ship. A senior admiral or general has found himself put down when appearing before Vinson and his thirty-seven fellow committee members. The senior officer would hear himself addressed by Vinson as "Boy, what did you say your name was?" Junior committee members fare no better; they are treated as children who should be seen but not heard.

In the spring of 1964, President Johnson told a press conference:

"Carl Vinson one time, after I served on a committee about eight years, was presiding and I asked a question about the Corpus Christi Navy Base. He said 'Admiral, we must go on and get other matters taken care of.' I said, 'It looks like after a man has been serving on this committee for eight years he would be entitled to one question.' And he [Vinson] said, 'All right, but just one.'"

Under Vinson's chairmanship, Armed Services manages to report out unanimously an amazing number of bills on controversial matters—unification of the armed services and the RS-70 airplane program, among others. There have been recent exceptions, as in the matter of four Republican dissents to the 1963 civil defense fallout shelter program. And on the floor in 1962, Vinson lost a fight to Representative George Mahon of Texas over a disputed provision in the fiscal 1963 Defense Department appropriation bill. Senior members found this more interesting than the bill itself. Vinson, as a skillful and powerful chairman for thirty-three years, has vast influence within the Defense Department. He tends to support one of the armed services, Army, Navy, or Air Force, in any disputes it may have with its parent, the Defense Department. Shortly after the Department was established during the Truman Administration, it was suggested that Vinson would make an outstanding Defense Secretary. "Shucks," Vinson was quoted as commenting, "I'd rather run the Pentagon from up here." By "up here" is meant Vinson's third-floor Capitol Hill office in the Cannon House Office Building which a four-star general or a Secretary of the Army, brief case in hand, can be seen entering as early as seven-fifteen or seven-thirty in the morning during budget-hearing weeks in the early spring.

Vinson does not hesitate to lay a barrage on a President. In 1958 President Eisenhower, who had some familiarity with military matters, recommended a reorganization of the Defense Department. Vinson didn't like it. "I do not profess to be a military leader, I do not profess to know the technical aspects of strategy and tactics, but I do know," Vinson said on the House floor in April, "that as one Member of the House of Representatives I shall fulfill the obligation imposed upon me by the Constitution of the United States with reference to our national security. . . . Space ships, satellites and guided missiles cannot abrogate the Constitution of the United States. Scientific advances and technological progress may frighten some people into unwise and hastily considered decisions, but I do not believe they will stampede the House of Representatives. . . . The actual result of the President's proposal is a supreme Prussian-type general staff." And that ended that.

Such instances as this, combined with tactics of baiting witnesses, have created the myth that Vinson terrorizes the Defense Department. The truth may be somewhat less than that. It is conceivable that many a military and civilian official of an Executive department pays lip service to the myth and the man behind it as a sort of ceremonial rite, tolerating the boorishness and slights and at the same time picking the chairman's pocket.

Vinson's critics contend that he never lets national interest interfere with his power and prestige. They claim the committee should more properly be called the Military Installations Committee or the Committee on Military Real Estate on grounds that much of its effort is spent parceling our military installations, large and small to districts of deserving Members.

Vinson's remarkable staying power has meant that his viewpoint cannot be discounted if he shows interest in any piece of legislation, no matter what its character.

Although considered a southern moderate, Vinson voted increasingly with the conservative coalition in the Eisenhower years. At one point Rayburn said, in exasperation, "That old fool. You can't get him to vote for anything any more." An analysis of his votes cast on major legislation when Rayburn was Speaker shows that if Vinson actively supported Rayburn's position, the measure would carry. If he was opposed, the result was uncertain.

The lesson was clear, then, when John Kennedy, who had won a narrow victory, sat down late in 1960 to count the strength in the House for his legislative program. The liberals had elected a President but had suffered a net loss of approximately twenty House votes—pro-Kennedy votes on most issues—at the 1960 November election.

Additional supporters were needed. In February 1961, Rayburn forces met with Lawrence F. O'Brien and other members of the White House congressional liaison staff. At the conference I emphasized that Vinson was the key. I do not know the inside story of what ensued. Perhaps only John Kennedy could have told it. However, during the first session of the Eighty-seventh Congress, the "Admiral" was on the Kennedy team. In the majority lobby one day, an old-timer remarked aloud, "My God, Vinson even made a New Frontier speech down home in Georgia."

With Vinson's co-operation, increases in the minimum hourly wage and an extension of these minimums to previously uncovered categories of employees were passed. Of course, the benefits did not apply to the exploited employees of commercial laundries in the South.

Another peer among the seniors until his death at eighty-five in May 1964 was Clarence Cannon of Missouri, who, as Appropriations Committee chairman, brought to his job the air of a man smelling a rotten egg. He was a crusty loner in the House. For that reason, in subtle, tangential ways he did not have the influence of Smith and Vinson.

Cannon fulfilled in a lifetime two vocations, either of which most persons would settle for. Television viewers may remember his pinched, prunelike face as he carried out his role as parliamentarian of the Democratic national conventions. When accused by an opponent of being two-faced, Cannon is supposed to have retorted, "Don't you think if I had two faces I'd use the other one instead of this one?"

Cannon came to Congress early in this century as a clerk to Representative Champ Clark of Missouri. When Clark became Speaker in 1913, Cannon became House Parliamentarian, a little known but influential post he held for about ten years. At each new Congress Members still receive an updated small volume of Cannon's "Precedents." Cannon also wrote the manual of rules for nearly a dozen national conventions of the Democratic party.

However, most of his congressional career was occupied, not with details of parliamentary procedure, but in ruling the Appropriations Committee since he first became chairman in 1941. He served as chairman longer than any predecessor, although his rule was interrupted when the Republicans held a majority in the House in 1947–1948 and 1953–1954.

To this committee must be given nearly all presidential recommendations for the expenditure of funds. In a sense the committee stands as a "little Congress" in itself. A new highway, health, or foreign-aid program is first authorized by the proper legislative committee, such as Public Works, but the program is a paper one until the appropriations committtees of both House and Senate approve the funds to operate the program and, of course, Congress as a whole approves the programed expenditures.

With fifty members, thirty Democrats and twenty Republicans, the committee has been overwhelmingly conservative in outlook, indeed more so than the House itself. The Congress has authorized an extensive program of low-cost public housing. But the committee has approved funds for only a fraction of it. Legislation thus becomes a two-step process—authorization and appropriation. In some subject areas of legislation Members profit by this procedure. A Member can point out to constituent supporters of foreign aid that he voted for a large authorization bill that passed. Then he can point to opponents of foreign aid that he supported the curtailed appropriation recommended by the committee. A Member can play this double game because weeks and sometimes months elapse between passage of authorization measure and passage of the related appropriation measure.

Sometimes it has not been a double game at all, but simply a Member's fear that Cannon and his fellows on the committee would retaliate if the Member voted against the committee recommendation. One form of retaliation is to veto funds for civil works projects in the offending Member's district.

An example of the Appropriation Committee's power can be cited in an episode that occurred in 1962. Representative Michael J. Kirwan of Ohio, a ranking member of Appropriations, wanted $10 million for a pet project, the construction of an aquarium and marine science center in the District of Columbia. Kirwan's interest in it was said to have grown out of his friendship with the late official of the Fish and Wildlife Service. Members of the Oregon delegation opposed the project on the grounds that the money should be used to improve the marginal municipal services of Washington, D.C., the Nation's Capital. Kirwan, also chairman of the Appropriations subcommittee that handles the budget of the Interior Department, angrily denounced the Oregon delegation. When the Interior Department budget was reported out by Kirwan, most of the projects requested for Oregon were missing. It took President Kennedy's personal intervention to have them restored before Congress adjourned in October.

Kirwan is a rough-and-ready self-made legislator, who holds another trump card in his capacity as chairman of the Democratic Congressional Campaign Committee, which supplies campaign funds to Members.

I believe that a study would reveal that the conservative-dominated Appropriations Committee has favored conservative Republicans and Democrats in the House by approving funds for projects in their districts. It has thus been a hidden buttress for the conservative coalition. A study would probably reveal also that the conservative coalition, rural in character, has designed farm subsidies, military construction and federally aided hospital construction to benefit rural areas most.

Cannon's successor is Representative George Herman Mahon of Texas, a youngish-looking sixty-four. Prior to becoming chairman, Mahon headed the subcommittee with jurisdiction over the annual Defense Department budget, which in recent years has reached

$50 billion. Defense expenditures are the largest individual component in the federal budget, and Mahon is, unlike Cannon, favorably inclined toward Robert McNamara, the Secretary of Defense. On social and economic issues, Mahon, quiet, able, and diligent, votes as a conservative.

One noticeable episode underlined the new leadership shortly after Mahon became chairman. It involved the foreign-aid bill, which Representative Otto Passman of Louisiana, as the subcommittee chairman in charge, mangled regularly each year. In 1963 Passman's shrill demagogic attacks had wound the foreign-aid bill into a legislative and parliamentary tangle that was not unsnarled until almost Christmas Day. Speculation that Passman was more a creature of Cannon than a formidable figure in his own right received confirmation during mid-1964. Passman's subcommittee outmaneuvered and outvoted him to report a foreign-aid bill generally conforming to President Johnson's request. Tightfistedness as an end in itself seems to have relaxed in the early months of the Mahon chairmanship.

Mahon, of course, as did his predecessor Cannon, typifies the group of oligarchs whose power is based on the standing committee system and the inviolable rule of seniority.

An exception among the older committee chairmen was Brent Spence of Kentucky of the Banking and Currency Committee, who retired in 1962 at the age of eighty-seven. He possessed high intelligence, deep conviction, and a strong commitment to the public interest. However, these did not suffice to make him a powerful or influential chairman outside his own committee room.

Time after time his committee would report out a bill only to see it drastically altered or completely defeated on the floor. Some of these bills, such as those on public-housing and price-control legislation, might have been dealt with harshly in any event. Spence's lack of success may have been due partly to his concept of a committttee chairman's role: he seemed to believe that his committee should report out the best bill possible. Then if the House cut it down, the public record was there for all to see. But the more successful committee chairmen devise bills that have a reasonable chance of passing.

It has been observed that a Member has not earned the title of legislator until he has had his head bloodied; but, as Rayburn said, "if you get beaten too often you will not be an effective legislator." This was Spence's misfortune. Committee conservatives baited him with open contempt; even fellow committee members who shared his economic views began to snipe at him. I used to be shocked and embarrassed at the way in which certain senior members of the Rules Committee bullied Spence when he appeared to request a rule for one of his bills.

Spence as chairman of the committee had as ranking minority Member Jesse Wolcott of Michigan, the shrewdest of all Republican floor managers. Personally charming, he played the legislative game ruthlessly. He never broke the letter of an agreement, but woe to the Member who did not understand the fine shadings of his words. On economic matters he was to the House economic conservative what Taft was to the Senate. He was a conspicuous example of how a skillful minority Member can shape a committee and its works.

The Committee on Banking and Currency now has as its chairman a Texan, Wright Patman, seventy-one, whose Populist views of financial affairs chill the financial community. He has been a consistent critic of the Federal Reserve System. Recently, on the issue of branch banking he became an ally of the small banks, usually state-chartered, against the banks with large resources, usually federally chartered, and their ally, James J. Saxon, Comptroller of the Currency.

His constant repetition of certain of his unorthodox views on money and banking has lost him influence in the House. This was reflected in the budget cuts applied to his committee by the full House in 1963. It is a case of an able man of incredible industry and many economic insights decreasing in influence as he has risen by length of service to top positions on committees. For many years, Patman and Rayburn were professionally and personally closely aligned. In Rayburn's last years, a certain coolness developed in respect to legislative matters.

Youngest of the committee chairmen is Wilbur D. Mills, fifty-five, of Ways and Means. Arkansas-born, educated at Harvard Law

School, Mills is admired for his vigorous, lucid explanations of complicated bills on the House floor that have brought Members of both parties to their feet in applause. This happened during the major expansion of the President's tariff-setting powers in 1962 and during the tax-reduction bill in September 1963.

Mills as chairman of Ways and Means has twofold power: first, through his committee, which handles tax, trade, and social security legislation; and second, because the Democratic members of the committee, including Mills, constitute the Committee on Committees that makes recommendations on appointments of Democrats to standing committees.

His unquestioned ability and personal charm would logically lead to expectations that Mills might become Speaker. However, the race issue is a ball-and-chain attached even to his nimble political legs, just as it is to other able and skilled southern legislators. No House Member from the old South, excepting southwestern states (including Texas), could survive at home by taking a position on the race issue that would make him acceptable to the northern Democrats. Mills signed the segregationist Southern Manifesto in the 1950's.

The Arkansas delegation, with only four Representatives in the House, includes still another Member who is chairman of a powerful committee, Interstate and Foreign Commerce. Oren Harris at sixty-one presides over a thirty-three-member committee that has wide ranging jurisdiction—hospital construction, air and land transportation. Most importantly, the committee has legislative control over most of the regulatory commissions, such as the Securities and Exchange Commission, Federal Communications Commission, and Federal Power Commission.

This is the committee that Rayburn chaired from 1931 to 1937. Harris maintains the same consistent protective attitude that Rayburn had in respect to the oil and natural-gas industries—an attitude that earned the bitter condemnation of consumer-interest groups.

Interstate and Foreign Commerce is often criticized for reporting favorably a great deal of legislation that helps specific economic interests, but not always the public interest.

The Merchant Marine and Fisheries Committee is criticized on the same grounds. Its chairman is Herbert C. Bonner of North Carolina, a former secretary to a Member from the same state. He knows his subject well, though he indicates a bias toward the views of management. His pleasant temperament is such that he does not attempt to extend his influence beyond the limits of his committee and whatever appearances on the floor are necessary in behalf of committee legislation.

Harold Cooley, also of North Carolina, as chairman of Agriculture, presides over the committee that is perhaps the most bitterly divided in a partisan sense. At one time, the farm bloc presented a united front on the committee. However, in recent years this has broken into two rival groups. On the one hand, there are the cotton, tobacco, peanut, and rice interests represented by the Southerners; and on the other hand, the wheat and corn interests represented by the Republicans, although this is a bit oversimplified. The effective legislative work of the thirty-six-member committee has tended to reflect divergent crop interests, obscuring the national agricultural interests. This results in such ridiculous situations as developed on the floor in 1962 when the chairman accepted amendment after amendment in an effort to secure passage of the Administration's promising supply-management farm bill. At one point a Member offered an amendment to permit the Agriculture Department to have no more employees than there are farmers. The proposed amendment, foolish if offered seriously and disrespectful if offered in jest, was accepted by the chairman. Even so, the farm bill was defeated after as clumsy a display of floor management as has been seen in years.

The thirty-one-member Education and Labor Committee was chaired until recently by a Member from North Carolina who typified the conservative strangle hold on legislative channels.

Graham Barden regarded liberals and their legislation as a Moslem regards pork. He ruled the committee as he pleased, arbitrarily calling committee meetings and adjourning them when he wished. He would summon a dozen Chamber of Commerce witnesses to filibuster a federal aid-to-education bill. He would hector and heckle AFL-CIO witnesses who appeared before him. He treated the second-ranking Democrat on the committee, Adam

Clayton Powell, a Negro, as if he were an "invisible man." He was vocally and straightforwardly against trade unions; he strode backward into the future. However, by 1958, the Democrats so preponderantly controlled the House that the bipartisan conservative grip on the committee was broken, and a majority was assembled that was favorable to federal aid to education and to unorganized and organized labor. It may well be that this is the real reason Barden retired from Congress in 1960.

But the existence of a majority does not guarantee control. Rayburn and others before him said that "a determined majority can work its will." The liberals on the Education and Labor Committee became a determined majority largely because of the efforts of Representatives Lee Metcalf of Montana, now a Senator; Stewart L. Udall of Arizona, now Secretary of the Interior; and Frank Thompson, Jr., of New Jersey, still a committee member, despite a movement to draft him to run for governor. Each of these men, members of the Democratic Study Group, brought special talents, intellect, and energies to recasting the autocratically ruled committee into an issues-oriented, liberal one. It was a rare example of liberal vitality and purpose. Metcalf, formerly a State Supreme Court justice, possesses the first-rate intellect, deeply rooted conviction, and patience that made him the anchor man in the reconversion project. Udall provided a fanatic determination to achieve objectives once he completed his characteristic philosophical speculation on means and ends. Thompson contributed a sophisticated parliamentary skill acquired as assistant minority leader in the New Jersey General Assembly. He has a finely honed sense for anticipating opposition moves and a quick perception as to the direction behind an apparently innocuous opposition maneuver.

Udall hit upon what was to be the *coup de grâce*—the drafting of a set of committee rules, meeting majority approval, that when adopted would constrict the chairman so that his dictatorial scepter could be knocked from his hand. It worked. Barden retired, even though it was to mean the committee would be chaired by Powell.

At fifty-six, Powell, with his charm, good looks, and bravado, resembles a sixteenth century Spanish grandee. He possesses intelligence bordering on brilliance. He also suffers from recurring inability to apply himself consistently to committee work, although his first year as chairman was a fruitful exception. His attention span has been variously estimated as ranging between forty seconds to two minutes.

On Sundays, Powell, an ordained minister, presents himself to his congregation in Harlem at morning service—the most segregated hour in America in our churches—as an eloquent spokesman for his people. Criticisms, such as those directed against his foreign travels, he simply turns against his detractors by accusing them of being "anti-Negro." He points with truth to the deportment of other chairmen, white men, who are just as dictatorial, just as extravagant, and just as highhanded—usually more so.

His political base in the slums of Harlem seems unshaken. A newspaperman tells the anecdote about an opponent of Powell during a campaign several years ago. The opponent, making an unusually hard run at Powell's seat, took up his stand one hot August night at a crowded Harlem street corner. He criticized Powell's personal habits, claiming that Powell slept in air-conditioned splendor in summer, wintered in Puerto Rico, ate at fine, costly restaurants in Manhattan, and owned real estate. He pointed out that Harlem's poor sweltered and froze alternately, fought off rats in their slums, and scraped to keep body and soul together. As he reached the climax of this indictment, a voice from the audience cried out, "Man, does that cat really live!" The opponent's campaign went downhill from that moment.

Apparently the rank-and-file find a gratifying sense of identification and a vicarious pleasure in the leader who lives high off the hog, just as in the case of Jimmie Hoffa, the Teamster union boss.

And Powell's critics among House Democrats are somewhat disarmed because they balk at joining the motley collection of racists and reactionaries who attack him.

The other committee chairman who is a Negro operates differently. William L. Dawson of Illinois, chairman of the thirty-one-member Government Operations since 1949 except for a two-year Republican interlude, is a respected and liked machine politician from the South Side of Chicago. A Republican until the New Deal, Dawson moves quietly, fairly, and with some effectiveness. Early in 1949 when Dawson was in line for the chairmanship, Speaker Rayburn first made certain that Dawson could handle his political affairs in Chicago without slighting committee operations. Dawson gave this assurance, as I was told the story, and became chairman.

Beginning with the summer of 1963, the national spotlight focused on the thirty-five-member Judiciary Committee within which President Kennedy's civil rights legislation was being reshaped. The chairman, Emanuel Celler of New York, is at seventy-six an erudite and learned member of a large, prosperous New York law firm. Despite seniority based upon forty years' service, intellect, and his committee position, Celler often finds himself in the awkward position of a chairman who presides over, but does not command, a majority of his committee.

Celler previously had had difficulty in controlling his committee because of the power and prestige of a Member who ranked second in seniority to Celler among the Democrats. This was Francis "Tad" Walter of Pennsylvania, who died early in 1963. Walter had a three-pronged power base that outranked Celler's. He was chairman of the Judiciary Committee's subcommittee on immigration, which handled hundreds of private bills introduced by Members who wished to resolve the status of aliens residing in their districts and often belonging to politically powerful hyphenated-American ethnic groups. In addition, Walter was chairman of the House Patronage Committee, which allocates hundreds of managerial, custodial, and housekeeping patronage jobs in the Capitol that are allocated to senior Members who may fill them as they will. Third, Walter was chairman of the House Committee on Un-American Activities (HUAC), the most damned and most praised committee in the House.

Many a feebly endowed Member achieves applause from professional patrioteers in the Nation for wild-swinging, unsubstantiated charges against card-carrying members of the liberal establishment. The HUAC produces almost no legislation, and receives excessive funds—a record no other House Committee can match. Walter regarded his assignment, I think, with mixed feelings. Nevertheless he remained loyal to the HUAC in the sense that he could and did vent his displeasure on those few Members who voted against the committee's appropriations. Members were understandably loathe to offend Walter; and his power did not make Celler's task as chairman of Judiciary easier.

The civil rights struggle within the Judiciary Committee indicated that Celler did not have firm control. The committee was particularly incohesive in 1963 because, under the stress of civil strife, including Mississippi murder and Birmingham bombings, it had discarded its customary pattern of maneuver on civil rights legislation. In past years the subcommittee on civil rights within the full committee had reported out strong civil rights measures drafted by urban Democrats knowing well that the Republicans and southern Democrats on the full committee would appreciably modify the bill. But in this momentous year of 1963, the urban Republicans, such as William N. McCulloch of Ohio, John V. Lindsay of New York, and Charles McC. Mathias, Jr., of Maryland, were not playing patsies. Urban Republicans and urban Democrats joined to produce a strong civil rights bill in the fifth month of hearings and discussions. The subcommittee strengthened the Administration's measure to the point where President Kennedy and many strategically placed pro-civil-rights House Members judged that the strengthened measure could not be passed on the floor, even if it managed to escape the ambush the conservative Rules Committee would certainly lay. At one point, Celler and other key House Members found themselves meeting with President Kennedy at the White House. After the meeting, efforts were made to cut back the subcommittee's bill. Cellar and McCulloch, ranking minority Member whose support was vital to passage, managed to assemble a makeshift grouping of Members willing to modify the bill.

A plan was drafted. Representative Roland V. Libonati of Illinois was selected to make the necessary motions to temper the subcommittee bill. Libonati was selected reportedly because he did not need to worry about political repercussions in his machine-run Chicago district. Libonati obliged. However, a subsequent interview of Celler on a television program changed matters. Libonati saw the interview on television, and backed out. Libonati was quoted as explaining:

"So then I'm sitting down, just like you and me are sitting here now, and I'm watching television and who do I see on the television but my chairman (Celler). And he's telling 'em up there in his district that he's for a strong bill, and that he doesn't have anything to do with any motion to cut the bill down. So when I hear that, I says to myself, 'Lib, where are we at here, anyway?' And I think that if they're gonna get some Republican votes anyway, and if the chairman says he doesn't have anything to do with my motion, then certain representations that were made to me is out of the window. So I withdraw my motion."

This was a case in which a committee chairman did not rule.

An influential but seldom seen chairman is seventy-four-year-old Charles A. Buckley of the Bronx, New York, who heads the membership list of the Public Works Committee. This committee authorizes a wide range of legislation from interstate highways to remedies for poverty-ridden Appalachia and a host of Corps of Army Engineers' civil works projects.

Buckley, gruff and publicity-shy, appears more interested in the operation of his Bronx barony than in the detailed operation of the thirty-four member committee he titularly chairs. Much of the work is left by this absentee congressional landlord to John A. Blatnik of Minnesota, fourth-ranking Member, and George H. Fallon of Maryland, second-ranking on the majority side. At least this seems the case judging by the remarks following Buckley's primary defeat, after fifteen congressional terms, in June 1964 by a reform candidate, Jonathan B. Bingham. A veteran press-association reporter at the Capitol observed that he wished "Charlie Buckley had stayed around a few more years, I would have liked to have met him." A couple of members of Buckley's committee insisted they had never met him. And Republican members asserted that the fifty-three-member committee staff included nine persons that they, the members, had never seen in the committee suites. A highly respected Republican, Representative Fred Schwengel of Iowa, was quoted in the *Washington Post* on May 12, 1964, as saying: "It's a bad situation. Buckley has as many [committee staff] people in New York as Republicans have on the whole Committee staff."

The Constitution provides that the President shall make treaties "with the advice and consent of the Senate." This accounts for the prominent position of the Foreign Relations Committee in the Senate. But the thirty-three-member Foreign Affairs Committee of the House has no such exalted sanction. The State Department is not inclined to pay much attention to it. Its chairman has neither the prestige nor the recognition that accrues to the Senate committee. For years, the flamboyant, volatile Representative Sol Bloom of New York, was chairman. His pince-nez provided this brilliant Member with more public attention than his position as chairman. A later chairman, Representative Thomas Gordon of Illinois, was conspicuously conscientious, but a heart ailment caused him to step aside for the present chairman, Dr. Thomas E. Morgan of Pennsylvania, fifty-eight, a physician with a large industrial practice near Pittsburgh. A large, slow-moving man, with no eloquence or surface brilliance in his make-up, Dr. Morgan has shown a capacity for hard work and an understanding of the need for compromise and teamwork in matters of policy that require bipartisan agreement. As a consequence, he has become one of the most effective chairmen of this committee in many years. The position is most difficult to fill, and is a thankless one to boot, because a House Member's term is a two-year one, not six years as in the Senate, and because the congressional district is concerned with immediate benefits from its representatives.

Morgan has succeeded in producing effective foreign-aid legislation in a House that at best is temperamentally unenthusiastic about the program. He has shown skill at making the necessary trims and still protecting the heart of the program. Assisting him in this thankless task were first John Vorys of Ohio and then Walter Judd of Minnesota, both Republicans. Neither of these were the ranking Republicans on the committee. Representative Robert Chipperfield of Illinois outranked them, but for reasons of personal preference and apparent poor health, left the duties, if not the trappings, of leadership to his juniors—surely one of the most unusual situations that has existed in the House.

There are also what can be called special-interest committees. One is the thirty-four-member Interior and Insular Affairs, whose jurisdiction includes Indian affairs, federally owned lands, Puerto

Rico, Guam and Wake Island, reclamation, conservation, resources, and mining. Few House Members, except those whose districts or states have a direct interest in these matters, care to serve on the committee. A few who take objective broad national views, such as conservationist ideologues, may ask for assignment. Other Members, such as those from eastern coal-mining states, apparently consider it their main duty to defeat hydroelectric-power legislation.

Consequently, Representative Wayne N. Aspinall of Colorado, sixty-eight, chairman, and his senior assistants are deprived of the advantage of built-in, automatic majorities for much of their legislation. They must take more care to prepare the legislative pathway for their bills, which in the case of wildlife flyway refuge, wilderness and grazing fee matters, sound somewhat esoteric to many Members reared on asphalt pavements. Aspinall prepares the pathways quietly, patiently, and carefully. In part because he is trusted and respected he is persuasive. A Member may not understand Pacific Northwest regional power preference legislation but he will follow Aspinall because he knows him to be an honorable man.

Usually during the life of each Congress sensible Members will say a good-will prayer for the continued well-being and longevity of Representative Olin E. Teague of Texas, chairman of the twenty-four-member Veterans' Affairs Committee. His position is an even more thankless one than is Dr. Morgan's on Foreign Affairs. Too many Members hold to the myth that the veterans' organizations with their millions of members of record speak with one voice for the twenty million living veterans of our wars. Were it not for the courage of Teague, a wounded, decorated veteran of World War II, many outrageous and selfish raids would be made on the United States Treasury by means of ill-conceived legislation. The Veterans of World War I is a particularly offensive professional veterans' organization in respect to pie-in-the-sky nonservice-connected general pension proposals, which would reward all veterans who served ninety days in the service. Teague, on the other hand, fends off such bills, and works instead in behalf of carefully designed, beneficial bills to improve the financial circumstances of disabled veterans with service-connected disabilities and the widows and orphans of those who died in uniform. "Tiger" Teague has earned his sobriquet in saving Members of the House from irresponsibility due to unfounded fear of retaliation by veterans' groups. Happily, Teague has been honored by the few veterans' groups that have matured.

Representative Tom Murray of Tennessee, seventy, chairman of the twenty-five-member Post Office and Civil Service Committee, is another who fights the battles of others. In this case he is often fighting the battle of Republican and Democratic administrations against the ceaseless, unending lobbying of government employee groups for pay increases. These employees are reasonably well represented through unions, which have given up the right to strike. The postal unions are conspicuously effective. Each pay increase has to be pushed through the Congress. It is most difficult to argue that pay increases and survivor and retirement benefits are not deserved. Adequate salary, commensurate with comparable pay scales in private industry, is in large measure a fulfilled pledge of the Kennedy Administration. Nevertheless, national administrations resist the original demands of employee groups, mainly through the willing co-operation of Murray, a white-haired conservative who fights to keep the increases as low as possible by the widest use of his powers as chairman. In fact, it was generally believed that during the Eisenhower Administration Murray was rewarded for his services by being given the right to name postal personnel in his district—perhaps the only Democrat to have this privilege during this Republican Presidency.

Representative Omar Burleson of Texas, fifty-eight, a dapper, pleasant man, presides over the Committee on House Administration with nervous seriousness. The committee is the internal housekeeping organ of the House. It has attracted attention in recent years because of its duty to exercise financial control over expenditures of committees and their chairmen.

Somehow the Committee on the District of Columbia brings to mind the old saw that a "camel is an animal put together by a committee."

The District of Columbia—Washington, D.C., to the general public—is, as the seat of the federal government, an anomaly itself. Due to the ratification of a constitutional Amendment, the Twenty-fourth, legal residents voted for President and Vice-President for the first time in November, 1964. Since the 1870's, legal residents have not possessed the right of local self-government. It was taken from them by act of Congress ostensibly on the grounds that the city government had accumulated too large an indebtedness as the result of a much-needed, extensive public works program. A more compelling reason was the fear of the Southerners in Congress that the arrival of increasing numbers of Negroes would ultimately mean the Negro would have representation in city affairs. In place of home rule, the Congress authorized a three-member Board of District Commissioners to administer the city: two civilians, appointed by the President; and a commissioned officer of the Army Corps of Engineers, usually a general who would serve as the "public works commissioner." The real locus of authority, however, for the District lies on the Hill. The District of Columbia Committees of both House and Senate inadequately legislate for the city. The Appropriations committees of House and Senate appropriate. Thus the District government is balkanized. The city's affairs are managed in unimaginative, pedestrian fashion. An annual $50 million federal payment, supposedly in lieu of taxes lost because of the vast nontaxable federal holdings, is authorized. In fact, it does not begin to compensate. Indeed, the fully authorized amount is seldom appropriated, the fiscal 1965 appropriation being $37.5 million.

In recent years, the Senate District Committee has been the more enlightened. The House District Committee, politically unprofitable to most of its Members, is a segregationist-minded, southern-dominated committee. Blatant racists remain on it as a tithe to their cause. Judge Smith, as *éminence grise*, keeps a watchful eye on committee affairs. John L. McMillan of South Carolina is titular chairman.

The committee is given to vicious, reactionary outbursts. One example is the staff "investigation" undertaken in the late 1950's to discredit school desegregation in Washington public schools.

Until his resignation in 1962, committee power was wielded to an inordinate degree by its clerk, William N. McLeod, Jr., an alternately genial and wary type whose relations with his fellow

South Carolinian McMillan were not warm. McLeod conducted himself as a one-man board of aldermen. He proved politically agile enough to remain as clerk when the Republicans controlled the House in 1953–1954.

The committee has strong ties to the extremely conservative Board of Trade of Metropolitan Washington, which frequently calls the signals on District legislation. The three District commissioners show a marked passivity during their appearances as witnesses before congressional committees, even at such times in 1962–1963 when Senator Robert Byrd of West Virginia terrorized the Public Welfare Department.

In January 1963, liberals made an unsuccessful attempt to change the complexion of the committee when vacancies occurred. Two Members with eight years' service each, Edith Green of Oregon and Charles C. Diggs, Jr., of Michigan, and a freshman, Carleton R. Sickles of Maryland, offered to serve. Southerners, who know a curve when they see one thrown, astutely let Diggs, a Negro, become a Member, but blocked attempts of the other two. This left the committee balance little changed.

The present mode of governing the District of Columbia is a waste of time for the Congress. Self-government should be returned to Washington residents, with provisions that would protect the very real federal interest.

Over-all, the committee chairmen are not responsible to the Speaker. They are not responsible to the majority of their party's members in the House. Occasionally, they are rebuffed, but generally regroup to command as before. Their power is not coupled with institutional responsibility. From time to time most of them have acted in a way that shows they are more powerful individually than the sum of the parts of the House. Irresponsible power that is not called to account periodically is harmful to representative government.

According to the roster, Members from southern and border states, such as Tennessee, are chairmen of thirteen of the twenty standing committees of the House—Agriculture, Appropriations, Armed Services, Banking and Currency, District of Columbia, House Administration, Interstate and Foreign Commerce, Merchant Marine and Fisheries, Post Office and Civil Service, Rules, Un-American Activities, Veterans' Affairs, and Ways and Means. Moreover, on eleven of these same thirteen committees, southern Members are second-ranking, that is, next-in-line to become chairmen in a Democratically controlled House where seniority prevails. Of the eleven second-ranking Members, three are from Mississippi (District of Columbia, Interstate and Foreign Commerce, and Rules), two are from South Carolina (Armed Services and Veterans' Affairs), one from Alabama (Banking and Currency), one from Louisiana (Post Office and Civil Service) and one from Virginia (Un-American Activities). An analysis of the voting record of the chairmen on key votes, selected by *Congressional Quarterly* in 1961, during the first session of the Eighty-seventh Congress is significant. At that time southern and border-state Members held eleven of the twenty chairmanships during the first year of the Kennedy "New Frontier" Administration. Four of these chairmen were identified as being against President Kennedy's position on eight or more votes; eight of these chairmen held positions against the President five or more times; ten of these chairmen were against the President three or more times. The sectional character of this dissent is underlined because on ten of these dozen votes a majority of all House Democrats voted support of the President's position.

The disproportionate southern membership is also illustrated by the composition of the twenty-five-member Ways and Means Committee. In January 1964, of the fifteen Democratic members, eight were from southern or border states. On another key committee, Rules, five of ten Democrats are from southern states.

Many of these chairmen who stand astride the road that legislation must travel to reach the floor have an outlook that we formed in another era. Smith of Rules and Vinson of Armed Services are eighty-one; Celler of Judiciary is seventy-six; George P. Miller of California, Space and Astronautics, is seventy-three; Murray of Post Office and Civil Service, seventy; Charles A. Buckley of New York, Public Works, seventy-four; Patman of Banking and Currency, seventy-one; Aspinall of Interior is sixty-eight; Cooley, Agriculture, is sixty-seven; Mahon of Appropriations, is sixty-four.

This leaves only three chairmen of major standing committees who were born in this century—Mills, Ways and Means, is fifty-five; Harris of Interstate and Foreign Commerce, sixty-one; and Powell of Education and Labor, fifty-six. Vinson's likely Tory successor, however, L. Mendel Rivers of South Carolina, is fifty-nine.

The ages of the chairmen should not be surprising in view of the present organization of the House. The combination of standing committees and seniority practice favors those who wish to halt or delay legislative action. Once assigned to a committee, a Member with two or three re-elections under his belt can be assured that he will remain on the committee. And the Member, in turn, generally works to obtain a seat on a committee or committees that can affect major economic activities in his state. Such committees are those on Agriculture, Interior and Insular Affairs, and Merchant Marine and Fisheries, each of which has a majority of Members whose districts and states have a special interest in the legislation that comes under their jurisdiction. Of course, states such as Nebraska, Mississippi, or Georgia should have Members seated on the Agriculture Committee. But when the committee is dominated by Members with special interests, they have a disproportionate influence on national farm policy. Members on the Agriculture Committee have "tunnel vision" in respect to broad national agricultural policy. Their sectarianism seems excessive when legislative warfare breaks out among the partisans of three varieties of peanuts—Spanish, Virginia, and runner. The committees, creatures of the House, should be more representative of the Membership of the whole House. This is particularly true today when a committee's proposed legislation is often passed or rejected on the floor with little substantive modification.

Democratic and Republican Members on these committees are equally guilty of serving narrow interests. The seniors on these committees exercise their influence to assure that the new Members coming on the committee are sympathetic to the system, which becomes self-perpetuating. The system allows the special interest to supplant the general interest in any committee where policy is shaped. The consumer has a stake but little voice on special-interest committees that concern themselves exclusively with producing legislation that benefits the grower, the refiner, the distributor, the importer and the exporter.

Another tactic of the oligarchs is noted by Richard F. Fenno, Jr., of the University of Rochester, in his study of the Appropriations Committee: senior committee members force younger members, particularly freshmen, to conform to the standard committee practices. The junior member is quickly made to realize by a chance remark, gesture, or perhaps a Dutch-uncle talk that his rewards will come if he goes along with the seniors, behaves as a "good boy" who accepts the notion that "Poppa" knows best. The obverse implication is that if the junior member is brash enough to advocate views contrary to his seniors', he can expect to be a pariah at political harvest time. The powers of the elders can be fully appreciated when it is realized that able men and women in their thirties and forties and fifties bend to this system.

Thus the skillful seniors attain self-renewing power and influence. They carefully keep disputes among themselves within certain limits.

The mortar that binds the system consists largely of what has been called inelegantly but properly "boodle." Boodle includes the location of a military installation, with a construction payroll followed by a steady payroll of civilian and military employees who live and spend and pay taxes in a Member's district. It also includes a wide variety of public works—dams, rivers, and harbor projects, federal post office and office buildings, conservation and reclamation projects.

The boodle in itself is legitimate and productive. The hitch is in the way it is distributed. There are just not enough federal dollars to finance boodle for each of the 435 House districts simultaneously. So 435 hungry House Members jostle for projects adequate for, say, 200 districts. The conservative ruling elders maintain their power by determining in large measure which House Members will get the larger portions. Generally, the stay-in-line orthodox Member will come away with the fuller plate.

A great multimillion-dollar flood-control dam that affords protection to my congressional district plays a large part in my re-election over the years. My political reputation in my district is associated

more with this project than with many stands I have taken on substantive issues involving life, well-being, and national security in
our time. The same is true of a $32 million federal office building
under construction in Kansas City, which comprises most of my
district. Both these projects are worthy and needed. They went to
my district because I was an "insider," because I was a lieutenant
and confidant of Speaker Rayburn. Because of this special relationship I was also able to vote my convictions on national and international issues. I would have it no other way. But other Members
have fared less fortunately.

Besides the House committee barons, certain unpublicized individuals in the House exercise a special kind of influence that accompanies nonelective anonymous responsibility.

One of these is Lewis Deschler, House Parliamentarian since the
late 1920's.

The title itself conjures up a vision of a dried, parchment-paperlike blinkered figure narrowly looking at the House through the
prism of its general rules.

Deschler is none of these things. He is a large-sized man with
large-sized influence growing out of his encyclopedic knowledge.
He cultivates anonymity. He never speaks to the press for quotation.
There is little written about him. The one article that purported to
describe his functions included the incredible inaccuracy that the
Parliamentarian presides from the Speaker's chair when the House
resolves itself into the "Committee of the Whole," as it does when
the House as a whole discusses measures. Actually, this is just about
the only thing that the Parliamentarian does not do for the Speaker.
His knowledge is like that of a ship's engine-room boss who knows
the capacities of the boilers in all sorts of weather.

Hinds' and Cannon's Precedents of the House, the detailed set of
rules and procedures by which the House, unlike the Senate, operates, fills eleven large volumes. The rules are the Ten Thousand
Commandments of the House—thou shall do this . . . thou shall not
do that. Today's rules are the product of modification, change, and
codification. These rules state the nature of the legislative business
that is in order on specified days; what matters are "privileged,"
that is, have special priority rights; and the duties of everyone from

the Speaker to the Doorkeeper, who has many assignments but does not tend doors.

A detailed knowledge of the rules is a prerequisite of an effective legislative career. Wise Members spend hours studying the small black book that contains "Jefferson's Manual—the Constitution and the Rules." Jefferson, when Vice-President, then as always the student and scholar, compiled a manual that served in effect as the first rules of the House. Once a Member, while commenting to Rayburn that he had broken Henry Clay's record for length of service as Speaker, said, "I guess you know the rules better than any Member." Rayburn said, "One of us knows the rules: that fella that just left—Lew."

Many Members sit in the House for years without being able to tell just why something happened or did not happen on the floor on certain occasions. They should ask Deschler. He would probably know, but he might not tell.

And Lew Deschler does know the rules. He knows the practical application of them better than any group of Members ever have and probably ever will. Deschler, first appointed Parliamentarian at twenty-three by Republican Nicholas Longworth, has made himself the second most influential person in the House, during his service of more than three decades. Only the Speaker, at whose right hand he sits when the House is in session, has more influence. The word is "influential," rather than "powerful," because Members who hold the power are influenced in their exercise of it by Deschler. The influence to a point, of course, is derivative. He has the Speaker's confidence. He knows the Speaker's mind. He can act on this.

When consulted, Deschler can tell the inquiring Member just what can be done under the rules. Then, as always, deferential, he may suggest how a desired purpose can be attained within the rules. Perhaps the timing is discussed, and lurking in the background is perhaps an implication that the purpose of the Member may not really be a very good idea.

This kind of influence is substantial for a non-Member appointed by the Speaker. It is startling to circulate among Members of long service and realize that the great majority do not faintly realize

Deschler's stature as he operates either on the floor or in his small office that is closer to the floor than the Speaker's office.

I once cautiously raised with Rayburn the question of whose purposes Deschler really served. Since Speaker Longworth appointed him, there were grounds to believe his background was both Republican and conservative in attitude toward major issues. I suggested that these inclinations might be activated when Deschler was brought into discussions on major legislative issues. Rayburn, realizing exactly what I meant, said gruffly: "We will not discuss it further. He is loyal to me." For some time afterward I was not sure that Rayburn was correct. I have since decided that he was correct if "He is loyal to me" is translated "Deschler is loyal to the Speaker and the Speaker's decision." Deschler, the anonymous Parliamentarian, is the catalyst that makes the House function, rent as it is by partisanship, faction, personal jealousies, logrolling, rivalries, and hearty dislikes. Each Member in a position of leadership consults him about parliamentary procedure. So, too, does the perceptive Member of whatever rank who wants to have an amendment adopted. Deschler is available. His "open door" policy brings a flow of inquiring Members. Thus he knows more of what has happened, is happening, and will happen than any oligarch and, on occasions, more than the Speaker. He becomes the "Speaker's man," his adviser, his confidant, his sometime companion after hours, a major source of information and, if asked, advice. Thus a long shadow is cast by his formal role of Parliamentary Adviser to the Speaker as presiding officer.

In addition, Deschler has become the chief administrative officer of the House. I am not aware that such is part of the job description of Parliamentarian. But in practice it is Deschler, not the Speaker, who actually decides which bills will go to which committee. This is important if a bill conceivably could be assigned to either of two committees, one of which would probably be inclined to favor the bill while a majority of members or the chairman of the second committee would be unfriendly.

He can arrange, for example, for a bill to have a symbolic or fanciful number—H.R. 1776 for the lend-lease bill or H.R. 1, the first bill introduced in each Congress. It was not accidental that

Representative H. R. Gross of Iowa introduced a bill that was assigned the number H.R. 144, a play on his surname.

The Parliamentarian can find a precedent both for and against a proposed legislative action.

Some liberal Members distrust him, usually because of an encounter during which Deschler was not helpful, because these Members were attempting something of which the Speaker disapproved. In such circumstances, Deschler is faultlessly polite but totally uninformative and about as helpful as a deaf mute. He is amenable to the role of the Speaker's man, because he regards the Speaker as the first man of the House. And so the Parliamentarian acts, too, out of commitment to the House as an institution. He does not approve changes in the House. His immediate reaction to a substantive change in the rules is negative. However, should the Speaker agree to a change, he will dutifully dress the proposal in the necessary parliamentary language to achieve the objective.

Besides Deschler, there are other anonymous persons of influence —the staffs of each Member of House and Senate and the squads of specialists who form the staffs of many committees. In the House, the Number One position in the office of each Member is usually the "secretary." In the Senate the titular head of each Member's staff carries the title of "administrative assistant." In the Senate the abilities of the top staff member are generally superior to those of his counterpart in the House.

In the press galleries, some Senators are known as "staff-directed" Senators; another Senator possesses such independence that his staff, with much embarrassment and chagrin, do not always know his plans or on one specific day whether he will be in Washington or in Chicago to give a speech. In some cases, a Senator's legislative assistant is the staff heavyweight.

In the House, the quality of Members' top staff personnel is uneven. There are some extremely talented and capable "secretaries," upon whom their bosses rely heavily for political and legislative advice. One of them is now President—Lyndon Johnson. Capable secretaries usually move on to the Senate side or move to House or Senate committee staff assignments as did L. J. Andolsek, secretary to John A. Blatnik of Minnesota, later chief clerk of the House

Public Works Committee and now a United States Civil Service Commissioner.

Important constituents, other House Members, and the press soon learn to judge the caliber of secretaries. As one official of an executive branch department put it: "There is no sense in trying to convince Congressman Blank unless you convince his man first." A reporter once asked a certain Member about a bill he had introduced, and was told to check with the staff man, as "he gave it to me to introduce."

However, it is the staffs of committees that more often exercise decisive influence in respect to specific legislative matters. They are invariably anonymous. An exception occurred in the case of the Interstate and Foreign Commerce Committee. Bernard Schwartz had been hired by a subcommittee of the full committee to investigate reports about influence peddling within federal regulator agencies. Schwartz apparently soon came to the conclusions that his findings would be buried, so he leaked them to the press. He was fired, after refusing to resign. It turned out to be one in a trail of episodes, linked by political gunpowder, that led to Bernard Goldfine, a vicuna coat, and the resignation of Sherman Adams, presidential assistant to Eisenhower.

On the Senate side, publicized but unrepresentative committee aids were Roy Cohn and David Schine, the footloose malaperts hired by Senator Joseph McCarthy of Wisconsin to lead degrading terroristic forays against executive-branch liberals—all in the spurious guise of "anti-Communism."

The "wheeler-dealer" atmosphere was sufficiently publicized during 1963 and 1964, as in the episode of Robert G. "Bobby" Baker, Secretary to the Senate Majority, to preclude further discussion here. However, it is my view that Baker himself was somewhat a victim in the sense that he was thought to have wielded more influence than he actually did because the position he occupied was potentially an influential one.

However, in general staff members of the committees are exceedingly capable. They usually remain whether Republicans or Democrats control the House. One reason is that House Members are usually "amateurs" who need to be backstopped by such capable men as Leo H. Irwin, Chief Counsel of Ways and Means, and Colin F. Stam, Chief of Staff of the House-Senate Joint Committee on Internal Revenue Taxation.

Stam and Irwin and others like them suggest legislation, suggest troubled areas of public policy that need study, suggest prospective witnesses who would be helpful at hearings on legislation. They often are the blacksmiths who forge the reports and the bills that House Members vote upon, either in committee or on the floor.

Chapter 5

The Executive, Judicial, and Legislative Branches

"I am not a Whig"
—JOHN F. KENNEDY

The telephone has achieved little in shortening the distance between the White House and the Capitol, the seat of the Congress. That road is still the longest political mile in the world.

Early in 1963, a member of the White House congressional relations staff was quoted in a Washington daily newspaper as having said that the legislative and executive branches of the federal government operated in an "atmosphere of mutual suspect." There is some doubt that the remark, if actually made, was phrased so bluntly. However, there is scant doubt that the statement reflects a common attitude on the part of many senior Members of Congress and policy-makers in the departments and agencies of the executive branch.

The attitude arises, in part, from the nature of two highly competitive institutions and the highly competitive men who man them. In part, too, it stems from the notion, once inculcated in high school civics courses but now happily fading, that the executive, judicial, and legislative branches represent an unbroken separation of powers. In view of the Senate's constitutional right to accept or reject presidentially negotiated treaties and the President's right to veto congressionally passed legislation, any theoretical description of the federal structure would be more valid if the three branches were regarded as parts of a system of shared powers.

The executive and legislative branches, indeed, are constantly taking each other's pulse, whether for hostile or friendly purposes.

The observation of Mr. Dooley that the Supreme Court follows the election returns indicates that at least one component of the federal judiciary shows some interest in the legislative and executive moods.

Since the inauguration of George Washington, the pattern of shared powers has given way in practice to periods in which the legislative branch is sometimes the horse and sometimes the rider in its relations to the executive.

In a previous chapter, it has been shown that Alexander Hamilton was Washington's agent in the Congress and that President Jefferson hand-picked the House Speaker. The House then was cast in the role of the horse. Clay reversed the roles. But in later decades, prominent Members of Congress whose primary loyalty was to the body to which they were elected sensed that for the national legislature "to be anything," it must stand against the President. To follow presidential direction was to be diminished, according to their reasoning. In practice, the consequence of such an attitude was to dissipate rather than to integrate the strength of the federal system.

In modern times Members of Congress have had a truculent attitude toward the executive branch. It has been said of Senator Borah, for example, that he was constitutionally uneasy in support of any President. A close reading of speeches by congressional seniors makes it quite apparent that many do not, indeed, regard the legislative branch as part of the federal government. In their view, each congressional seat is in the nature of a bit of their transplanted home territory from which they conduct legislative and verbal forays against two alien bodies, the executive and judicial, that threaten the domestic peace and tranquillity.

John Sherman, who served as House Member, Senator, and Cabinet official, thought that the executive department should be subordinate to the legislative; the President should obey and enforce the laws, leaving it to the voters to correct any mistakes made by their representatives in Congress.

Sherman Hoar of Massachusetts, both Representative and Senator during his lifetime, noted that "the most eminent senators would have received as a personal affront a private message from the White House expressing a desire that they should adopt any course in the discharge of their legislative duties that they did not approve. If they visited the White House, it was to give, not to receive, 'advice.'" This view from Capitol Hill is complemented by an observation of Woodrow Wilson that "the informing function of Congress would be preferred even to its legislative function." And congressional seniors sigh nostalgically at the words of the Whig Calvin Coolidge in his autobiography: "I have never felt that it is my duty to attempt to coerce Senators or Representatives or to take reprisals."

Only a few years later, under the strain of the depression, the climate had become unrecognizable. When Democrat Franklin Delano Roosevelt was President, a Republican minority floor leader, B. H. Snell of New York, could take his seat among his colleagues without fear after having stood to support a New Deal emergency banking bill. In the course of approval Snell said that "the house is burning down and the President of the United States says this is the way to put out the fire."

Beginning with the New Deal, the dual role of the President—Chief Executive and chief legislator—became more apparent. When he has not fulfilled the latter role, either in domestic or foreign affairs or both, the national government and, therefore, the Nation has suffered. The Constitution itself gives the President the greatest single power over legislation possessed by any one elected official—the right of veto.

Active Presidents, believing government creatively capable of more than simply preventing crime and enforcing contracts, fulfill the permissible legislative functions assigned by the Constitution and by precedent and custom. Since Franklin Roosevelt, Presidents publicly state their positions directly to the Nation, as in the "fireside chats" or the appeal of President Eisenhower in support of the Landrum-Griffin labor legislation. President Kennedy had one eye cocked on the Nation when he sent a stream of messages to Congress in support of a variety of legislation. The establishment of a formal staff of congressional relations men during the Kennedy Administration is further recognition of the President's role as chief legislator.

The leadership of the President in times of crisis must extend to more normal times. His constituency is the whole Nation. He must propose policies and labor for them. As leader of his party he must deal with major issues in order to achieve a record that sets off his party from the opposition. The complex presidential role implies a high degree of interaction with the Congress. He must simultaneously be the Chief Executive, chief legislator, chief lobbyist, chief of his party.

In a caucus of House Democrats held during a notable period of presidential power—the first term of Franklin Delano Roosevelt—a party leader told his fellows: ". . . when the Congressional Record goes to President Roosevelt's desk in the morning, he will look over the rollcall we are about to take and I warn you new Democrats [there were 150] to be careful where your names are found." E. Pendleton Herring of Harvard University, writing in the *American Political Science Review* of the incident, noted that "hisses and groans greeted this admonition but the point struck home."

Activist Presidents are apt to regard Members of Congress, the House in particular, as persons whose habits and attitudes are conditioned by transitory public moods. This, it is reasoned, tends to create an environment in which the House Member makes his decisions in the narrowest possible context—what is pleasing to the most blustery segment of voters in his district. The President has a responsibility to lift his sights beyond the momentary condition.

In fact, Congress itself has pressed upon the President certain mandatory duties that have enlarged his role: the Railway Labor Act, the Taft-Hartley Act, the Atomic Energy Act, and the Full Employment Act of 1946.

Not that these statutory grants of authority ensure push-button operations. President Truman sympathetically speculated upon the frustrations that Dwight David Eisenhower was bound to suffer when the general exchanged the military command system for a civilian one. Eisenhower's memoirs published in 1963 confirmed Truman's speculations.

A newly inaugurated President soon discovers that the procedures of the House can thwart his efforts to obtain passage of major legislation.

The late President Kennedy said in a television interview in late

1962 that it is far easier to defeat than to pass legislation. A bill that is introduced in the House, he said, must receive favorable action by the subcommittee and its full committee, the Rules Committee, and the full House. The process is then repeated in the Senate. A single objection by a House Member to sending the bill to a conference to iron out Senate and House differences can send the bill back to Rules. Assuming it emerges from Rules, approval for the bill to go to conference must be given by the full House. Then if a mutually acceptable bill is agreed upon by the conferees, the House and Senate must each approve the conference report. Then there is always the presidential veto confronting some bills. Two-thirds of both House and Senate Members must vote approval if a bill vetoed by a President is to become law.

The President and his aides must keep up constant lobbying efforts in Congress to put through the legislation they need. FDR's men were Thomas Corcoran and Ben Cohen; Kennedy's were Larry O'Brien, Henry Hall Wilson, and Charles O. Daly. And it is not only the Congress that they must deal with. Sometimes the bureaucracy of the executive departments and even Department heads appointed by the President pursue courses that are inimical to his legislative program.

One instance of this occurred in 1962. The state of Mississippi lost one House seat as a result of the 1960 federal census, which showed the state had suffered a loss in population. The state legislature revised the congressional districts so as to place two incumbent Members in competition for one seat in a newly aligned district. One of these Members, Frank Smith, had been a supporter of President Kennedy even before the President was nominated. Smith was as moderate as the racist sovereign state of Mississippi would permit. The other Member was Jamie L. Whitten, an outspoken opponent of the President and his legislative programs. Whitten, in fact, had bolted the Democratic national ticket during the 1960 campaign. Whitten, however, was chairman of the Agriculture Subcommittee of the House Appropriations Committee. In that role, he had influence not only over the Department's budget but also was in a position to influence staffing of the Department.

As a consequence, certain employees of the Agriculture Department fed Whitten politically advantageous announcements of departmental plans for new projects to be built in the new congressional district. These actions gave the clear impression to the voters of that district that Whitten was in a position to do more for them, if elected, than was Smith. Actually, the situation was just the reverse. Smith, as a long-time Kennedy supporter, would have been in a far stronger position than Dixiecrat Whitten to help the district. But contrary to the ground rules, the bureaucrats in Agriculture played their own political game. Smith lost the election. He might have lost anyhow, since he did not hold to the ultra-Tory views of Whitten, a modern Charles X. This remarkable episode illustrates the manner in which the "down-town" departmental bureaucrats flout the power of men who are elected and accountable. Indeed, so independent a course does it pursue, that, in effect, an agency such as the Forest Service is attached to its parent organization, the Interior Department, only for rations and quarters.

Besides the guerrilla fighting within the bureaucracy, the President must confront the rural oligarchs on Capitol Hill. His emphasis is usually on persuasion rather than punitive measures. His men are on the Hill early in the legislative year, consulting with the leadership, talking to other key Members, bringing to both small favors and kind words. The President's men carry with them some of the aura of the Presidency, but they work at a disadvantage in the midst of proud, even arrogant elected politicians who have run the campaign gauntlet many times. The House Member is disinclined to submit to arm-twisting; and if it is attempted, it raises the risk that the Member will cry "foul" aloud—a cry certain to rally his constituents to his defense.

The President himself, or more usually, his subordinates, may hold out tangible rewards in the form of projects for a Member's district. The President can agree to appoint a Member's favored constituent to one of the numerous national and regional citizens advisory councils that assist in the administration and operation of federal water-pollution control and manpower training programs. Or the President can agree to accept an invitation to speak at a convention or banquet of a trade organization or a trade-union group in the Member's district, thus giving the Member the credit for having the influence to bring the President to the meeting. Or a Member may be given the privilege of announcing the approval of a federally assisted project—office building, juvenile delinquency program, or reclamation project—in his state if he supports the Administration, whether it is Republican or Democratic. One Democratic delegation is convinced to this day that a regional post office was moved from a large city in their state to a large city in another state as a reward to a Member from the latter state for his support of President Eisenhower's position against a hydroelectric power project. The proposal was defeated.

Sometimes, in return for his support a Member will ask the Administration to lend a hand on a bill he favors or to back off its support of a bill he opposes. Or more.

For example, during floor discussion in the House in August 1964, it seemed a fair assumption that perhaps as many as thirty Southerners, as a price for their support of the President's antipoverty legislation, demanded that Adam Yarmolinsky be denied an important role in the program. Yarmolinsky, bright and abrasive, had been regarded by Southerners as an aggressive advocate of racial nondiscriminatory programs and policies in his role as Special Assistant to Defense Secretary McNamara. Yarmolinsky was active in assembling the legislation submitted to Congress.

Of course, what can be granted can be withheld, but there is a law of diminishing returns in such a policy, because the President has dozens of legislative measures that he wants Congress to pass, and the number of enticements he can offer is simply not that large. So in the end the President has to use his own and his delegated powers of persuasion and leadership—appeals to the merits of policy or bill, appeals to party loyalty and personal loyalty. In addition, most of the House Members have a predictable position on most major issues. There is a group of fifty to one hundred Members who are swing votes—some urban Members who may leave the Administration to vote against a farm subsidy bill, a liberal Pennsylvanian who may well vote with the coal interests against the liberal issue of public hydroelectric-power development projects in the West, a liberal who will support urban renewal programs, but cannot be depended upon to vote in favor of the establishment of a federal Cabinet-level Department of Urban Affairs.

Nose-counting is done by the President's men before the head-hunting begins. If the measure at hand concerns foreign aid, then the State Department's congressional liaison staff may assist. During the 1962 fight on the farm bill, embodying the supply-management concept, many executive departments' congressional liaison men were put to work nose-counting and head-hunting. Secretary of Agriculture Orville Freeman came to the Capitol, cornered a telephone, and lobbied with religious fervor right up until the final roll call began. In this case, the big farm lobby organizations were heavily propagandizing—for the bill, as in the case of the Farmers Union, or against, as in the case of the American Farm Bureau.

During the nose-counting stage, Members will be graded as certain, probable, or possible "fors," or hopeless or probable "againsts." Then if the tally does not assure a comfortable margin for the Administration's position, the head-hunting begins. When the names of the possibles and uncertains are gathered, various means are employed to win them over. Someone suggests that the Speaker ought to talk to a particular Member. Someone knows that one Member is particularly a close friend of a labor leader or banker in his district, so a phone call is made to the banker or labor leader to ask him to call or wire the Member. The President is, of course, far removed from this kind of necessary painstaking detail. But if he lacks majority support on the eve of a vote, he may start telephoning.

"Hello," the presidential voice will say. "How have you been? I really have appreciated the support you've been giving us on some of these tough ones. I'm calling to see if you can help me out on the tax bill. It's very important. I know it may be tough on you politically, but if you can help us, we won't forget it. Thank you [John, or Mr. Jones, or Mr. Chairman]." Few men are inclined to deny a President, unless to agree would mean committing certain hara-kiri. And this, a President, himself a politician, will not ask. Such presidential telephone calls are employed sparingly. The technique is employed only on the most wavering Members—and it usually works successfully.

A President must often build his majorities for specific legislation out of diverse building blocks. He is confronted with requests by his Departments for legislative priorities for the bills that each wants. A particular Department may receive a lower priority on a bill. Chagrined, it may lobby within Congress to regain the edge for this bill over the President's preference.

The more publicized examples of executive-branch infighting have been the brawls among the three military services for what each considered its proper role and appropriation in the missile program. A service that feels that it has lost the budget battle within the executive branch takes its fight to sympathetic members of the Armed Services and Appropriations committees. The Government Operations Committee of the Senate under Senator John L. McClellan of Arkansas is frequently regarded as a "court of appeals" for an aggrieved Chief of Staff or Army, Navy, or Air Force brass whose views have been overruled by the civilian Defense Secretary. The experimental tactical fighter, the TFX of the newspaper headlines, is a case in point. The Air Force appealed to the congressional committee over the head of the executive department in protest over the way Defense Secretary McNamara decided the design of the aircraft.

Defense policy in recent years has been the object of pulling and hauling among the White House, the Defense Department, and the Congress. In 1959, Congress approved the so-called Russell amendment that required congressional approval for the primary-weapons programs of the three military services. Hitherto, the single focal point at which Congress, specifically the Appropriations Committees of both House and Senate, could attempt to impose policy decisions was the moment the annual Defense Department Appropriation came before it each year. The Russell amendment, taking its name from Senator Richard B. Russell of Georgia, chairman of the Senate Armed Services Committee, provided a second major confrontation.

Prior to 1959, Congress could attempt to force a shift in emphasis in weapons programs by appropriating more funds than an Administration requested for aircraft procurement or, as during Eisenhower's years, for the Nike-Zeus program. But the Congress could not force the President to spend the supplementary funds. The Russell amendment enabled Congress not only to secure primacy over the Executive in the area of weapons programs but also to exert its influence on defense strategy on a sustained basis.

Because of these complex interactions among the departments of the executive branch, the White House itself, and the major committees of the Congress, the lines between the executive power and the legislative power is often blurred. In his role as legislator-lobbyist, the President must sometimes woo the oligarchs in Congress. It amounts to courting those who are not his friends. It enhances their independence; they see no need to be compliant when an Administration comes seeking support.

It would be easier for a Democratic President to accomplish this legitimate legislative objective if the House were reformed. This is unlikely to happen unless a Democratic President decides to use his full powers as party leader and party spokesman to help bring about the necessary change.

The House directs its characteristic cries of conservative outrage against the federal judiciary, particularly the Supreme Court, as well as against the executive branch. Until 1937, after which time human frailty and three Presidents changed the situation, the Court was a joy to the conservatives and a bane to liberals. The attitudes are today somewhat reversed. Since its 1954 decision striking down enforced racial segregation in public schools, one House Member, a southern moderate, even avoids taking visiting constituents to the Court's showplace building while giving them a personally conducted tour of the Capitol Hill "campus."

The House, with its two-year term, is more prone to fits of outrage and panic over the Supreme Court than the Senate with its six-year term. The Court's decisions regarding national security and civil rights and liberties have particularly incurred the displeasure of the House. In the wake of such decisons, House Members introduce legislation to curb the Court's reviewing power. The most singular recent outburst of congressional distemper occurred during the summer of 1964. The purported issue was a Supreme Court decision that June. A majority of the Court ruled that districts of both houses of state legislatures must be "substantially equal" in population. Otherwise, the majority said, citizens are deprived of equal protection of laws under the Fourteenth Amendment.

The decision cannot be read without the knowledge of one shaping transformation that has occurred in the United States. Seventy-five years ago, two-thirds of the American people lived in areas of a rural nature. Today, two-thirds of the 190 million Americans live, conversely, in areas of an urban character. However, the apportionment of more than 40 of the legislatures of the 50 states in the year 1964 did not reflect this change. In a dozen states one-third or less of the people can elect a majority of the legislature. In Connecticut, for example, 12 per cent can elect a majority in the state house and 32 per cent can elect a majority in the state senate.

Senator Dirksen introduced a bill that would have granted a mandatory stay of execution of court orders for reapportionment for a period of two to four years. In mid-August, Senator Mike Mansfield of Montana, majority leader, joined Dirksen in a compromise for temporary stays. The Dirksen-Mansfield amendment was tacked onto the pending foreign-aid authorization bill.

In the House, the Rules Committee, by a 10 to 4 vote, simply cleared for floor action a bill introduced by Representative William M. Tuck of Virginia. The conservative majority on Rules just took the bill away from Judiciary. After a bitter wrangle, on August 19 the full House approved, by a 218 to 175 vote, an amended Tuck bill that, in effect, would prevent federal courts from hearing complaints that rurally oriented state legislatures were apportioned unconstitutionally. Decisions in the area of racial matters and two decisions involving the composition of both congressional and state legislative districts had brought out the vengeful spirit in those members whose sources of power stood to be most drastically shaken by such decisions. Among these were all the southern and border-state chairmen and even one from the West.

The congressional foray against the Court envenomed an election campaign that already had as one of its principals Senator Barry Goldwater of Arizona, the most conservative candidate of a major party since William Howard Taft in 1908.

Still another example is that of the "tidelands" oil controversy.

Congress passed the Submerged Lands Act of 1953 as a consequence of a Supreme Court decision that had upset a long-standing rule that the states held possession of marginal lands under the sea.

Other instances of congressional response have not been successful. For example, in 1957, Representative Katherine St. George of New York introduced a bill denying to the Supreme Court jurisdiction to review any case involving practices or jurisdictions of congressional committees, school board regulations in respect to subversive activities of teachers, state action in respect to admission of candidates to practice law, state control of subversive activities within its own borders, and the enforcement by the national government of security regulations applicable to federal employees. A similar bill was introduced by Senator William Jenner of Indiana. Fortunately, neither bill made any progress. Even the American Bar Association, whose leadership of recent years has been directing injudicious comments at the Court, opposed the bills.

The same year, Representative Mendel L. Rivers of South Carolina introduced a bill to preclude jurisdiction of federal courts over actions growing out of state statutes and regulations governing public schools. It, too, failed.

The interaction of Court decisions and subsequent legislative ambushes arises primarily because of the constitutional provision that provides an affirmative grant of appellate jurisdiction to the Court, yet simultaneously authorizes the Congress to restrict that jurisdiction.

Section 2 of Article III states in part:

"In all Cases affecting Ambassadors, other public Ministers and Consuls, and those in which a State shall be Party, the supreme Court shall have original Jurisdiction. In all the other Cases before mentioned, the supreme Court shall have appellate Jurisdiction, both as to Law and Fact, with such Exceptions, and under such Regulations as the Congress shall make."

From time to time opponents of the current judicial position of the Court have introduced measures to change the Court in some way. One such effort would place a limitation on the length of service by the Justices. Another would require a specified number of years of judicial service, perhaps five or ten, in order to be eligible for appointment to the Court.

One relevant observation is germane in the face of uncritical attacks upon the Court. Alexander Hamilton in the seventy-eighth *Federalist* paper observed:

"Whoever attentively considers the different departments of power must perceive, that, in a government in which they are separated from each other, the judiciary, from the nature of its functions, will always be the least dangerous to the political rights of the Constitution; because it will be least in a capacity to annoy or injure them. The Executive not only dispenses the honors, but holds the sword of the community. The legislature not only commands the purse, but prescribes the rules by which the duties and rights of every citizen are to be regulated. The judiciary, on the contrary, has no influence over either the sword or the purse; no direction either of the strength or of the wealth of the society; and can take no active resolution whatever. It may truly be said to have neither force nor will, but merely judgment; and must ultimately depend upon the aid of the executive arm even for the efficacy of its judgments.

"This simple view of the matter suggests several important consequences. It proves incontestably, that the judiciary is beyond comparison the weakest of the three departments of power . . ."

The image of black-robed judicial Samsons pulling down the pillars of the Republic is somewhat at variance with facts.

A Government Printing Office publication, printed in 1936 under the title *Provisions of Federal Law Held Unconstitutional by the Supreme Court*, reported that from its inception to 1936, the Supreme Court has decided approximately 40,000 cases. In the process it rules invalid in some respect 84 provisions of law. Twelve of these invalidations occurred from mid-1933 to mid-1936 during Franklin Roosevelt's first Administration. Between 1936 and 1957, another three federal statutes, none of great significance, were ruled unconstitutional in some respect.

The Court's record is equally modest in the field of Executive orders. Until 1957, the federal courts had struck down in some measure 38 orders, of which the Supreme Court accounted for 14 adverse decisions. The most spectacular in recent times was the lecture read to President Truman by the Court in 1952 after he had ordered government seizure and operation of most of the steel mills in the country.

In respect to congressional investigating committees, which the Court is accused of subverting, the Court until 1963 had decided fewer than two dozen cases that challenged in any way the authority or procedure of such committees. All these occurred since 1949. And the Court has challenged in some respect about a dozen cases arising out of state legislative investigations.

The Court has held to the general proposition that the power of the Congress to conduct investigations is inherent in the legislative process. However, far-reaching as this writ is, it has limitations—namely, that there is no general authority to expose the private affairs of individuals without justification in terms of the functions of the Congress.

The Court's box score in its lifetime, in any event, caused a professor of constitutional law at Columbia University, Noel T. Dowling, to remark that only when it is driven to the wall does the Court turn and stab the statute to death.

Fortunately, the Court may remedy the pernicious distemper of the volatile House. If the Court doesn't follow the election returns, it does, in the words of Lord Bryce, feel "the touch of public opinion. Opinion is stronger in America than anywhere else in the world, and judges are only men. To yield a little may be prudent, for the tree that cannot bend to the blast must be broken."

James A. Bayard of Delaware, a Member of the House in its fledgling years, remarked in 1802 that a constitution unaccompanied by a judicial system to enforce its provisions remains a homily on political morality.

"How vain is a paper restriction if it confers neither power nor right," Bayard said. "Of what importance is to say, Congress are (cq) prohibited from doing certain acts, if no legitimate authority exists in the country to decide whether an act done is a prohibited act? Do gentlemen perceive the consequence which would follow from establishing the principle that Congress have the exclusive right to decide on their own power? This principle admitted, does any Constitution remain? Does not the power of the Legislature become absolute and omnipotent? Can you talk to them of transgressing their powers, when no one has a right to judge of those powers but themselves?"

Chapter 6

The Lobbies

One dictionary defines the verb "to lobby" in these words: "to address or solicit members of a legislative body in the lobby or elsewhere, with intent to influence legislation."

The definition is a useful one, because it provides an objective description of a technical term that has become distorted by value judgments that, depending on the source, characterize as good (or bad) the lobbies of the AFL-CIO, the American Medical Association, and the Widgetmakers Association for a National Tariff (WANT). A conspiratorial theory of lobbies may be useful as a whetstone for honing one's moral superiority, but it provides scarcely any other advantage.

Lobbying is desirable; indeed, it is an indispensable adjunct of the legislative process. If the press claims the title "the fourth estate," or fourth branch of government, then the lobbyists are certainly the fifth.

The AFL-CIO and the United States Chamber of Commerce find themselves in this position on occasions when other than broad social issues are at stake. The AFL-CIO is, predictably, opposed to the cleverly misnamed national "right-to-work" bill. The "Chamber," of course, is in favor. However, in the late summer of 1963, while Edwin P. Neilan, the outspoken Chamber president, was denouncing such federal threats to private interests as the operations of the Area Redevelopment Administration and the accelerated public works program, the president of the Millsboro, Delaware, Chamber in Neilan's home state was welcoming the award of a $250,000 federal sewer-system grant to the community. Pending legislation to expand federal aid to hydroelectric facilities will result in the sometime AFL-CIO-affiliated United Mine Workers siding with the coal industry in opposition, while other AFL-CIO affiliated unions and even individual members of the AFL-CIO high command will support it.

The shadowy sutlers among the lobbyists are the ones that provide fodder for the syndicated columns of Drew Pearson. These are the lobbyists whose maneuvers—tapping telephones of rivals in downtown Washington hotel rooms, for example—explode into headlines. Their interests are as narrow as the lapels on their expensively tailored suits. These are the lobbyists whom the general public associates with lobbying. Their unsavory objectives are usually apparent. There is no reasonable excuse for any except the most befuddled Member of Congress not to discern them—unless the Member is a compliant accomplice, in which case the problem is not one of lobbying.

During a television interview with Edward R. Murrow in 1958, President Truman estimated that about 15 million Americans are represented by lobbies of some sort, while 150 million Americans are unrepresented. The President, he said, has the job of representing these, and if he doesn't, the American people are in trouble.

The President and his men lobby the Members. So do Senators, Cabinet officers, governors, state legislators, political leaders, bankers, trade-union officials, professional groups, veterans' organizations, pensioners, libertarians and antilibertarians, dealers and anti-dealers, snake-oil salesmen, ideologues, as well as racists and bigots and others beyond the fringe. Unfortunately, too, often on the outskirts of the thirsting throng is just plain Joe Doakes, the tongue-tied Everyman. In addition, Members lobby other Members—perhaps the least noticed but the most effective of all lobbying efforts.

A fascinating insight into the anatomy of lobbying is provided in a book, *The Real Voice*, published in 1964. The author, Richard Harris, skillfully assembles testimony and interviews into an authentic recapitulation of the Senate drug hearings, under Senator Estes Kefauver of Tennessee, out of which came the Kefauver-Harris Drug Act of 1962. The measure provided the Food and Drug Administration with extended control over effectiveness and safety of new drugs.

Lobbyists are within their rights. The First Amendment to the Constitution declares that "Congress shall make no law . . . abridging . . . the right of the people . . . to petition the Government for a redress of grievances." The right of petition is as important a civil liberty as the other provisions of the amendment, which encompasses freedoms of speech, religion, press, and peaceable assembly. The right of petition is the right of a citizen to present his views to those who govern.

There is something commendable in the idea of a horny-handed yeoman petitioning for relief against the unjust tax collector. There are few such sympathetic characters in the lobbying fraternity. It was inevitable that lobbying eventually would lose its amateur standing. Organized groups have found that their interests are better served if they are represented by expert advocates—for example, the lawyer and that artful dodger the public relations man. Lobbying is now "big league."

Three hundred and four organizations filed spending reports in 1962 under the Federal Regulation of Lobbying Act that took effect in 1947. Their declared expenditures totaled $4.2 million. Under the Act, which the Supreme Court ruled in 1954 applies only to lobbying organizations that have "direct communication" with Members of Congress, quarterly expenditure reports must be filed by anybody who indirectly or directly collects, solicits, or receives money or anything of value that is used to influence the passage or defeat of legislation.

Twenty-two of the 304 organizations reported expenditures in excess of $50,000. First was the National Committee for Insurance Taxation, $181,766; second, the AFL-CIO alone (not counting affiliated international unions), $149,212. Others included the American Farm Bureau, $118,957; American Legion, $102,931; American Medical Association, $83,075; and the National Rivers and Harbors Congress, $50,177. However, much more is actually spent on lobbying in Washington than is declared, as one can surmise in reading the Supreme Court decision.

The lobbies are as diverse as our society. Some of them may limit their efforts to working in behalf of one specific agricultural crop or natural resource, such as cotton or copper; or one finished product, such as domestic cotton textiles and steel; or one specific policy

—free trade, universal disarmament, or establishment of national "right-to-work" legislation. Other lobbies attempt to influence whole areas of national policy. The Air Force Association, the Navy League, and the Association of the Army are closely tied to the viewpoints of the chiefs of these respective armed services. The Air Force Association reflected the hostile viewpoint of the Air Force toward the limited nuclear test ban treaty ratified by the Senate in September 1963. The Rivers and Harbors Congress has close ties to the Army Corps of Engineers, which administers the federal civil works program—dams and river and harbor channel improvements.

Education has its lobbies. The American Council on Education, representing more than a thousand colleges and universities, maintains headquarters in Washington. Universities, such as the University of Pittsburgh and the University of California, maintain Washington offices for the purpose of maintaining close liaison with the research and grant programs of the federal agencies. Different lobbies within one area of interest frequently conflict. An example occurred in the education field in late 1962 when the American Council on Education lobbied strongly for a bill to provide federal construction funds for academic facilities. The measure that emerged from a Senate-House conference also included a provision for student financial assistance. The Association for Higher Education, a division of the negatively powerful National Education Association, was obliged to stand by while its parent group, the NEA, flew its state representatives into Washington to help lobby against the bill on the dubious grounds that it is not constitutional to provide federal assistance to church-related institutions of higher learning. The measure was defeated.

Other lobby groups comprise many diverse constituent member organizations, and at times their position on a legislative issue is so broad as to be ineffective. Or the leaders simply take no stand, and let the constituent organizations or members take their own conflicting positions.

The Representatives lobbyist works openly. For example, he requests an appointment with a Member. If it is granted, he appears, presents his business card, and states his case by legitimate means—

argumentation and documentation. Charm, persuasiveness, and special knowledge are his accouterments. The Member realizes that this is a special pleader, and may judge accordingly.

More often, the lobbyist, whose business card identifies him as a public relations adviser or consultant or special or legislative representative, circulates among those Members who already favor his position. The representative of the American Medical Association, whether his home office knows it or not, seldom visits a Member who is unalterably committted to a hospital and nursing home care bill to be financed by social security taxes. However, a representative of an insurance company or of an existing private, nonprofit medical-surgical program may visit this Member to persuade him to support an amendment to provide an alternative. This amendment might permit federal financing of part of the cost of a private health coverage plan to the individual who may elect to purchase a private medical-surgical plan instead of depending on social security.

Collectively, the lobbyists play an important role in the legislative process. They provide a great deal of factual information to Members. The fair-minded lobbyist will often state his position, and then candidly inform the Member of what the opposition's argument is, and what its strength is. There is a symbiosis between Members and lobbyists. If they have a common interest, one may alert the other to a legislative maneuver by the opposition. Late in 1963, it became known in one House Member's office that the conservative Ways and Means Committee leaders planned to offer legislation in 1964, a presidential election year, to increase social security and other benefits by perhaps 5 to 10 per cent. This was regarded as a counter to a publicized liberal push to pass President Kennedy's social-security-financed hospital benefits bill, a typically shrewd maneuver by the conservatives to split the supporters of the President's legislation. Eligible social security beneficiaries would be more inclined to support a bill to increase existing benefits, however small the increase, than to keep ranks in support of legislation that had been blocked for a long time. The lobby groups in favor of the President's legislation were promptly notified that this conservative maneuver was in the wind.

An example in reverse occurred when the Education and Labor Committee was considering in executive session the National Defense Education Act. Sitting in as technical advisers were members of the Federal Office of Education. At one point, a committee member suggested a change in one section of the bill that would provide less business to certain suppliers of audio-visual teaching equipment. Within hours after the committee meeting ended, it became apparent that the lobbyist for these suppliers had been informed of the proposal. Signs pointed to the Office of Education representatives as having leaked the information. They were barred from subsequent committee meetings on this bill.

Lobbies operate in different styles. Some operate in nothing less than sybaritic fashion in swanky office buildings along the fashionable lower end of Connecticut Avenue near the hotel district. Others operate out of small offices whose door discreetly carries only a personal name or some innocuous organizational title such as the Association of Associations in the National Interest. Some lobbies operate largely by newsletters to Members, with many of the items cribbed from the Washington newspapers and scuttlebutt in the legislative corridors. These groups do little more than verbalize support for some issue, visit friendly (but not always the most effective) Members, and function, inadvertently or otherwise, as conduits of secondhand information of a not very high caliber.

One category of lobby might be called the nonpartisan one. It includes the League of Women Voters, the Business and Professional Women's Association, the American Association of University Women, and many social-action divisions of churches, as well as the National Council of Churches itself. They are generally favorable to free trade, foreign aid, and improved efficiency and operation of the government. On such specific issues as the United Nations bond issue in 1962 or the civil rights legislation in 1963–1964, their newsletters may handle the matter gingerly because of the varied political faiths of their members. Their principal influence does not stem from skill in intensive lobbying. The members of such organizations have wide-ranging interests beyond their immediate day-to-day problems. They are anxious and willing to learn. The leadership of such organizations, rather than exerting pressure in behalf of their members' views on legislation, as the typical lobbying groups do, stimulates knowledge and awareness of issues among the members by means of publications, forums, and special projects. In other words, the leadership educates. The impact of such lobbies is sometimes imperceptible, but they help to create a public opinion that in the long run has an influence on the great public issues of a decade. They bring into the mainstream of legislation vast numbers of Americans who otherwise would not be involved at all.

In contrast is the "one-man" lobby, such as Benjamin Marsh's "The People's Lobby," which had ideological ties to the Progressive movement of Senator Robert M. La Follette of Wisconsin. However, the more conventional lobbies represent the large and small economic and social power groups of our society. They are knowledgeable, aggressive, and always well briefed on each Member of Congress—"we'll get him . . . he's on the fence . . . we'll lose him." Usually these lobbies represent clients who have a direct economic stake in legislation.

Broadly speaking, on most of the major legislative issues of domestic policy—taxes, aid to education, medical care, labor-management relations—two great coalitions of lobbies are at work. The core and main strength of one is the conservative business community, with which is usually allied the professional community. Export-minded or import-minded industries may disagree among themselves on aspects of foreign policy, but domestically they tend to agree. This coalition is represented by such organizations as the Chamber of Commerce, the National Association of Manufacturers, and the American Farm Bureau. The heart of the other great coalition is organized labor, liberal in inclination. Part of this constellation are the Americans for Democratic Action, the National Farmers Union, and the National Association for the Advancement of Colored People. Sometimes the co-operative movement and the conservationist organizations are involved. The prominence of their roles varies from issue to issue. The NAACP may lead the way if the legislation at hand is civil rights; the ADA may provide the oratorical flourishes; while organized labor provides much of the muscle backstage.

Each of the coalitions furthers its ends in the same general way.

First, each one tries to nominate and elect candidates favorable to its viewpoint, and works to defeat unfriendly candidates. The amount of effort and financial assistance varies. These coalitions concentrate their efforts on congressional districts where the outcome of an election is uncertain. An entrenched incumbent is usually let alone by interest groups opposed to his views.

During primary and general election campaigns, these groups recruit campaign workers and supply a variety of other services—researching issues and opponents' backgrounds and views, distribution of campaign propaganda, staffing offices, running mimeograph machines, and transporting voters to the polls. Both business firms and trade unions provide abundant hidden services. The publicity department of a large firm may be assigned to develop campaign material for a Republican candidate, and a printing company may print at cost the resultant handbills and bumper stickers. The staffs of union locals and internationals are loaned to national, state, and local candidates, usually Democrats. A building owner who favors a candidate may provide him with convenient, free campaign office space. A furniture store may provide floor-sample furniture, and utilities concerns may supply telephones, electricity, and heating at cost or free to favorite candidates. In the West, where congressional districts take several hours to cross by car and the communities are widely scattered, a friendly business interest will provide a candidate with a rented airplane or an unmarked company airplane.

These and other campaign contributions, which do not have to be reported under the inadequate 1925 Federal Corrupt Practices Act, led *Congressional Quarterly* to estimate that the actual total cost of election campaigns for all offices in 1962, a nonpresidential election year, amounted to almost $100 million. Actual expenditures reported under the Act for congressional election campaigns totaled $18.4 million: $6.6 million by candidates and $11.8 million by political committees. Contests for House seats that year may have cost an average of $40,000 each. President Kennedy, a newspaper editor wrote in 1963, estimated that Republicans and Democrats spent a total of $175 million on the 1960 presidential primaries, conventions, and election. The exact figure is not known. The 1925 Act does not require reports of contributions or expenditures in congressional primary campaigns or in connection with a party's presidential nomination. The Act's disclosure provisions apply to funds received and spent by the candidate himself, and therefore do not require reports of political committees that confine their activities to a single state or committees that are not subsidiaries of national political committees. Neither do the costs of gubernatorial campaigns have to be reported.

There are many other ways in which lobbies and friendly groups may boost a candidate. They help him to develop as a politician by giving him a base. A former House Member from California, Jerry Voorhis, has written in his autobiography of "the inner warmth" generated by the knowledge that there are friends who can be relied upon, and the need for a "political 'home' in the bosom of some strong group, whose interests they would always protect and who could then be depended upon to go all out for the candidate for re-election whenever the need arose."

Business, professional, labor, and civic organizations may offer their favorite candidates an opportunity to appear at regularly scheduled general membership meetings. Sometimes, a fraternal, veterans', professional, or ethnic organization can find its way, with the proper lobbying, to make some sort of "distinguished service" award to a favored office seeker. A governor of a western state has managed to have a rose named after him. An unfinished public works project unexpectedly is dedicated or a cornerstone laying of a public building is scheduled during campaign time in order to provide an opportunity for an incumbent candidate to appear at the ceremony and thereby be identified with it. These events do not occur just by chance. Someone lobbies to have such honors and awards bestowed at the proper time.

Even while the winning candidate reads his congratulatory telegrams and the loser ruefully reads his bills, lobbyists assess the results. Soon enough the winner will be visited by the lobbying groups that supported him.

At the same time, the President and his men are considering what measures to propose, what priorities shall be assigned to individual items in the legislative package. Executive-branch Departments—State, Commerce, Interior, Health, Education, and Welfare, for example—jockey for presidential priority for their pet legislation, such as less restricted foreign aid, more money for the national park system, increased appropriations for interstate highways, and comprehensive education legislation.

Meanwhile, lobbyists and their friends in the House, as well as the President and his men and the majority and minority leaders, are noting vacancies on committees. Each wants to see these filled by "friendly" members. Lobbyists also prepare for the assault on the Congress—it is in the nature of an assault because most Members are strong in conviction, strong willed, and steeped in skepticism.

When the President and his men and the outside lobbyists approach the new Congress as it convenes, they find among the Members both cohesive blocks and shifting alliances, each connected to social and economic interests.

There is a hard-core labor bloc that goes right down the line with the wishes of labor leaders—more because they think along the same lines rather than because they are political hostages. There is also a corresponding business-minded bloc, a portion of which is a disaffected splinter concerned with the plight of the small businessman in a corporate economy. There are Members highly responsive to the interests of sugar producers, both beet and cane, the oil and gas producers, giant combines or relatively small domestic independents, and maritime shipping interests.

Each special interest has its intramural conflicts. In 1962, for example, private shipbuilding interests were simultaneously supporting the Navy's request for ship repair, conversion and construction funds, and fighting the Navy over the percentage of naval repair and conversion contracts that should be allocated to them and to the Navy's own yards. In the same year the East Coast private shipyards were successfully fighting to remove the 6 per cent shipyard differential traditionally allowed the West Coast private yards in competitive bidding on ship-construction contracts.

There is a certain degree of mutual help within the brotherhood. One lobby with no particular interest at stake helps another that has a definite interest at stake. During the Korean War the Office of Price Stabilization was under heavy attack by business and agricultural interests that were trying to weaken its power to control prices. One Member of the Banking and Currency Committee tells that he received a call from a constituent who was an old friend and a prominent businessman. He urged the Member to vote for an amendment strongly pushed by the cattle-raising and -feeding interests. The Member expressed surprise that his friend was interested in such a matter. The friend replied, "No, I'm not; but didn't you know we all work together on this kind of thing?"

Legislation is shaped by broad coalitions or by a few men, or even by a single individual. Highly controversial housing legislation, for example, has had one common factor over the years—provisions that neutralized or overcame the opposition of organizations representing mutual savings banks, savings and loan companies, mortgage bankers, and residential contractors and suppliers.

On the other hand, in 1955 the trade restrictionists in the House came within one vote of turning aside legislation to extend the Reciprocal Trade Act. This did not happen because of exceptionally skilled leadership or because dominant economic interests wanted the Reciprocal Trade Act scuttled. Rather the near victory was the result of almost single-handed lobbying and organizing effort by O. E. Strackbein, a veteran vocal leader of protectionists in the Washington lobbies. His well-conceived and tirelessly executed effort nearly succeeded because he organized opposition forces first outside and then within the House, while proponents of the Trade Act extension paddled along unconcernedly.

Within committees, proponents and opponents of legislation jockey for position—each complementing the activities of their alter egos in lobbies outside. Adverse witnesses can be kept to a minimum, for example, or they can be sandwiched among friendly witnesses in scheduled appearances so that their testimony does not receive as much attention from the press as it deserves. Scant attention will be given, for example, to a knowledgeable opponent of the federal fallout shelter program if he is scheduled to testify on such legislation on the same day as are Dr. Edward Teller, an Assistant Secretary of Defense, and a three-star general. The opponent is neatly boxed in. Unversed in the arts of publicists, the witness may come prepared only with notes or bring only one copy of his formal testimony. No copies, therefore, are available for the press table during the committee hearing. Meanwhile, the Defense Department's battery of duplicating machines provides a corps of grateful reporters copies of the testimony of the Department's witnesses.

With conservatives controlling most committees, the odds are much in favor of the *status quo*, the established economic and social patterns and the nay-sayers.

How does a Member react to these pressures and stresses? In the April 1964 issue of *Challenge* magazine, Representative Clarence D. Long of Maryland, once a professor of economics at Johns Hopkins University, wrote:

"... All these efforts have won me a reputation as a hard-working Congressman, who helps people. As a result, my strongest potential opponents have backed away from running against me. I have discovered—or think I have—that most voters are not greatly interested in national legislation. They have problems and needs of their own, and if you help them with these, they allow you great freedom in voting on national legislation. Put it another way, a solid base of popularity with the ordinary voter gives a Congressman sanctuary from pressure groups who want things inimical to the national interest. As a consequence, I can vote solidly for civil rights in a basically Southern State with a white constituency drawn increasingly from the deep South."

The reference here is to another class of constituent—the regular constituents, unlobbied and invisible except when they step into the polling booth and mark their ballots every two years. These constituents are found at all levels of economic, social, and cultural life.

They are often more acted upon than acting. They seem passive, gullible, and even bewildered as to the meaning of the major issues of the day. Studies have shown that many do not recognize the names of their Senators, their representative in the House, or even the President. Their interest in politics is erratic, fragmented, and vulnerable to irrelevant influences. They demand too little of themselves. They demand both too little and too much of their House Member.

Yet these constituents, too, play a vital role in the democratic process. If, for example, they were willing to make a small contribution of $10 to the national party of their choice, candidates for office would be freed of dependence upon the open or disguised campaign contribution from an economic interest with an ax to grind.

A little "savvy" would permit them to look intelligently into the substance of a Member's voting record. Legitimate parliamentary techniques permit a Member to claim he voted "for" a bill his constituents favor, while actually, since he was personally against the bill, he opposed it until its final passage.

Before the final roll call, a motion may be made to recommit a bill with or without instructions to the committee from which it came. The razzle-dazzle occurs particularly on a motion to recommit with instructions that are designed to direct the committee to modify the bill in a particular way and return the altered bill to the House floor for another vote. A Member may vote to recommit. If the motion fails, the Member then votes to pass the bill, since passage is usual once the recommittal motion has failed. Thus this Member can return to his district and claim he voted against or for a bill—whichever accords with the viewpoint of the constituent who asks him how he voted.

By means of another piece of chicanery a Member may vote to authorize a program and then vote against the subsequently proposed appropriation to finance the program. On rare occasions this is justifiable, but in most cases, it is double-dealing.

Few newspapers give a meaningful analysis of the votes cast by Members in the paper's circulation area. Passage or defeat of a bill is treated in such general terms that an individual Member's role is totally obscured, unless he happens to have been the sponsor or a main proponent or opponent of the bill.

This lack of information puts all constituents at a disadvantage, even those who are represented by lobbies. Lobbying organizations and leaders tend to develop interests quite apart from those of their membership. One of their goals is simply self-perpetuation. The rank-and-file members of such organizations often have little control over their leaders. Certainly it is surprising how little control physicians, who are able, well informed, and public-spirited, exercise over that giant among trade unions, the American Medical

Association. The rank and file of the Teamsters Union locals in Kansas City have been badly served by their national leadership. And certainly something is amiss when a veterans' organization lobbies for a multibillion dollar general nonservice-connected pension bill and at the same time urges an end to wasteful government spending.

Constituents on all educational levels are similarly ill informed on legislative matters, the functions of their Congressmen, even their identity. A woman Member of the House receives letters on watermarked stationery as well as on dime-store paper beginning "Dear Sir." A newspaper editor, writing to his Representative in the House, sent the letter to the State Capitol. Sometimes House Members are addressed as "Senator." A university professor writes to congratulate a Member on a bill, showing in the context of his letter that he does not know the difference between sponsoring a bill and voting for it. There are few constituents, whatever their business or professional skills, who have even a rudimentary knowledge of how a bill becomes a law. This is a commentary on the educational system and the quality of information on public affairs rather than a reflection on the intelligence of individual constituents.

Members want to see constituents, to know their needs, and to advance their interests. But to be a ceremonial figure or an errand boy is to substitute a shoddy imitation for a really effective Representative. Often a Member can do more for a constituent by having a few minutes' conversation with him or a leader of his lobby group than by spending several hours in a noisy banquet room on a Saturday night.

Democracy is the worst form of government, but the best yet devised, to paraphrase an observation of Winston Churchill. The whole process of democracy must be improved, and the improvement must begin among those enlightened voters who are skeptical of campaign oratory and noisy political hootenannies. They need more and better information, and they can have it if people in politics and communications and political science make the most of their educational functions. As constituents understand more of political processes, they will participate in them to a greater degree.

Chapter 7

The Politician and the Press

"That compound of folly, weakness, prejudice,
wrong-feeling and right-feeling and newspaper paragraphs."

—Sir Robert Peel on Public Opinion

The public officeholder and the press continuously negotiate
with each other over the spoils of free publicity and free news.

Outwardly, their relations are correct, sometimes friendly, and
occasionally cordial.

The House Member wants favorable mention, including the correct spelling of his first name and his last name. The reporter for
newspaper, magazine, television, or radio "wants the story." The
House Member, orally or by mimeographed statement placed in
the press gallery, gives the reporter a story that the Member wants
his constituents to know. The reporter insists there is more to the
story than the House Member is telling. This is very probably true.
The reporter seeks additional information. The Member withholds
it or offers a harmless generalization. Neither is entirely satisfied
with the result.

The House Member is at a disadvantage with the press, which has
a bias in favor of the 100-Member Senate, because mechanically it is
easier to cover. The 435-Member House is too large for neat coverage. Power in the House is diffused, and its struggles are more
difficult to identify, isolate, and analyze than in the Senate. Tactics
and strategy are more closely concealed. The stricter rules of discussion, regulating the substance and time of debate, blunt the
moments of high drama on the House floor. From the Senate press

gallery, reporters can look down on a hundred men and women and see the personification of forces and philosophies. From the House press gallery, they see only a sea of heads. Therefore reporters have concentrated on the Senate and the White House for the bulk of the news.

Although House Members have a passably good relationship with correspondents from the newspapers in their own districts, most Members mingle with them warily.

Shortly before his untimely death in an airplane crash during the 1962 campaign, Representative Clem Miller of California published a sensitive and perceptive collection of his letters under the title *Member of the House*. In commenting on the press, he wrote:

"I have talked to them in the Speaker's lobby, but it is difficult for me to talk to newspapermen. I don't seem to have the hang of it. I don't like to talk in clichés and the headline phrase does not come easily. Since the press operates under terrifying time pressures, many newsmen think in clichés. They want Congressmen to talk in clichés. They become uneasy if you tend toward too much 'background' talk, or if your thoughts are tentative.

"This, of course, is due to the modern demand for slogans. Everything is compressed. People have no time to attend, to listen. We have become a nation of headline readers. It is not at all surprising that the working press has come to require the same of politicians in its day-to-day reporting. The result is distortion, the inevitable distortion that comes from oversimplification and compression. . . .

"What all this means in terms of Congress is that the congressman who tailors his speech and remarks to the strictures of modern reporting is going to get in the news; and he who doesn't is going to have difficult sledding. It means that many capable legislators operate fairly silently, while others who might be of inferior competence are heard from quite frequently."

Wire-service editors impress upon their staffs that somewhere in the world a client newspaper is "going to bed"—that is, going to press. Every day hundreds of thousands of words are shoveled into the wire-service teletypes to satisfy harassed editors. This accounts for the fact that almost any mimeographed statement placed in the gallery is seized upon for news copy. City-reared Members, whose only view of a cow has been on a can of condensed milk, can get their names quoted in the press as experts in agriculture. A House Member whose travels consist of a triangular course between West Wetdrip, Washington, and the Army-Navy game in Philadelphia can make the news with outrageous remarks about our foreign-aid program simply by getting a press handout to the gallery early in the morning. A Member who can't keep his family accounts in balance can be quoted on the President's economic message to the Congress provided he looks at an advance copy and sends a statement to the gallery first thing in the morning. Thus, much of the wire-service copy is unselected and inconsequential.

The stories are gathered quickly and written quickly. The emphasis on speed brings with it a tendency to accept all statements of all House Members as being of equal merit—the press calls this "impartiality" or "objectivity." The insistence upon frozen formats such as this helped Joseph McCarthy's bully-boy career in the Senate. The concept of objectivity, superficially plausible, rules out the informed interpretation, the "in-depth" piece that explains why such a vote is meaningful and how Representative X's voting record on a given issue may be keyed to certain pressure groups.

The Capitol Hill bureaus of the press associations are staffed by able, knowledgeable men and women, but the compulsion to make a deadline blunts their effectiveness. It is not uncommon for a wire-service reporter to cover two or three committee hearings in a morning. He does this by going to the first hearing just before it opens, picking up available mimeographed copies of witnesses' prepared testimony, then going to the second and third hearings, where he also collects prepared testimony. He may stay a few minutes in each of the hearings, but he depends on being backstopped or "filled in" by the more fortunate reporters from daily newspapers who have just one hearing to cover. It is impossible to obtain an adequate story in this fashion. It implies that the once-over-lightly story will do for the "average reader." But instead there are blocs of readers, and some of them want considerable technical detail in news stories about their field of interest. An overly generalized story on higher education means that a college president in Oregon must make a call to Washington or await the next newsletter of his professional association in order to find out necessary details of a bill.

Compounding the wire-service reporter's problem is the wide variety of opinions held by the subscribers to the press associations. The reporter in covering a hearing on civil-rights legislation will be writing for the editors in Birmingham, Alabama; Oxford, Mississippi; and New York City and Chicago.

This results in what Ralph McGill calls "wood pulp pablum." The two major wire services, Associated Press and United Press International, are the sole source of news of the House for most newspapers and for almost all radio and television stations. Although there were 890 newspaper, magazine, and radio and television correspondents accredited in 1964 to the press galleries in House and Senate, there is too little continuous perceptive and accurate reporting. What scant commentary on the House there is is largely found in the syndicated columns and editorials.

One of the puzzling characteristics of newsmen is their tendency to report legislative business in terms suitable to a police story. Possibly this stems from the practice of training reporters on the police beat. The orthodox line of progression on the daily newspaper, which for some unexplained reason is supposed to produce first-rate reporters, is from police reporting to obituary reporting to general assignment to special assignments or "beats," such as city hall and the state house. After hanging around police headquarters long enough, the reporter often carries with him a policeman's view of events in which every man is so crooked he must screw his socks on in the morning. It makes for a simple cops-and-robbers picture of the world. It accounts for the concept of "the scoop"—for example, the Member's wife who is on his pay roll—and the righteous hunting down of petty misdemeanors. It is not surprising that a newspaperman known for his aggressive reporting can say that when he sees a door shut on Capitol Hill "he wants to break it down." This is the attitude of the voyeur, not the reporter.

Newspapers thrive on wrack and ruin and catastrophe. Sweeping social changes in the world are converted into a scorecard of crises. If X number of bills are not passed by the House by a certain month, then it automatically follows that the House is "tied up" or "lag-ging" or "doing nothing." If a complex bill is held in a committee for a prolonged, legitimate discussion, then the bill becomes "con-troversial," "under fire," and "threatened with defeat."

In his formative stage, the reporter is pushed to master technique and develop an eye for minutiae. The middle initial of a man's name is regarded as of equal importance with the main point of a story. Once, in the house organ of the American press, *Editor & Publisher*, an editor was quoted as saying he would fire a reporter who used the word "however" instead of "but." There have been silly experi-ments with sentence lengths—one Chicago paper once adopted a "14-W" formula—no opening sentence or "lead" could contain more than 14 words. At an eastern journalism school a former news-paperman turned teacher would each year proudly tell the story of the occasion when, before the telephone was common, his city editor sent him back to the scene of a collapsed church steeple, an hour's journey, because he had not found "how high was the steeple." It may have been such pointless anecdotes as this that prompted A. J. Liebling in *The Wayward Pressman* to exclaim with impatience that this particular journalism school "had all the intellectual content of a school for A & P clerks."

Such is the outlook and experience that many reporters bring to Washington. It accounts for the condition of the American press—long on facts, sometimes trivial ones, but short on a sense of facts. Americans may have available the most numerous sources of in-formation, as press people claim, but whether Americans are the most informed is debatable.

Much of the effort of the Washington press corps is expended in the area of "nonnews." Or what Daniel J. Boorstin at the University of Chicago calls the "pseudo-event," usually an interview scheduled simply to get the subject of the interview into the news columns. Probably more than one-half of any daily newspaper consists of pseudo-news. The proportion of actual events that occur without prompting by the press is decreasing. The Washington, D.C., press corps can be the most aggressive fight promoters in the world. There is many a report of a "feud" or "clash" or "row" within the House that exists only in the newspaper. One West Coast correspondent, covering the presidential signing of a major bill, reported that two Members of a state delegation jostled for position behind the President at the start of the White House ceremony. This story, with overtones of feuding, made the headlines back home. In fact, the two Members were escorted to their position behind the chair by a White House staff member before any other Members invited to the ceremony were admitted to the President's office.

Correspondents in Washington for out-of-town newspapers tend to compound the provincial character of the House by introducing into news stories the "local angle," emphasizing the views, opinions, and votes of the Member from the district in which the newspaper is located. When a local accent is given to a major foreign-aid story, the national issue inherent in the story becomes obscured and distorted. Often, Washington correspondents are closely attuned to the editorial position of their newspapers back home, and this gives a further slant to political stories.

In the American way, when reporters became correspondents or "journalists," they may acquire "clients." Spoilsmanship reaches its highest development in the cases of such Washington journalists. Their clients are an improvement over the usual panel of newsroom favorites that reporters can reach for that desperate on-deadline comment, the enlivening quote, or the controversial opinion to help brighten a light Monday-morning newspaper. These clients are House and Senate Members who are on the make with the press, radio, or TV men. These Congressmen are frequently seen on the Sunday-afternoon and early-evening panel shows; they are the source of the crutch story—the overnight wire-service story written for the first editions of the next day's afternoon newspapers. If the House passes a bill to bring peace on earth, the reporters doing the crutch story can turn to his client in the Senate for the quotations, often anonymous, that will permit the story to start out, "The peace-on-earth bill, passed overwhelmingly by the House, faces rough sledding in the Senate, key legislators said today. . . ." These clients are usually entrenched powers in the House and presidential aspirants in the Senate. In this state of symbiosis with a newsman, the Member of Congress can get his own ideas before the public. If the Member comes under attack, the correspondent can be relied upon to defend him. For example, Charles Halleck, John McClellan, and Barry Goldwater each has his Boswell.

A variant of this type of reporter is the correspondent who collects executive departments. A story out of the White House as to possible disarmament moves is certain to be followed by dire, anonymous warnings from well-protected scientific sources in the Defense Department. If these scientific sources get wind of what is up at the White House, their favorite science reporter will be called to shoot the disarmament moves out of the water even before they are launched. In the Senate in August 1962, George McGovern of South Dakota rose to suggest that the Soviet Union and the United States had acquired such an awesome nuclear arsenal that each had the potential to kill off the other's populations many times over—the so-called "overkill" concept. To those knowledgeable in the Byzantine ways of the Washington press corps, it was a reasonable certainty which reporter on which newspaper would quickly appear with a rebuttal to McGovern from unidentified sources.

Unlike Members of the Senate, relatively few House Members are beneficiaries of the "client" system. In any event, clientism is a disservice to the Congress and the American people. It understates the crucial role of issues and grossly exaggerates the power of individuals to shape situations and circumstances. It discourages a vigorous approach to news coverage. Not long ago, a newcomer to the Washington bureau of a major daily newspaper commented despondently that his fellow bureau members had protested his suggestion that the newspaper prepare a story on legislative conflicts of interest among Members of Congress. The reporter said his fellows pointed out that it had taken years to build up confidences and contacts with important Members and that such an exposé story would "rock the boat."

A capable newspaper man, Peter Lisagor of the *Chicago Daily News* explains the hazard of "psychological undertow." This, he explains, is the consequence of a reporter's frequent association with a particular important government official—a Cabinet office or a President. "You tend to soften the edges of criticism. . . . You tend to obscure, minimize things that the public generally ought to be hearing about, ought to know," Lisagor said. Newspapermen, too, like to be greeted affably and by first name by important persons.

Alan Barth, editorial writer for the *Washington Post,* phrased his thoughts on the matter in his acceptance of the Oliver Wendell Holmes Bill of Rights Award in 1964:

> "I do not mean to make light of the threats which reckless journalism may pose to rights of privacy, to the right to a fair trial and to other individual rights. These are serious problems. I am more concerned, however, with a different danger—with the danger that the press in the United States has become excessively responsible—has become, in fact, to an alarming degree, a spokesman and partner of the Government, rather than a censor."

A minor example occurred recently when reporters regularly covering the State Department unexpectedly appeared in print as motion-picture critics assailing as prejudicial to the American image overseas the offbeat film *Dr. Strangelove, or How I Learned to Love the Bomb.*

In 1963, Senator J. William Fulbright of Arkansas turned up distressing indications that the line between news and propaganda can be breeched. The Foreign Relations Committee, under Fulbright's chairmanship, held hearings on lobbying and public relations carried on in this country on behalf of foreign clients. The hearing record shows that International News Service, eventually purchased by United Press, for a fee assigned its own news-gathering reporters to gather material for commercial clients, such as General Rafael Trujillo, the Dominican Republic dictator. There were further indications that the material gathered for Trujillo was also sent to INS newspaper clients, mostly Hearst papers, as "news."

The Fulbright hearings also paid attention to the Special Services Bureau of United Press International (UPI). The following question-and-answer passage appears in the hearing record between Fulbright and the UPI Special Service manager, C. Edmonds Allen:

FULBRIGHT: You take no responsibility as to who their clients are?

ALLEN: That is correct, Sir.

. . . .

FULBRIGHT: And therefore, certainly your reporters could not know who they are working for in performing an assignment given to them by Special Services, could they?

ALLEN: That is correct, Sir.

. . . .

FULBRIGHT: And also, therefore, the person whom the person [reporter] is contacting in the course of his assignment naturally wouldn't know either, would he?

ALLEN: That is correct.

Writing in the fall issue of the Columbia Journalism *Review*, Ben Bagdikian commented that "No one brought up at the hearing a major danger in selling reporters' entrees: the power to make things happen merely by asking questions. UPI charges its private clients $50 a month retainer and a per-assignment fee. It could be worth several times $50 for private parties—corporations, business associations, labor unions—to have a national wire service ask a pointed question of a key government official."

Another kind of correspondent regards the House and Senate as hallowed legislative museums rather than as viable organs of government to which major problems are brought for resolution. The emphasis upon form rather than context favors the entrenched powers and gives the American people a false sense of security about their national assembly.

Television and radio stations have occasionally cast longing glances at the House, where, unlike the Senate, television and radio coverage of committee proceedings is not permitted.

In 1952, Speaker Rayburn ruled that microphones and cameras would be prohibited at most full sessions of the House and at committee hearings. Joint sessions of Congress held in the House chamber have been an exception. Rayburn felt that TV coverage had made ham actors out of ambitious Senators.

Broadcasters argue that modern equipment is unobtrusive. In their view its exclusion from committee hearings in the House is discriminatory. Rayburn's rule is still in effect, but there will plainly have to be some modification if the full news-gathering force is to focus on the House.

One indication that House Members feel they are not being adequately "covered" by the Washington press is the widespread use of periodic newsletters that Members send to constituents and the increasing utilization of home-district television and radio for two, five, and fifteen minutes by Members.

Over-all, the press coverage of the Congress, particularly the House, is inadequate. The "big name" Members are not necessarily the most competent or the most powerful or the most influential. They may be big names because they have big mimeograph machines, or a staff member with newspaper experience who knows that the way to get the boss a precious half-column of news, instead of a couple of paragraphs, is to time releases and speeches for publication in Monday-morning newspapers, when news is scarce.

Some of the most perceptive reporting is being published in the trade and specialty press, such as the *Wall Street Journal*, or magazines such as *Commentary*, *The New Yorker*, and *Science*. Our cluttered newspapers, with their lack of focus, makes one appreciate the *London Sunday Observer*, the American Survey section of the *Economist*, or the American reports of the Manchester *Guardian* with their organized, lucid, and knowledgeable coverage of American domestic affairs.

The American press is not yet the adequate machinery of knowledge of which Walter Lippmann has spoken. Adequate coverage of politics would take account of that complex three-cornered interaction of the event itself, the reporting of the event, and the human reaction to it.

A reporter who knows the House well once said, "The only reform the House needs is full disclosure." A brilliant scholar has remarked that basic research, not reform, is the answer to what is wrong with the House. There is truth in both observations. Until the press systematically begins to reveal the weaknesses of the House as an institution, it cannot stimulate enough public interest to support a popular movement for reform.

The American press, a privileged institution with constitutional protections, has the opportunity to make known to voters the facts about how the House functions, where the true centers of power lie, the significance of seniority and the committee system, and the long dominance of the South and of rural Representatives in the House. The seasoned reporter knows that it is forces, not individuals, that ultimately underlie political struggles. Until the press gives its readers accurate information and analysis and a true perspective on the character of the House, it shares a responsibility for the present condition.

Chapter 8

The Landrum-Griffin Labor Bill

"So ends the bloody business of the day"
—ALEXANDER POPE

In March 1958, the Senate Government Operations Committee issued a report on its first year of work—a seminal report that generated one of the major legislative battles since World War II. The committee, whose chairman is John L. McClellan of Arkansas, took aim at the labor movement by proposing legislation to establish safeguards against mishandling of union funds and to ensure democratic intraunion operations. The committee made other proposals designed to remedy improper practices it reported it had found during its investigations of labor-management relations.

The hearings of the committee had often been dramatic proceedings. They revealed that within the then 16-million-member trade-union movement certain unions at the local and national level were disloyal to the trust American workingmen and workingwomen had placed in them. In 1957 the Teamsters Union had been expelled from the AFL-CIO on charges of internal corruption.

The findings, translated into headlines, shocked Americans, including friends of organized labor. Demands grew inside and outside the Congress for a legislative remedy.

Two Kennedy brothers were prominent in the hearings. The McClellan Committee counsel, Robert, became as well known as his brother, Senator John, who even then was easily recognized as a strong candidate for the Democratic presidential nomination two years hence. John F. Kennedy was at that time chairman of the Labor Subcommittee of the full Senate Committee on Labor and

Public Welfare. The subcommittee held jurisdiction over the type of legislation proposed by the McClellan Committee. The two brothers, fiercely blood loyal, provided a means for the two committees to lockstep.

The McClellan Committee report materially changed the climate for labor legislation. Before the report was issued, it had seemed unlikely the Senate would act on a major labor bill that year, 1958. However, the impact of the McClellan report changed that. Within a three-month period, extraordinarily brief for such major legislation, the Senate passed what was popularly known as the Kennedy-Ives bill that called for disclosure and reporting of certain aspects of labor-union operations, as well as those of management in respect to its relations with its employees. The bill came from the Kennedy subcommittee. It was debated and amended during a five-day period on the Senate floor. On June 17 the Senate passed it by a vote of 88 to 1.

When the bill arrived in the House, Speaker Rayburn held it up until July 28, six weeks later, when he referred it to the House Education and Labor Committee. Quite rightly, Rayburn declined to refer the bill to the committee before that date because the committee already had a bill before it aimed at safeguarding administration and operation of pension funds. Rayburn reasoned that both bills would be endangered if he referred the Senate bill to the House Committee before the pension bill was reported out. Once the pension bill came out of the committee, Rayburn immediately referred the Senate labor-union reform bill to it.

In the interim, however, Rayburn was publicly and privately criticized. He was subjected to considerable pressure to send the Senate bill to committee before the pension measure had cleared it. The stress bothered him little. In private he would occasionally growl about "those damn fools who were trying to get him to make a bad situation worse." He was well aware that many in both management and labor circles did not want the federal government to be equipped with statutory authority to prescribe standards for the management of pension funds. He was not going to help them block the pension bill by creating a situation in which the committee, with adjournment only a few weeks away, might be forced to sidetrack it in order to deal with the Senate bill for which there was a public clamor of support. Rayburn's strategy worked. The pension bill, the Welfare and Pensions Plans Disclosure Act, became law on August 28, 1958.

Shortly after the House Education and Labor Committee received the Kennedy-Ives bill, it became apparent that it would be kept there unless it could be sprung by some unusual parliamentary tactic. A number of friendly House Members asked me to help persuade the Speaker to call up the bill under suspension of the customary House rules. This procedure allows only forty minutes of debate, no amendments are permitted, and a two-to-one majority is required for passage. The Speaker was understandably reluctant to go this route, if for no other reason than that the measure was so controversial. In fact, at first he flatly refused to attempt it. Pleas and pressures mounted. Rayburn finally was persuaded to attempt the maneuver, because many Members let it be known that they had to be on record on the bill before the 1958 fall campaign, a few weeks away. Rayburn knew before the votes were cast that it would be a legislative miracle if the measure mustered the necessary majority. He made it clear that he doubted it would even receive a simple majority, much less a two-thirds. He was aware of two factors: House conservatives, representing a management point of view, wanted a bill much more anti-labor than the Kennedy-Ives. They could not toughen it unless the bill came to the floor open for amendment, and this could not be done under suspension of the rules. On the other hand, labor-minded House Members were violently opposed even to the Kennedy-Ives bill, and many of the most responsible and honest of trade-union leaders were reluctant to support it. Prior to the vote, however, President George Meany, speaking for the Executive Council of the AFL-CIO, sent a telegram to each Member of the House. Meany urged them to support the bill. The measure came to the floor. After a short but violent debate the bill not only failed to receive the necessary two-thirds majority; it also failed to receive a simple majority. The vote was 190 in favor and 198 against.

Shortly afterward, in August, the Eighty-fifth Congress was adjourned. In the ensuing congressional elections in November 1958, the Democratic party scored its greatest success in a nonpresidential year since 1936. The Eighty-sixth Congress that would convene for its first session in Washington in January 1959 was clearly the most liberal and pro-labor in twenty years—283 Democrats and 154 Republicans.

During the campaign I had spent some time in different sections of the country, including my own district. Everywhere it seemed that there existed genuine public concern about labor racketeering. It was apparent that public concern was focused only on defects within the labor movement. The McClellan Committee's hearings had also revealed racketeering within management, but the public, taking its lead from the one-sided headlines, overlooked this.

Returning to Washington in December 1958, I made some checks within the labor movement on the national level. There was obvious confidence that the Eighty-sixth Congress would be friendly to organized labor. This sprang from the liberal hue of the fall elections, which, in turn, was interpreted as meaning that any reporting and disclosure bill that labor opposed could be successfully blocked. Such confidence even led labor leaders to believe that if pressure should compel Congress to pass a reporting and disclosure bill covering labor unions, it would be possible to incorporate into it amendments that would pull the teeth of the despised Taft-Hartley Act. At the same time, House conservatives and their cheerleader lobbyists were determined to battle not only for a bill designed to curb "labor racketeering" but also to extend its scope to include restrictions on legitimate trade-union activity.

As the Congress opened, it was immediately to be plunged into what *Time* magazine correctly forecast as the "roughest, bitterest brawl of the 86th."

In the opening stages, I made a point of checking with three friends, Stewart L. Udall of Arizona and Frank Thompson, Jr., of New Jersey, both Education and Labor Committee members, and Lee Metcalf of Montana, who had just left the committee to take a seat on the key Ways and Means Committee. We found that our views on labor legislation coincided. Udall, in particular, was convinced that if this Congress did not pass at least a reporting-disclosure bill, the Democratic party ticket at all levels would encounter stormy political trouble in the 1960 presidential election.

I went to the Speaker and told him that for this reason, as well as for the primary objective reason of need, a bill had to be passed at this Congress. Rayburn agreed, but this did not clear away an obvious hazard.

The hazard was this: Assume, as was likely, that the Senate passed a bill not entirely acceptable to organized labor, whose leaders were feeling quite bullish. The bill would come to the House, where it would be referred to the Education and Labor Committee, whose complexion had changed from anti-labor to pro-labor in recent years. This would make it difficult to wrest from the committee a bill that was both fair to trade unions yet sufficient to serve the public interest.

Rayburn now asked a number of questions about the membership of the committee, as a means of confirming my judgment. Finally he nodded agreement and then seemed to invite additional comment. I first expressed my misgivings at the storm ahead, but offered my services to work on this legislative problem to the exclusion of any but routine duties. Rayburn inquired as to other major legislation—education, housing, depressed areas, and minimum wage. I suggested that nothing much could get done anyway until the labor bill had cleared the House. Rayburn accepted my offer, saying as I left, "Keep me informed."

The coming weeks proved the most difficult, most hazardous, and most unsuccessful in my experience as a House Member. In the events that followed, both liberals in general and labor types in particular—the "lib-lab" lobby—and managements' lobbyists simultaneously denounced my role.

Metcalf, as leader of the Democratic Study Group, and Thompson and Udall were my main touchstones. In March a special subcommittee of the Education and Labor Committee began its work, which was to take thirty-nine days.

However, the Senate was the first battleground. The scope and depth of the Senate version of a labor bill would not only influence the House action but also, and more importantly, would affect the final compromise between the House and Senate versions.

Secretary of Labor James Mitchell was carrying the ball for the Eisenhower Administration. It had proposed a bill more far-reaching than the straight antiracketeering measure co-sponsored by

Senators John Kennedy and Sam J. Ervin, Jr., of North Carolina, to supplant the now dead Kennedy-Ives bill. The Administration bill included strengthening amendments to the Taft-Hartley Act. These were anathema to many of the most respectable labor leaders. If the Kennedy-Ervin bill withstood assault to emerge as the Senate version, then prospects would be improved for the House to adopt a legitimate antiracketeering measure without deliberately punitive anti-labor sections. If, however, the Kennedy-Ervin bill were amended to include anti-labor provisions, then the House's version would correspondingly take on such a coloration.

Labor lobbyists were ever busy and still optimistic. They predicted the Senate would pass a bill they could accept, even though they might not find it desirable. Essentially, labor wanted no bill at all on the grounds that there was little evidence of wrongdoing, and, anyway, labor could police itself. I was disturbed at this attitude, not only because their assessment was incorrect but also because I sensed they had misjudged the public mind and the balance of the forces engaged in the struggle.

It seemed evident that the majority of concerned Americans were aghast at the findings of the McClellan Committee. They supported a more or less "tough" bill. The Eisenhower Administration had sent to Capitol Hill a bill that could properly be described as more stringent than the Kennedy-Ervin bill. Management's lobbyists were working incredibly hard. They had many sympathizers for their position in the Senate; more, I feared, in the House.

The Kennedy-Ervin bill was reported to the Senate on April 14. Debate began the next day. In several tests of strength, proponents of the bill won handily. However, on April 22 the Senate adopted by one vote an amendment sponsored by a Member whose name in these circumstances was magic—McClellan. It provided for a so-called "bill of rights," designed to protect the rank and file of labor-union members against the autocratic actions of their leaders. McClellan's move provoked surprise because the year before he had supported the Kennedy-Ives bill that had passed the Senate before it was killed in the House. With the adoption of McClellan's provision with the catchy title, the line was breached. The struggle continued. Fifty-five votes, sixteen by roll call, had been cast on amendments. The Kennedy-Ervin bill had been reshaped. Before final passage of the over-all bill on April 25, the McClellan amendment was modified. However, the damage had been done.

The Senate-passed bill now entered the lists in the House. At hand was the situation Rayburn had been warned about. Labor wanted the Senate bill reduced in scope—or no bill. A sounding led me to believe that a bill, without any of the Taft-Hartley amendments the Senate included, could be brought from the committee. But labor wanted some of these amendments. I reported to Rayburn that if labor-favored Taft-Hartley amendments were retained in committee, it would be an invitation to management to add its pet anti-labor Taft-Hartley changes. However, some of the Taft-Hartley amendments in the bill as it then stood were regarded as "sweeteners" that would help the labor movement—that is, the AFL-CIO but not the Teamsters and Mine Workers—to swallow the other sections of the bill. As my explorations of opinions continued, I became convinced that a bill confined to "antiracketeering" provisions would be insufficient. Support had developed, as well, for prohibitions on refusal of nonstriking union members to handle goods from a struck plant and picketing designed to persuade an employer to permit his employees to be organized by a union. Management and the Adminstration called these "hot cargo" and "blackmail picketing" provisions a standard technique of racket-ridden union locals.

Building these provisions into the bill, on the other hand, would goad the labor movement, which felt that these tactics were perfectly legitimate weapons used by perfectly legitimate unions. As opinion within the House began to coalesce around a more stringent bill, the AFL-CIO high command decided to accept an antiracketeering bill without any of its sweeteners. However, the shift in position was already too late.

At about this time, the AFL-CIO held a dinner "rally" for a number of House Members friendly to organized labor. Labor leaders also attended, making a gathering of about two dozen. The atmosphere was quite unrealistic. Several Members of Congress, with connections running into the labor movement, gave passionate locker-room speeches. The speeches were pretty. They were also gravely misplaced, resembling as they did the kind of speech given union members about to "hit the bricks," that is, strike. I spoke my piece, and explained that the House was veering toward passage of a punitive anti-labor bill. I suggested that the group had better drop the exhortations, and concentrate on cutting losses. Better to devise a bill that, while being as close as possible to an antiracketeering measure, still could pick up sufficient support with fringe changes to fend off labor-busting amendments. In sum, the discomforted diners were told to be prepared to accept a mildly distasteful bill in order to avoid a bill they would gag on.

As I spoke I had the impression that everyone was listening politely but that no one was concentrating sufficiently to hear the warning. After the meeting, one AFL-CIO leader took me aside to ask if I had "really meant" what I said. I hoped the apprehension would spread among his colleagues.

Simultaneously the Teamsters Union was operating in what seemed to me a most peculiar fashion. While all its representatives were flawlessly polite to me during our discussions, stories began to circulate that they were not so courteous to other Members. The Teamsters were using methods that may be effective in state and local legislative bodies but not in the Congress of the United States. Few Members of Congress permit themselves to be treated as if they were either for sale or could be intimidated by loudmouthed bullying. The Teamsters' techniques became a major unearned asset to management forces. At times it seemed that the Teamsters actually wanted a patently anti-labor bill enacted into law. One Teamster representative persistently attempted to visit Rayburn. I advised the Speaker to refuse, on grounds that this particular Teamster man was moving about Capitol Hill as if he were some sort of headless horseman.

Meanwhile, the lobbyists, whatever the persuasion of each, had allies within the then thirty-member Education and Labor Committee. Twenty Members were Democrats. Ten were Republicans, all of whom, from the most to the least reactionary, supported so-called "tough legislation." Of the twenty Democrats, two, Barden and Landrum, basically took the Republican position. Of the remaining eighteen, ten supported the position of the AFL-CIO. The other eight, all favorably inclined toward the goals and aspirations of the trade-union movement, held commonly to the view that a bill as close to an antiracketeering measure as possible should be reported. Of the eight, five were particularly to play a crucial role. Their collective efforts were employed on many occasions to redress the imbalance when the bill, as it was being stitched together, seemed to veer in the direction of impairing labor's legitimate objectives or to veer toward ineffectiveness. The five—Udall, Thompson, Carl Elliott of Alabama, James O'Hara of Michigan, and Mrs. Green of Oregon—became known as the "fearless five" because each represented districts wherein organized labor had substantial political power. Each faced volley after volley of heavy political barrages from these labor forces. Conversely, to hotheads in organized labor the quintet were the "faithless five"—or worse.

Thompson, Udall, Metcalf, and I formed an impromptu command post to receive, assess, and act upon the stream of truths, half-truths, rumors, counterrumors, and advices that came our way. At the same time, the AFL-CIO Executive Council had delegated to a four-member committee the right to make decisions in dealing with the day-to-day problems involved in the fierce legislative struggle. Selected to serve with AFL-CIO President Meany were three vice-presidents of the labor federation, each, in turn, a president of an international union—George Harrison of the Railway Clerks, Al Hayes of the Machinists, and Walter Reuther of the Auto Workers. They invited Thompson, Udall, Metcalf, and me to dinner. Up to now, the communications and daily encounters between us four and numerous labor lobbyists were friendly in tone, whatever the disagreements. Some labor men, whose unions, in effect, the McClellan Committee, had cleared, agreed with us four that efforts should be directed at assuring that any bill reported should be as free as possible from punitive provisions. However, there were other labor men from equally unbesmirched unions who violently felt that we four Members were defeatist if not disloyal. A bill was unnecessary; efforts to bring out a bill should be thwarted. Their slogan: It shall not pass!

I have never quite understood the reason for this dogmatic attitude. Proud and honest men who temperamentally could not tolerate being lumped in with crooks? Internal pressures, structural rents or rivalries within the AFL-CIO itself? I do not know.

In any event, this was the background of the dinner meeting between the AFL-CIO command post and us four.

As it turned out, Reuther was absent. However, we were a little surprised to see that, in addition to Andrew Biemiller, former House Member and now AFL-CIO's chief legislative representative, and labor lawyers, the company included James McDevitt, director of COPE, the Committee on Political Education, the political arm of the AFL-CIO. We recognized the significance of McDevitt's presence.

Meany, Hayes, and Harrison were three representatives of the 16-million-member labor movement. We spoke for ourselves alone, although it was assumed, correctly, that I represented Rayburn's views. However, only Rayburn could speak for himself.

As at the previous dinner, I had the impression no one was listening carefully to our explanation. Labor's men were told that the time had passed when their friends in the House could do whatever labor wanted done. It was stated again that in order to prevent a harsh anti-labor bill from becoming law, efforts should be made to bring out a bill that would satisfy the articulated public demand for labor reforms, even if this meant including features objectionable to organized labor—and to us four personally.

The conversation washed back and forth across the table. The atmosphere became tense at one point when someone set out to make political threats against us. Wiser heads among labor soon recognized, however, that we had arrived at our position with due regard for the possibilities of labor's retaliation at the polls. Near the evening's end, I reiterated that while we knew what we proposed did not please them, we were not certain we could hold even that position in committee or on the floor. At this point, Meany said something to the effect that, rather than compromise, labor would prefer to go down to defeat in a clean fight for a position it believed in. I said with a smile that such an attitude would make it easier on all of us. And, while Meany did not say it, I think he realized that what I meant was that his position was beyond maintaining. The meeting broke up on the note that Meany had better talk to Rayburn. I agreed.

Soon Meany visited Rayburn in the Speaker's office. He made his argument; not unexpectedly, he heard in return Rayburn's position, which corresponded to the one we four had outlined at the dinner.

The AFL-CIO opened up its big guns. Metcalf, the "fearless" five, and I stood alone. We were in trouble outside Congress. We were in trouble inside Congress for similar reasons—we were settling for too much (labor's view) or we were settling for too little (management's view).

Labor's offensive focused on the five committee members—Thompson, Udall, Mrs. Green, Elliott, and O'Hara. All of them had courage and character. Many legislators more accustomed to pressure than these five would have collapsed, I was convinced. The only relief from their anguish was the knowledge of their conviction and that Rayburn would support them. Curiously, some important leaders of certain large AFL-CIO unions were strangely silent, even to the point of seeming sympathetic to them.

Within the committee, the five would vote on one occasion with outspoken AFL-CIO supporters among the Democrats to beat down the efforts of the ten Republicans and two Democrats who were the core of the intensely anti-labor movement within the committee. On others, the five would vote with the conservative twelve to provide a majority to keep the bill's teeth from being entirely pulled.

The stratagems worked. On July 23 the committee voted 16 to 14 to send the so-called Elliott bill to the floor. On this carrying vote, the five, all Democrats, were joined by three other Democrats, two anti-labor Democrats, and six of the ten Republicans on the committee. Minority Leader Charles A. Halleck corraled these six party fellows on the grounds that this was the only way to bring a bill to the House floor.

When the report, a printed explanation of the bill, and the assents and dissents of the committee members, was issued, the accomplishments of the five became startlingly clear. Of the sixteen who voted for the Elliott bill, only the five themselves stood without reservation behind the bill.

Four days later, Representative Phil M. Landrum of Georgia, a Democrat on the committee, and Representative Robert P. Griffin of Michigan, a Republican on the committee, introduced another bill, H.R. 8400. They designated the bill as a bipartisan measure that they would attempt to substitute for the Elliott bill at a proper time on the House floor. It contained many more anti-labor provisions than the Elliott bill. On July 30, Representative John F. Shelley, now mayor of San Francisco, and a former president of the California Federation of Labor, introduced an AFL-CIO-supported bill.

Endorsements followed. Senator Kennedy and his brother Robert, counsel of the McClellan Committee, endorsed the Elliott bill. So did Rayburn. President Eisenhower and McClellan himself publicly supported the Landrum-Griffin bill.

At this point, I telephoned Biemiller and invited myself out to his home for a drink. Although we were friends of long standing, I was uncertain about his current attitude because of the deep passions aroused by the labor struggle. Pleasantries behind us, I set out to win his support. It seemed probable that the choice had narrowed to one between the Elliott or the Landrum-Griffin bills. There was no way to block any and all bills. Biemiller listened, seemingly unconvinced, as I suggested that unless the AFL-CIO representatives and the "fearless five" supporters shook hands and worked for the Elliott bill, the schism would result in an easy triumph for Landrum-Griffin. It was clear that the Elliott bill was the more palatable. I suggested a group of counters be established, to keep track of the potential votes for the Elliott bill; Metcalf and I would operate in co-operation with Biemiller and his men.

Biemiller said nothing for a while, and then remarked: "For God's sake don't let Thompson and Udall show up. Some of our people are awfully bitter about them."

The counters began meeting in Metcalf's office. Labor men were present. Understandably there was some strain, but this soon eased. Systematically we determined how wavering and uncommitted House Members should be approached—how and by whom—a House leader, labor lobbyist, an influential friend or constituent, for example.

Each Member was classified and followed for any indications of a change of mind or heart. After a while we could call the roll of Members by states from memory.

One afternoon Thompson appeared. Feeling was so high that Metcalf and I had to ease him out of the room as gently as possible.

The result of the first count sobered everyone. The Elliott bill trailed, but not hopelessly so. The information soon reached us that the Landrum-Griffin supporters had selected about fifty to sixty House Members upon whom heavy pressure would be maintained continuously. Their muscle, as best we could figure it, was being furnished by the United States Chamber of Commerce, the National Association of Manufacturers, and the American Farm Bureau. The American Retail Federation and other lobby groups within the business community apparently were detailed to do specific assignments. Their efforts were successful. Strong Members blanched under their pressure. One Member from Georgia, Erwin Mitchell, was subjected to round-the-clock harassment. He stuck with us, but at an awesome toll. His first full term became his last, and he retired from Congress with his health impaired. The legislative struggle is a most ungentle one.

We ran into a series of unexpected setbacks. In a close fight over controversial legislation, the Member whose name is associated with the bill often assumes a decisive importance: we had hoped for this when Elliott agreed to give his name to the committee bill. Elliott, a sincere, respected, and intelligent man, was an asset. He represented a rural district in northern Alabama, and found himself in the middle because of the anti-labor forces that are inclined to dominate rural areas. But he wore no man's collar. It took courage for him to sponsor the bill, and he was an effective advocate. We had counted on his leadership to hold votes and win votes. This strength was knocked from under the bill when Elliott was put out of action by a severe gall-bladder infection requiring surgery.

Shortly after the Elliott bill moved easily out of Rules to the floor, President Eisenhower threw his enormous popularity behind its rival, the Landrum-Griffin bill. In a nation-wide television and radio appeal on August 6, the President urged Americans to bring pressure on the Congress to pass the Landrum-Griffin bill. He had never injected himself with such vigor into a legislative fight. It was really out of character. It must have been due to the influence of his business friends and legislative leaders and the essentially conservative nature that lay behind his affable exterior. As we watched the televised speech we were shocked by the one-sidedness of the presidential presentation of an issue that was many-faceted. We had no hope that the intense bias of the speech would redound to our favor. This speech of a President, whose first Cabinet contained nine millionaires and a plumber, was probably decisive.

The countermove was by Rayburn. Efforts were made to obtain equal time for him to reply to the President. All the networks, except one radio network, refused to allow the time to Rayburn alone. The Speaker made his speech, essentially a plea for fairness, over the one available radio network. He asked that punitive legislation, the Landrum-Griffin bill, not be passed, and stated the case for the Elliott bill as one that would provide effective curbs against the relatively few cases of racketeering, without hurting legitimate trade-union objectives. It was a good speech. But no Speaker, even Rayburn, has the impact on the American people of any President.

On August 11, debate began on the House floor. The Shelley bill, supported by the labor federation, was crushed the following day. The debate was conducted informatively and soundly, but if it ever changed a vote I have never discovered it. The flow of battle was against the Elliott bill. However, we still had a long-shot possibility.

During detailed examination Archibald Cox, a Kennedy adviser, a member of the Harvard University Law School faculty, and in 1964 Solicitor General of the United States, discovered a "sleeper" in Section 609 of the Landrum-Griffin bill. Language in the section, if pursued through a series of references in the bill, was susceptible of being interpreted as a strong civil rights provision. Told of this, we decided to exploit the discovery. It involved a delicate parliamentary maneuver. The Elliott bill was the basic bill under discussion in the "Committee of the Whole," a parliamentary sleight-of-hand whereby the whole House converts itself by a resolution into the committee wherein the time for debate is limited, the quorum is only one hundred members, there are no recorded votes, and other rules help to expedite discussion of a bill. Assuming the Landrum-Griffin bill would be offered as an amendment to the Elliott bill, the Committee of the Whole would then "rise" and become by another parliamentary sleight-of-hand the House again. At this point all amendments, including the Landrum-Griffin ones, would be frozen into the labor bill. But now a roll call could be demanded on the amendments adopted by nonrecorded votes in the Committee of the Whole. At this juncture we would make known the existence of the civil rights provision. This should cause sufficient Southerners to desert Landrum-Griffin. They could explain voting for a milder labor bill, the Elliott measure, by stating that they preferred Landrum-Griffin, but "when I discovered that it contained a civil rights provision surely I could not stand by and see dear old Dixie hurt." We would make known the sleeper provision by circulating one hundred marked copies of the Landrum-Griffin bill that revealed the implied civil rights provision. Ten non-southern House Democrats, sworn to secrecy, were to be given a list of Southerners to whom at the crucial time they were to hand a marked copy of the bill, and explain its significance. If the maneuver were skillfully executed, the Elliott bill might win. But we never had an opportunity to find out. On August 12, Representative James Roosevelt of California, for reasons I have never been able to discover, rose in the House and gave the show away. He announced to the whole House that he had discovered a "silver lining" in the Landrum-Griffin bill. He then told the Southerners just where the sleeper provision was. The Southerners panicked, but had plenty of time to remove the offending provision. They did.

The climactic battle was to come the following day, August 13. That morning I reported to Rayburn that our count showed there was still an outside chance of getting as many as 215 votes for the Elliott bill—if a high percentage of Members listed as "probable" supporters actually cast their votes as indicated. During the morning pressures from proponents and opponents of each bill became so enormous that a number of Members actually hid so as not to be found by those persistent trackers, the lobbyists. Using as up to date a list as could be compiled, I explained to Rayburn each Member's position based on what the individual had told us directly or on indirect sources of information. The Speaker listened, asked questions occasionally, and sometimes made a brief comment. At the end, he said: "You and the boys have done the best job that could be done in this situation. And I have done everything I thought would help. But we're going to get beat."

The final stage was, in Rayburn's phrase, "raw and bloody." In Committee of the Whole, the Landrum-Griffin bill was adopted by a teller vote of 215 to 200—415 Members out of 435 being present, an extraordinarily high vote.

The Committee of the Whole dissolved itself into the House. The roll call began. Meticulous plans had been made to keep track of the voting as it proceeded, in hopes of corraling those Members who were considered tentative in their positions before the roll-call results became officially announced. However, about halfway through the first call of the House roster, I told John Brademas of Indiana, who was at that point keeping the tally, "not to bother, it's a waste of time." It was apparent we were not garnering the high percentage of "probables" needed for victory. The final key vote was 229 to 201 in favor of Landrum-Griffin. Even now I remember quivering when I looked over the final vote and realized that if those we miscounted as "probables" had indeed voted with us the vote would have been a tie, 215 to 215. Speaker Rayburn would then have voted against Landrum-Griffin to break the tie.

Carl Elliott's diseased gall bladder, President Eisenhower's nation-wide speech, and Jimmie Roosevelt's premature disclosure had wrought defeat.

At once, of course, the twenty-twenty hindsight speculation from the sidelines began. Rayburn hadn't really been for the Elliott bill or why would sixteen out of twenty Democratic Members in the Texas delegation, his delegation, have jumped the traces and voted for the Landrum-Griffin bill. Therein lies not one tale but two.

The outcome of the vote was to bear heavily on Lyndon B. Johnson's chances to be his party's presidential nominee in 1960. It also showed that under his flinty self-control Rayburn was subject to bitter personal disappointment.

After the House had adjourned and the hurly-burly with the

press had ended, I went to the back office of the Speaker. I found him chatting with an acquaintance from Texas who was interested in the labor bill. I complied with his request to give a rundown on the "probables" who never came home. Later the friend left. I then said to Rayburn: "Mr. Speaker, I have never asked you to do this kind of thing before, but could I bring Metcalf, Thompson, and Udall to your hideaway this evening for a drink? They fought hard. They feel as badly as we do. It might cheer them up." Rayburn declined. My surprise apparently showed, because Rayburn, who spent nearly every evening of his life with a group that included two or more favorite Texans, elaborated. "No, not this evening. Tomorrow. I can't stand to be with those Texans tonight." The next evening we four—Metcalf, Thompson, Udall, and I—did sit in with the Speaker and several Texas Members, over a drink. John W. McCormack, majority leader, entered. He looked in exaggerated surprise at the faces of the men, strangers to the hideaway—Metcalf, Thompson, and Udall. "John," said Rayburn, "this time I thought for a change I'd like to be with the boys that are with me."

The shrewd reporters did not buy the story that Rayburn was half-hearted about his support for the Elliott bill and his opposition to Landrum-Griffin. They began rooting around to discover why only four of twenty Texas House Democrats—Jack Brooks, Patman, Al Thomas, and Clark Thompson—had stayed with the Speaker on the vote. These reporters knew Rayburn had pushed the Elliott bill farther than he had pushed a major bill in many years. They recalled his radio appeal on the eve of the floor debate. They came to the same answer—Lyndon B. Johnson, majority leader of the Senate, and a Texan. Johnson had said that it would be politically ruinous for Texans in the House to vote for anything less than the toughest labor bill available. Most of the delegation responded favorably to the Johnson hustle.

At one point before the vote, labor men came into possession of a letter, probably—to be fair—a routine release from Johnson's office in answer to a flood of constituent mail on the subject of labor legislation. This letter satisfied the labor men that Johnson was very much a proponent of Landrum-Griffin. From then on, many powerful labor men swore to get revenge. The labor movement cannot nominate a presidential candidate any more than another single group. However, labor is too large a group to be ignored by a nominating convention. Labor held a negative power—the ability to veto Johnson as the candidate at the 1960 Democratic convention.

One more legislative battle remained. The Senate and House had passed differing versions of labor legislation. As is customary, conferees were named from each body to meet jointly in an effort to agree upon a compromise. Under the courageous and infinitely determined guidance of Senator Kennedy, the conference produced a compromise that significantly lessened the blatant, deliberate anti-labor sections of the House-passed Landrum-Griffin bill. Kennedy on this occasion convinced his critics that he possessed great qualities of mind and strength of being. Nevertheless, the end product was still decidedly less Kennedy or Elliott and more Landrum-Griffin. These three bills were strikingly alike in their respective provisions that dealt with racketeering. The difference lay in the Landrum-Griffin provisions that erected further obstacles to the proper and just objectives of American labor.

Kennedy, as chairman of the House-Senate conference, produced a bill both bodies accepted. If he had failed, would his uphill journey to the White House have been blocked?

Thus, ironically, the most pro-labor House in twenty years enacted a bill with numerous anti-labor provisions. The Speaker, leader of the Democratic party in the House, strongly supported a fair bill, but he did not have available enough institutional power to force to the floor the bill which he and a majority of his party regarded as essential to the public good, and incidentally to the good of the party. Indeed, Congress came perilously close to being unable to act at all on a matter of great national importance. There would have been no bill at all, and hence no law, except for the "fearless five" on the Education and Labor Committee.

Yet in the end, for all the poor judgments, miscalculations, accidents of time and place, human frailty and prejudice, a law was fashioned out of need, though distorted by conflicting interests, with each of the antagonists believing that his cause would triumph.

Chapter 9

Civil Rights—1956 and 1957

"The triumph of hope, over experience"
—Samuel Johnson

Although the Civil Rights Act of 1957 was far less comprehensive than that of 1964, strategy evolved to enable the earlier act to pass gave advocates invaluable experience in getting the second bill through. For years prior to the enactment of the Civil Rights Act of 1957—the first law enacted on this subject since 1875—Democrats and Republicans in Congress had been engaging in fruitless civil rights maneuvers. Each party accumulated an increasing file of noble statements, but every effort to frame a law collapsed in a scramble for partisan advantage.

However, the legislative war of nearly two years that culminated in the 1957 Act was to be successful. In the bitter struggle, the formulation of strategy was often the critical factor. For, while the combat may be compared to a chess game, it is one in which the chessmen constantly change value. And there are many steps from the conception of a strategy to its successful conclusion. There were skirmishes and battles, victories and defeats, all manner of crises. Each of these engagements was integral to the process of passing the bill.

Over the years the Senate had stood like a wall against all efforts to enact civil rights legislation. Manning the battlement was a small band of Southerners armed with the filibuster, the most effective parliamentary delaying tactic a legislative minority has ever had. It is sanctioned by Rule 22 of the Senate Rules, which require a vote of two-thirds of the Senate Membership to shut off debate. Repeatedly, the filibuster, or merely the threat of one, had prevented the Senate from giving civil rights legislation serious consideration. The House, with stricter limitations on debate, would pass bills only to have them struck down in the Senate.

In 1956 both parties had fundamental problems. The Democrats were bitterly divided. There were perhaps slightly more than 100 Democratic Members who really showed any genuine concern for civil rights legislation. Of the other approximately 130 Democrats, some have voted regularly but cynically for such legislation, assured the measure would be slain in the Senate; others, unshakable segregationists, opposed such a bill.

The Republicans seemed less divided. Often more Republicans than Democrats voted for civil rights legislation. Despite this, the problem among House Republicans was the general lack of steady, strong commitment.

During the 1956 congressional session there were probably fewer than 150 Democrats and Republicans in the 435-Member House who possessed a strong and sincere desire to push for passage of civil rights legislation.

In view of this, it seemed that a strategy should be conceived that could create an effective coalition of public opinion, presidential advocacy, supporting House Members, and lobbying groups with a particular or exclusive interest in civil rights. Because only 35 per cent of the House, 150 Members, could be relied upon as a base for legislative success, it was essential that leaders of each party in each body of the Congress be convinced that they would gain political advantage for themselves and their party as a result of civil rights legislation.

During the year 1955, it was increasingly recognized that Congress would soon feel pressure to make more than a mock drive for legislation. This was partly due to the Supreme Court's decision in May of the previous year that enforced public school segregation was unconstitutional. Outside the Congress, the National Association for the Advancement of Colored People, the NAACP, was driving for a bill, now that its attorneys had successfully fought school segregation through the courts.

For years most of the civil rights bills had been across-the-board affairs that attempted to settle all problems with one legislative blow. President Truman had recommended far-reaching proposals. So had Republican Members of the House. However, some civil rights leaders thought that most of the advocates were mainly concerned with bringing credit to their party by holding commendable views on a righteous cause.

In 1953–1955, the first three years of the first Eisenhower Administration, the President had submitted no substantial civil rights proposals. Nor had the Republican Eighty-third Congress, which met in 1953 and 1954, taken any action in this area. The Democratic-controlled Eighty-fourth Congress did nothing about civil rights in its first year, 1955.

As public opinion built up, leaders of both parties were concerned with the future political allegiance of American Negroes. Liberal organizations and segments of the trade-union movement were becoming increasingly vocal in support of effective civil rights measures: No more posturing—pass a bill.

Late in the fall of 1955, Clarence Mitchell, able and intelligent lobbyist for the NAACP, asked that sympathetic House Republicans and Democrats meet with him. They met in one of the two House Office Buildings. Few appeared, partly because many were back home, and some who had agreed to attend canceled their plans because of bad weather.

Nevertheless, the meeting was held. Some Members sent a staff representative. Various proposals were offered—a federal fair-employment-practices program, establishment of a federal civil rights commission, anti-poll-tax and anti-lynching legislation.

I was inclined to support legislation to guarantee the right to vote. I took the position that such a bill would underscore a fundamental issue in American life. If the Negro's right to vote were protected, he would achieve political power that would permit him to move toward other legitimate goals. Furthermore, I pointed out, voting legislation was far less susceptible than school desegregation to inflammatory opposition by racists. Perhaps, I even speculated, the southern opposition in Congress to voting rights could be reduced to a beleaguered group of fanatics who would be placed in the unenviable position of opposing legislation to provide effective legal guarantees that all Americans, properly qualified, be allowed to register and vote. A number of Southerners, even if they could not vote for the bill, would not fight it. And a few border-state Democrats would be able to see their way clear to supporting it.

I suggested that the President might be persuaded to propose such a bill. His initiative would recruit votes among his own party members in Congress who otherwise would doubtlessly be apathetic. Most importantly, militant groups, such as the NAACP and some labor unions, if persuaded of the wisdom of a step-at-a-time legislation, would not propose or support tough riders to the basic voting-rights bill that might lead to its defeat.

Any voting-rights bill had to be designed so as to reduce the possibility of a Senate filibuster that would kill it. The attitude of Speaker Rayburn would be important if this trap were to be avoided—not so much because of his influence in the House itself but because of his prestige and influence among Southerners in both House and Senate. And, in the Senate, his principal advantage was his protégé, Lyndon Baines Johnson, then majority leader.

In view of the factors that could be controlled, advocates of a voting-rights bill felt that it could be passed. Hard work and a little bit of luck would carry the day. The prospects seemed so favorable that it was tempting to me to travel to Bonham, Texas, to discuss the matter with the Speaker. Instead, I held off and awaited his return to Washington for the opening of the second session of the Eighty-fourth Congress in January 1956.

After the Speaker returned to Washington, the situation was discussed with him. He listened to the description of pressures for legislation, political implications, and the direction I thought the legislation should take.

Rayburn neither gave nor withheld his approval. He did say: "I'm not against the right to vote. Every citizen should have that." And, at the end of a long conversation, he simply thanked me.

Nevertheless, I walked from his office in relief and delight. I was certain that if certain preliminary tasks could be performed, the Speaker would step in at the critical time in order to give the bill the push that only he could effectively give. My hunch that the Speaker would ultimately play a crucial, favorable role could not be mentioned. As in the past, to involve him too soon in a legislative matter would probably be to lose him or to reduce his effectiveness.

A group of House Members met soon to make plans. Among them were Representatives Adam Clayton Powell of New York, Charles C. Diggs, Jr., of Michigan, both Negroes, James Roosevelt of California, all Democrats, and a key Republican, then a House Member, Hugh Scott, Jr., of Pennsylvania. Scott had been chairman of the Republican National Committee. He knew Attorney General Herbert Brownell, whose office would presumably be responsible for the drafting of the legislation. Scott was the logical person to persuade the Administration to propose voting-rights legislation. Scott promised to do his best. In spite of his best efforts and those of other Republicans, the Justice Department under Brownell moved slowly.

One reason may have been the difficulty of drafting effective language for the bill. Or there may have been deliberate delay within the Administration in the hope that the Democrats would become embroiled in an intraparty dogfight over the issue before the national conventions of both parties that summer or during the presidential campaign. In such an event, naturally the Republicans would benefit. Meanwhile, I set out to persuade labor and civil rights organizations to support the type of civil rights legislation that I anticipated would eventually be put forward by the Administration.

The measure came to the Congress on April 9, 1956—three months after the opening of the second session. The Democratic National Convention would begin August 13, four months later. By that time Congress might probably have adjourned or recessed subject to recall later in the year after the nominating conventions. However, in an election year, the latter seemed unlikely.

Timing, therefore, became a central factor. Unless House action could be completed by the end of May, there would be so little time left that the Senate opponents would be able to fend off the legislation by delaying tactics. This would be disastrous to the Democrats—the backwash from this outcome would engulf the party's presidential nominating convention in internecine warfare. The fortunes of the Democratic presidential nominee and congressional candidates would be imperiled.

Many difficulties could be foreseen in the Senate. For one thing,

Johnson, sympathetic to the legislation, concluded that there would not be time enough to pass the bill through the Senate. In view of this, he seemed to dread even the arrival of a House-passed bill.

The House moved slowly. Delays occurred in the Judiciary Committee. The bill was not ordered reported to the House from the committee until April 25. It is one thing for a bill to be ordered reported and another to report it. In the first instance, it signifies a majority of the committee has agreed to a finished version. But a report explaining the provisions of the bill has to be written. The opponents are entitled to have their dissent included in the report accompanying the bill. This provides an opportunity for opponents to dawdle along in preparing their written dissent.

After that, the bill would have to pass through a hostile Rules Committee with its bag of delaying tactics. At this point, it seemed that at best the House could not pass a bill that would arrive in the Senate before early July. Taking into account the Fourth of July recess, only three weeks would remain for the Senate to act. Johnson's premonition would be realized. The bill would be cut to pieces by Southern filibusters and the Democrats would suffer at the polls.

After an agonizing reappraisal I decided that the time factor could be used for the benefit of the bill. If the opponents could use delaying tactics, then the proponents could utilize delay for their purposes. To do so would involve a certain deception of friend and enemy alike. If I were exposed in the course of this process, I might forfeit my chances for re-election to a fifth term. More importantly, I believed in the bill. I had played a role in the legislative strategy and tactics established for the bill. If nothing were done, the bill would go to the Senate in time for it and my party to be mangled. Future events vindicated my decision.

First, I went to Rayburn and gave him my analysis of the changed situation. I suggested delaying the bill unobtrusively so that, while it would pass the House, there would be simply no time for the Senate to consider it before adjournment. This would avoid the much-feared Senate brawl. House approval at this session, the final one, of the Eighty-fourth Congress would hopefully give it priority in the first weeks of the first session of the Eighty-fifth Congress. The House would inevitably repass the bill early in 1957, thereby leaving up to eighteen months for the Senate to act before the Eighty-fifth Congress ended in August 1957.

I emphasized to the Speaker that Johnson had to be made aware that he was gaining only temporary relief—the Senate would inevitably receive a House-passed civil rights bill in 1957. Impatiently, Rayburn said, "I understand what you are saying."

The tactic of delay was never discussed again with Rayburn, but the Judiciary Committee did not report the bill until May 21, nearly one month after it had ordered the bill reported. Smith, the Rules Committee chairman, delayed a hearing on the bill until a committee vote of 8 to 3 forced him to schedule hearings for June 20. On June 21 some of the Rules Committee members left town expressing impatience because the session seemed to them to be dragging on. Whatever their reason, their departure enabled Smith to destroy the plan of bringing hearings to an early close—while one part of the plan involved getting the bill to the Senate too late for any action this session, the other integral part involved getting the bill through the House at the same session. Smith adjourned the meeting for lack of a committee quorum. That day, five of us initiated proceedings under committee rules to force another meeting to continue the hearings. One sidelight to the Rules Committee hearings seemed to me most uncommon evidence of psychological warfare by Southern opponents. As each one testified he looked, not down the length of the long committee table at Chairman Smith, but obliquely to his left at me, apparently to unnerve me. Another sidelight was the matter of absences. It was the liberal members of the Rules Committee who were not staying at the hearings, thereby permitting Smith to adjourn the hearings at one point. Once the liberals learned their lesson, they returned to compile a record of faithful attendance.

Getting a rule for the bill was like pushing a boulder uphill. It was finally obtained on June 27. Because of the Fourth of July recess, debate on the House floor was not scheduled until July 16.

One of the most curious features of the floor debate was a speech by Representative William E. Miller of New York, subsequently chairman of the Republican National Committee and vice-presidential nominee in 1964. After sponsoring the bill and voting for it as a member of the Judiciary Committee, he rose on the House floor to offer a motion to kill it:

"I must in good conscience state . . . this legislation in its present form will destroy more civil liberties than it will ever protect," Miller told the House.

The speech so upset his Republican colleague, Representative Joseph W. Martin, Jr., of Massachusetts, minority leader, that Martin urged Republicans not to be trapped into voting to kill the bill!

". . . this bill has been jockeyed into position where the one group that will be blamed for [its] defeat . . . is the Republican party," Martin said, "I just want to point out to the Republicans not to fall into this trap."

They didn't.

The independent whip system of the Democratic Study Group proved highly effective, and it helped to foil several of the opposition's clever tricks. On one occasion, a crippling amendment, supported by Southerners, was before the House. A particular hour had been set for closing the debate and taking a vote on it.

Supporters of the Southern amendment rose one after the other to receive their share of the debating time. However, instead of using the time to speak, each simply "yielded back their time," that is, did not use it. This shortened the actual time spent on debate, thereby bringing the amendment to a vote far in advance of the scheduled time. This is a frequently used device. Sensing what was happening, the DSG called its whip system into play. Within minutes, the required number of opponents of the amendment were brought from their offices and elsewhere to the floor in order to block the tactic. On another, similar, occasion, I was rushing along a corridor to the Democratic cloakroom and I nearly collided with the Speaker. As I pulled up to avoid him, Rayburn said, "You'd better get your boys here quickly." He was aware of the trick. I knew then for the first time that I had been correct in believing that Rayburn would be a supporter of the civil rights bill to guarantee voting rights to Negroes.

Finally, the bill, H.R. 6127, passed the House on June 18 by a vote of 286 to 126.

As we had planned, there was no time for the Senate to act before adjournment, but the Democrats and Republicans could go to the country and state that the House had passed a civil rights bill.

Civil rights did become a major issue during the ensuing 1956 presidential campaign. As President Eisenhower rolled over Adlai E. Stevenson, he pulled a larger percentage of the Negro vote than he had four years earlier. However, the party alignment in the Congress was little changed. In January 1957, the Eighty-fifth Congress would open with 49 Democrats and 47 Republicans in the Senate and, in the House, 234 Democrats and 201 Republicans, representing for the majority party a gain of two House seats. Politicians understood. Negro voters were no longer beguiled by soothing words in support of civil rights. They wanted performance. As a consequence, party leaders spoke up. For example, Senator Hubert H. Humphrey, Jr., of Minnesota, whose credentials as a civil rights supporter were unquestioned, warned after the election that "Democrats are digging their own grave by inaction in the field. . . ." Republican leaders took a similar cue from the election results.

When a new Congress opens, partially completed action on bills in the previous Congress is wiped out. The legislation must start all over again. So it was with the civil rights bill that had passed only the House in the last session of the Eighty-fourth Congress.

However, now it was the Democrats who were on the spot if no civil rights bill emerged from the new Congress. Republicans had only to point to the position of their President. Any blame for failure could be placed upon the Democrats.

The elements for success were all present. Everyone except the Southern die-hards understood that the Democrats must produce a civil rights bill. Here was an example of the pressure of "politics" working in a good cause.

The key, in my view, was Lyndon Johnson. Unless he was in favor of the bill, it could not be passed in the Senate, no matter how aggressively the bill was supported by Senators Paul H. Douglas of Illinois, a Democrat, and William Knowland of California, Republican and minority leader. There was ample time to deliver a workable bill from the Senate. It would, however, take the utmost exercise of Johnson's unsurpassed skill to avert a filibuster. He could do this by convincing the Southerners that a filibuster on a voting-rights bill might at some undetermined time generate overwhelming pressure for other civil rights legislation that would be even more "offensive" to southern segregationists. Johnson was going to have to assemble a satisfactory compromise that at every point in its progress through the Senate would be precariously balanced on the legislative rails.

Johnson's commitment to a civil rights bill involved his deserved prestige as the most effective Senate majority leader in many years. Also involved was his desire to become President—an objective he unexpectedly achieved under dreadful circumstances seven years later. Johnson certainly knew that his chance for his party's presidential nomination was dimmed at the outset by the fact of his being a Southerner. He had to shake off the incubus of being a sectional political figure. He knew that if he even attempted secret opposition to the bill, his tracks would be discovered by those in Congress who regarded him with distaste.

Often damned by liberals in Congress, Johnson, nevertheless, had always taken a constructive and positive approach to problems. While he might have hoped that the civil rights problem would go away, he knew it would not.

And so Johnson set out to pass a law, and Rayburn helped him to an undetermined degree. The Speaker often spoke about Johnson's concern over the Senate problems that would develop when the House bill came over.

The President's State of the Union message urged enactment of the same bill proposed the previous year. The Judiciary Committee of the House, dodging skillful southern opposition, reported the bill on April 1, 1957. Two of the eight Southerners who dissented in the committee report accompanying the bill were Republicans, indicating that on an emotional social issue party label meant nothing.

On April 7, I told reporters that when the Rules Committee met the next day I intended to press for immediate hearings and clearance of the bill for full House action. I told them about a rumored deal between Republicans and southern Democrats on the Rules Committee to delay the bill until next year, 1958. I indicated there might really be a deal, considering southern opposition to any bill and a desire among Republicans to set up a situation in which the Democrats' differences on civil rights would be put on record during an election year.

My statements were made with two purposes. First, I hoped that my motion would garner sufficient Republican votes to carry in Rules Committee. If so, this would enable the bill to arrive on the House floor before the Easter recess and to pass by early May. Second, should my motion be defeated, the Republicans might feel obliged to put pressure on Smith to call early hearings in order to get them off the spot.

I made my motion in Rules Committee. It was defeated April 8. Smith scoffed at reports that northern Republicans and southern Democrats had joined forces for the purpose of throttling the bill. Yet, on April 9, he scheduled hearings to begin immediately after the Easter recess. Thus he managed a month's delay, but it was an inadequate reprieve. Hearings began May 2. On May 21 the Rules Committee by an 8 to 4 vote granted the bill a rule. Four northern Democrats and four northern Republicans provided the majority.

The rule clearing the way for discussion of the bill on the floor of the House was adopted June 5. The next day Smith made a surprise point of order against the bill. He had not, according to custom, notified the Parliamentarian and the Speaker beforehand. Rayburn overruled the point of order. Had it been sustained, the bill would have been returned to the Judiciary Committee and been forced to repeat its arduous journey.

As the debate began, it became apparent that southern tactics were based on adoption of amendments guaranteeing jury trials to persons charged with contempt for violating injunctions issued by federal courts. As debate progressed, Southerners argued their case so well that at one point Rayburn growled at me, "Why shouldn't that provision be in there?" I told him only part of my reasons for objecting to the jury-trial amendments. The standard argument is that in most contempt proceedings the judge decides the case without a jury. I suggested that some southern juries would refuse to convict. However, my real, but unstated, reason was that I had become convinced no law would be passed unless the House sent the Senate a bill that was more than a minimal or acceptable bill. The House bill must contain provisions at which the Senate Southerners could take aim and quite likely hack away, still leaving an effective bill for the President to sign into law. This would enable the Senate Southerners to tell their constituents that the bill ultimately passed was far weaker than the House version. Thus they could soothe their inflamed segregationist constituencies and possibly feel satisfied enough to refrain from a filibuster.

I urged labor and civil rights groups to maintain the pressure to defeat my jury-trial amendment. The lobbyists proved enormously effective, and so did the White House. Also helpful was a statement, adhered to by eighty-three House Democrats, that warned against adoption of "crippling amendments," and said that the bill would be maimed or killed "only if a deal is worked out between southern Members and some Republican Members." The DSG whip system again proved its worth.

Representative Emanuel Celler of New York, chairman of Judiciary, ably led the proponents of the bill. It cleared the House on June 18, 1957.

The final test remained. The bill went to the Senate. There, it faced two possibilities of defeat: One was that without amendment the bill would raise a filibuster. If, however, the bill were amended so as to reduce it to meaninglessness, then it was predictable that Republicans, joined by outside civil rights groups, would rather have the issue than the law, and there would, therefore, be no law.

There were three discernible groupings in the Senate. Senator Richard B. Russell of Georgia, respected and skillful, led the southern forces opposed to any bill. At the other end stood a coalition of Republicans and northern Democrats who pushed for the strongest possible bill. Douglas and Knowland were conspicuous in this effort. Johnson held a middle ground. As the battle proceeded, few mistakes were made by any group. However, Johnson held the balance of power throughout.

At times it seemed as if the bill would never survive. Once, Johnson had to make three passes at the trial-by-jury amendment. On June 20, Vice President Richard M. Nixon, presiding officer of the Senate, materially assisted the Douglas-Knowland forces. He ruled that the House-passed bill could by-pass the Senate Judiciary Committee and be placed directly on the Senate calendar.

Two major modifications were made in the House bill. One effectively limited Title 3 of the bill to the enforcement of voting rights by the Justice Department instead of permitting the Department through the Attorney General to intervene in all cases of constitutional infringements. The other amendment adopted on August 2 guaranteed jury trials in all criminal contempt cases, not just those arising out of the civil rights statutes. If the Senate adopted the amended bill, the House and Senate versions would go to a conference of both bodies that would attempt to design a bill both House Members and Senators could accept.

I dreaded that the bill would die in conference because of a deadlock between the Senate conferees, led by Senator James O. Eastland of Mississippi, a violent racist, and House conferees under Celler of New York, each chairman of the Judiciary Committees of the respective bodies. Moreover, I could already foresee claims of some Republicans that the Senate, controlled by Democrats, had crippled the bill to the point of ineffectiveness. They would expect the bill that emerged from conference to resemble the House version—or be useless.

Nevertheless, it seemed apparent that civil rights forces would do no better next year. It seemed that the civil rights advocates outside Congress faced a decision whether to accept any bill, however short of their high-powered desires, or accept an issue steeped in partisanship.

Personally, I thought the Senate version represented an important accomplishment—for the first time since the Reconstruction Era following the Civil War the President and the Congress had intervened to protect Negro rights. The Senate version might carry the day if the aggressive civil rights proponents outside the Congress could be prevented from saying publicly that no bill was preferable to the Senate one. In this connection, four persons, one a Senator, could play a role in persuading civil rights groups to refrain from undiluted public disparagement. They were Joseph L. Rauh, Jr., spokesman for the Americans for Democratic Action; Senator Paul H. Douglas, one of the purest spirits in the history of American

politics; former Representative Andrew J. Biemiller, chief legislative representative of the AFL-CIO; and Kenneth Birkhead of the
American Veterans Committee, later an aide to Secretary of Agriculture Orville L. Freeman.

Then began what may be called swimming-pool weekends. I
telephoned Rauh. He agreed to see me on a Saturday afternoon if
I would come out to his home for a swim. Rauh and I had known
each other in New Guinea and the Philippines during World War
II. We had kept in touch since. Rauh, an outspoken liberal in the
orthodox liberal establishment, was a close friend of both Roy
Wilkins, executive secretary of the NAACP, and Walter Reuther,
president of the United Auto Workers.

After a plunge, I hesitantly broached the subject to Rauh. He
agreed there should be a law—representing the best compromise
achievable between the Senate and House versions. He agreed
that a positive statement of encouragement from civil rights supporters would be crucial, and said he would work to obtain support
for a statement which, while criticizing the Senate bill, would
make it clear that some sort of bill would be preferable to no bill.

Later the same weekend, I visited Douglas. Once again a swim
preceded my opening the subject. However, Douglas was visibly
outraged by the Senate action. He was adamantly opposed to the
course I advocated. I soon left without his support.

In the remaining days prior to the final Senate vote, I talked to
Biemiller and Birkhead. They felt as Rauh did. On August 7, the
day the Senate was to act, a statement was issued by civil rights
supporters that described the Senate bill as a "bitter disappointment." However, it acknowledged that the bill "does contain some
potential good," and went on: "Unless the efforts to improve the
bill are handled with skill and devotion, there is danger of winding
up with no bill at all. We call upon friends of civil rights, in both
political parties, to place the goal of some progress in this area ahead
of any fancied political advantage." The statement urged the Senate
to adopt its version. The Senate did so on August 7 by a vote of
72 to 18.

I thought the statement was most helpful. Rayburn stunned me
by remarking, "You didn't get much." I disagreed. At that stage, I

am certain he was interested only in persuading the House to agree to the Senate version.

A week later, it became clear that an acceptable compromise would be difficult to find. Efforts to have the House and Senate accept each other's versions of the bill failed. Martin, the Republican minority leader in the House, conferred with the President and then gave the advice, "Wait three months and get a real bill."

After the bill was passed through the Senate, nightly conferences were held at the hideaway office of the Speaker. The regulars of the House attended. Senator Johnson often attended. Two troublesome aspects of the situation recurred in the conversation. The newspapers seemed to agree with Martin's suggestion to put off final action. We surmised that Vice President Richard M. Nixon and his close friend Deputy Attorney General William Rogers favored keeping the issue alive rather than settling it that year.

As a result, each of us drew assignments to talk with editorial writers and columnists. Johnson and his staff drew the majority of assignments. To those with whom I talked, I emphasized the statements of men such as Wilkins in support of obtaining a law. In time, the trend of opinion in the newspapers reflected our position— not because we could order the change but simply because we gave convincing arguments.

The night meetings were devoted to seeking a compromise on the jury-trial amendment. We sought not only a formula but the joint support of influential people. Johnson suggested Knowland, who, he said, saw the issue as above partisanship. Johnson regarded Knowland as honorable and sincere, and knew he enjoyed the confidence of the President.

Johnson talked to Knowland on August 14; subsequently, Knowland talked to the President; and on August 21 the President at a press conference proposed a compromise on the jury-trial amendment. It would limit the right to jury trial to those cases wherein penalties exceeded $300 in fines or ninety days in jail. Eisenhower told the press that the Senate bill wasn't as strong as he would have liked. However, he indicated the compromise would still provide a sufficiently effective bill while quieting any "justifiable alarm that others might have as to excessive punishment of any kind." The

President, hoping the bill would be enacted before adjournment, made this crucial observation: "I can't conceive of anything worse than making the basic right of so many millions of our citizens just part of a political snarling. . . ."

This dealt a blow to the hope of some Republicans that the civil rights issue would remain unresolved, to the discredit of the Democrats. Martin, on behalf of the Republican minority in the House, presented the compromise the same day the President spoke out. Rayburn indicated on August 22, the following day, that House Democrats would be willing to consider an agreement based upon the Republican proposal.

The next day, Rayburn, Martin, Johnson, and Knowland talked for a long time. At one point, Knowland walked across the Capitol to the House floor to discuss the matter with Martin. That day was the only time I ever saw Rayburn display strong outward signs of how it feels to be in the "pressure cooker."

Then, late in the afternoon, he confided: "We've got it wrapped up. Lyndon, Joe, Senator Knowland, and I are going to announce it in my office in a few minutes." They carried out this unusual procedure.

Four days previously, August 19, three northern Democrats had joined with me to force a meeting of the Rules Committee. Judge Smith, as chairman, did not act. At this point, seven committee members, including Hugh Scott, the valued liberal Republican member, instructed the clerk of the committee to call a meeting on August 26. This was most uncommon procedure. However, the meeting was called and held. The resolution embodying the compromise was adopted. The House adopted the resolution on August 27.

In the Senate, an arch-segregationist, Strom Thurmond of South Carolina, spoke for twenty-four hours. Southern colleagues called it a "grand-standing" speech. His efforts were unavailing, and the Senate adopted the compromise. The first civil rights act in eighty-two years was sent to the White House for the signature of the President.

One night soon afterward, Johnson brought Knowland to the hideaway for a drink. As I looked at them I said to myself, "What punishment each of them has taken to serve his country as he saw best." It was quite a trio—two rocks and a rapier. Stocky Rayburn, bull-like Knowland, and the skilled, volatile Johnson.

Now, no one believed that the Civil Rights Act of 1957 would satisfy civil rights groups or liberal Members of Congress for long. Pressure for further legislation mounted. On February 28, 1963, President Kennedy sent a civil rights message to Congress. His proposals were fairly mild ones, and the message itself was partisan. In April and May a new nation-wide wave of civil rights demonstrations compelled the Administration to review its proposals. Shootings, slayings, and fatal bombings of Negroes created urgency in the minds of many for a truly comprehensive bill. Meanwhile, pro-civil rights Republican Members of the House were countering the partisan moves of the Democrats by a series of statements and legislative proposals.

At this time, the Administration did not seem to realize that no significant civil rights legislation could be enacted without the formation of a genuine bipartisan coalition of Republicans and Democrats in Congress that would work in harmony with the Democratic Administration. Within the Democratic party there were two pro-civil rights groups that disagreed fundamentally on the scope of legislation. One, which seemed to include most members of the Administration who were involved in the matter, seemed to feel that it would be impossible to pass a law that contained strong fair-employment-practices provisions, or one that would provide for the withholding of federal funds from any federally supported program in which there was racial discrimination. This group favored sending to Congress a fairly mild bill, of which the most controversial section would have been the one dealing with public accommodations.

The other group, of which I was a member, included many middle-rank Democrats in both House and Senate, who, with support from the outside by civil rights and allied organizations, felt that the strongest possible measures should be proposed. We had three reasons for this: Objectively it was a matter both of conscience and of the actual need for strong legislation. From a legislative point of view, it seemed sensible for the House to pass the strongest possible bill to allow for the Senate whittling away some of it without making the final version worthless. And from our partisan viewpoint, we knew that if the Democrats proposed a weak bill, the minority of Republicans who were traditionally in favor of civil rights laws would quickly top it with a stronger bill of their own.

A great deal of backstage maneuvering went on before President Kennedy, in June, sent a message on civil rights to Congress that did not entirely satisfy either group. The provisions for withholding federal funds brought cries of rage from the South but were considered too weak by the strong civil rights proponents. Fair Employment Practices (FEPC) were endorsed, but as a separate measure, since it was already pending before the Education and Labor Committee, while the rest of the proposals would be considered by the Judiciary Committee.

The Republican House Members felt that they had not been consulted enough during the drafting of the proposals. In this I believe they were justified. In June the Administration still did not recognize how much they would have to depend on Republican support.

Meanwhile hearings had begun before House Judiciary Subcommittee Number 5, which has jurisdiction over civil rights bills. As the hearing went on to great length, it became apparent that it would be difficult to frame a bill that would be supported by a bipartisan coalition. Agreements between the chairman, Democrat Celler and William M. McCulloch of Ohio, the senior Republican on the Judiciary Committee, who had played a major role in the 1957 Act and its 1960 amendments, were already breaking down. Neither the Republicans nor the Democrats could agree within their own parties on strategy. There was a constant undercurrent of conflict between two pro-civil rights factions: one leaned over backward to assure passage of any bill, however weak; the other realized that a strong bill, including provisions on public accommodations, FEPC, and withholding of federal funds, was possible, and in fact the only practicable kind of bill.

On October 2 Judiciary Subcommittee Number 5 reported a bill that represented the views of the most ardent civil rights advocates. It could not possibly be enacted into law without Republican support—and McCulloch, a recognized leader of Republican forces, was violently opposed to some of its provisions.

On October 15–16, Attorney General Robert Kennedy testified before the full Judiciary Committee and asked that the subcommittee's bill be modified to eliminate its more extreme provisions in order to win broader support in Congress and in the country at large. It was a courageous stand to take for both objective and political reasons. On October 22 the Judiciary Committee adjourned in time to prevent the reporting of the strong bill.

At this stage President Kennedy stepped into the negotiations. Some of these were carried on by him personally, some by his deputies. The constant liaison between Robert Kennedy, his deputy, Nick Katzenbach, and the Judiciary Committee, particularly with Republican Members such as McCulloch, was important to the final passage of the bill.

A bipartisan agreement was finally reached; the modified version retained the strong FEPC provisions, the withholding of federal funds, and other sections advocated by those of us who felt that a strong bill could be passed.

On October 29 the Judiciary Committee reported this compromise bill approved by Speaker McCormack, GOP Minority Leader Halleck, Chairman Celler, McCulloch, and many civil rights advocates inside and outside Congress. There was a good deal of speculation as to whether the Republicans would really support the fair-employment provisions.

Late in 1963 Chairman Celler of the Judiciary Committee introduced a resolution to bring the bill to the floor. I used this resolution as a basis for the rarely used and rarely successful discharge procedure to bring the bill out of the Rules Committee. My purpose was first to get the bill to the floor before Christmas if Republican support could be obtained for the discharge petition. Second, I used the threat of discharge to put pressure on Clarence Brown and other Republicans on the Rules Committee to persuade Chairman Smith to hold hearings soon. The hearings before Rules were held early in January; the bill was reported to the floor and passed virtually intact February 10—the most comprehensive civil rights legislation in this century. The final vote, 290–130, is deceptive. The bill did not have an easy passage. It required vast labors on the part of pro-civil rights Members in the House, members of the White House staff, the Attorney General and his principal assistants, the numerous legislative agents of the labor movement, various civil rights organizations, and religious groups to keep the bill from being gutted in the amendment stage. The task force of the civil rights Members was the Democratic Study Group Committee on Civil Rights of which I was chairman. It played a central role in dealing with policy problems as they arose during debate. It further kept pro-civil rights Members on the floor and ready to vote during the amendment stage. This is a crucial point, since it is easy to lose major portions of a bill to crippling amendments simply because Members become bored or distracted and leave the floor. There were critical moments during the debate, but the Celler and McCulloch forces, including several able younger members of both political parties, doggedly kept control on the floor. Disasters of past years were avoided with the assistance of outside civil rights sympathizers, notably clergymen and trade-union representatives.

Expectedly, southern Democrats in the Senate conducted a filibuster. The filibuster was broken June 10, the seventy-fourth day after the bill had been put before the Senate. The end came by means of a 71 to 29 vote that adopted a petition for closure of the debate. It was the first time since cloture had been adopted in 1917 that this technique was successfully employed in respect to civil rights legislation. Senator Everett McKinley Dirksen of Illinois, Republican minority leader, should be considered the chief senatorial architect of this feat. The dying gasp did not come from a Senator representing one of the Dixiecrat states—as was the case when Senator Strom Thurmond of South Carolina spoke against the 1957 civil rights bill for 24 hours and 18 minutes, a record. The last opponent to be heard from at length in 1964 was Senator Robert C. Byrd of West Virginia, who spoke for 14 hours and 13 minutes during the night of June 9–10.

Cloture applied, the Senate went on formally to pass the bill itself by about the same voting margin. The measure had miraculously emerged from the Senate without major alterations. Its comprehensive features included sanctions against racial discrimination in public accommodations, employment, and federally assisted programs and voting rights, as well as authorization for the Attorney General to intervene in certain civil rights suits and to initiate school desegregation suits.

When the bill came to the Rules Committee before going to the floor for final approval of the House bill as amended by the Senate, I made a motion to by-pass Chairman Howard Smith and place Ray Madden of Indiana, a liberal Democrat, in charge of further action on the civil rights bill. This met with violent protests from Smith and from William Colmer of Mississippi. However, I was supported by Clarence Brown, conservative Republican from Ohio, who voted against the chairman on the grounds that further delay on the bill would disrupt the national conventions of both parties. The motion to by-pass Smith was carried 8 to 5, and the amended bill was given a rule and passed in the House. President Johnson, who had supported it from the start, signed it into law on July 3.

There is a postscript. Several men in the Congress had their own angle of vision in respect to the civil rights bills, and they deserve credit. However, most of the credit belongs to the leaders of the American Negro. After miserable decades of disappointment, affront, and worse, they displayed the statesmanship, grounded in their high purpose, to support and work in behalf of legislation that was achievable.

Chapter 10

The Committee on Rules

The Committee on Rules of the House of Representatives was once considered so unimportant that no Members were appointed to it in five early Congresses—the Fifteenth, Sixteenth, Eighteenth, Twenty-first, and Twenty-eighth, which covered a period from 1817 through 1845.

Today, major battles out front and behind the scenes are fought over the selection of a House Member to fill a vacancy on the committee. When it became known in 1963 that John Young of Texas would succeed Homer Thornberry, also of Texas, who had been appointed to a federal judgeship, House liberals publicly expressed displeasure because Young's voting record had been hitherto quite conservative. Some of them conveyed this feeling to Speaker Mc-Cormack. Only indications that McCormack would regard efforts to dump Young as a no-confidence vote in McCormack himself prevented disgruntled liberals from making a stiff fight over the selection.

In addition to rows over the highly prized assignments to the Rules Committee, its size and powers provoke violent arguments.

Today, the committee can and does obstruct and block bills of which a majority of its members disapprove. Sometimes the chairman himself forestalls action by refusing to hold a meeting. In that event, committee members can force the chairman to hold a meeting by the procedure that was used to obtain hearings on the civil rights bill in 1956. Three members formally request him in writing to hold a meeting. If the chairman does not agree within three legislative days or seven calendar days, then a committee meeting can be held if a majority, at present eight members, vote to hold one.

The mistaken but common view of the committee is that it exercises the role of a "legislative traffic cop." Increasingly over the years, the committee as "traffic cop" has turned on red lights, erected barriers, and impeded the flow of legislative traffic. If the light was not always red, it at least seemed forever amber, and the "cop" has become a "commissar."

How has this situation come to pass?

The Committee on Rules was originally authorized as a select committee, that is, a committee authorized to be established at the beginning of each Congress. Its responsibility was to report a system of rules to govern the procedures of each Congress. It gained authority in the late nineteenth century as the legislative load increased. Until then there was no committee to decide upon the order in which bills reported from legislative committees should be discussed and voted upon on the House floor. In general a bill reported from a legislative committee took its turn in line to be acted upon by the full membership. Major bills sometimes became backed up on the regular calendar order. There arose a need for a power of selection, although the Speaker did exercise the power to select bills for floor action simply by his power to recognize a Member who wanted a major bill brought up. Later, Rules Committee was given the assignment of reporting to the House recommendations as to when a bill should be brought up or when a bill should be voted upon.

In 1880 the committee became a standing (permanent) five-member committee. Between 1890 and 1910 it gained privilege after privilege, particularly under the Speakerships of two Republicans, Thomas Bracket Reed of Maine and Joseph Gurney (Uncle Joe) Cannon of Illinois. The Fifty-second Congress (1891–1893) adopted the rule that it shall always be in order to call up for consideration by the full House a report from the Rules Committee. The House also adopted a procedure whereby proposals touching on the rules of the House must be referred to the committee.

The Speaker named himself chairman of the Rules Committee. He also named the other members. He controlled it. The committee at the time of the "revolt against Cannonism" in 1910 was an efficient organ. Cannon defended it with the observation that much of the progressive legislation during the Administration of Theodore Roosevelt would not have been passed by Congress if the committee did not have a right-of-way onto the floor at all times.

The 1910 revolt against the Speaker drastically altered the status of the committee. As responsibility for leadership in the House became diffused, the power of committee chairmen, and especially the power of the chairman of Rules, was enhanced. It became an elective committee, and the Speaker was barred from membership on it. A disappointed insurgent during the 1910 revolt, Representative John M. Nelson of Wisconsin, remarked that the uprising was largely offset by the pocket veto of the Rules Committee chairman. One historian of the period has said that the committee was known to have reported bills never referred to it for consideration. And more than once it brought in a special order for a bill, the ship-purchase bill in 1915, for example, which had not even been introduced. A more recent example occurred in August 1964, when Chairman Howard Smith and like-minded members reported to the floor the Tuck bill, designed to curtail the decisions of the Supreme Court in respect to apportionment of seats in state legislatures. The measure was simply removed from custody of the Judiciary Committee.

A point of order was raised on the House floor by opponents of this action. Speaker McCormack rejected the point of order. The basis for rejection was a ruling in 1895 by then Speaker Charles F. Crisp of Georgia. The nut of the Crisp ruling is: ". . . the Committee on Rules had jurisdiction to report a resolution fixing the order of business and the manner of considering a measure, even though the effect of its adoption would be to discharge a committee from a matter pending before it, thereby changing the existing rule relative to the consideration of business." The effect of the rule was to take legislation out of the hands of balky committees unresponsive to the majority.

This caused the *Washington Post* to comment editorially on August 24, 1964:

"It is important to note, however, that in 1895 the Speaker was a member of the Rules Committee, and the Committee functioned as an arm of the House leadership. Who is in control of the Committee today? It usually responds to the domination of Howard Smith who, more often than not, is out of sympathy with the leadership. So we have the remarkable spectacle of a potentially great tool of leadership being wielded, not by the Speaker or the Majority Leader or a central policy-making committee, but by a hostile faction which is not infrequently bent on malicious mischief as in passage of the Tuck bill."

Today, in sum, the Rules Committee has the power to sit while the House is in session—other committees must obtain special permission. It can report matters not previously introduced, reported, or committed to the Committee. It can have its own reports considered immediately. It can consider and report special orders.

A special order—commonly called a "rule"—determines the manner and length of debate on a bill. It also can restrict the opportunity to amend a bill.

The committee, equipped with such powers, is able to sift the bills that come from the legislative committees. Most bills do have to come before Rules before going to the floor. Rules can also determine which bills shall have the right-of-way to the floor, as well as the order of priority. Thus the committee can and does substitute its own judgment as to the substantive merits of a bill for that of the legislative committee. Although the latter is the organ duly assigned to receive testimony as to the merits and demerits of the bill, discuss it, alter the bill as introduced in any way, even substitute a completely different version, Rules Committee can report a rule on a bill that is markedly different from the bill reported by the legislative committee. In recent years, Rules has seldom done this. Instead, it has preferred to use this power as leverage to compel the legislative committees to report bills more closely tailored to the wishes of a majority of the Rules Committee.

Once the Rules Committee has reported to the floor a special order or rule to accompany a bill, the House can approve, modify, or defeat the rule, but this is very difficult to do. There are two parliamentary procedures established to circumvent the delaying tactics of the Rules Committee.

One is that of the discharge petition. Any Member of the House can file a discharge petition. Such a petition "discharges" a committee—Rules or any other standing committee—from consideration of a particular bill if the bill has been before a committee a certain number of days. The discharge petition must be signed by a majority of the full membership of the House; at present, it requires 218 signatures. At various times in its history, the petition had needed only 145 or 150 signatures. A Member may withdraw his signature at any time before the requisite number of signatures is obtained. According to a compilation by *Congressional Quarterly*, there have been 808 discharge petitions filed since the Sixty-first Congress (1909–1911). Of these, twenty-two obtained sufficient signatures. Of the twenty-two bills thus discharged, eighteen passed the House. However, of the eighteen, only two, the 1960 federal pay bill and the 1938 Wage and Hours Act, also passed the Senate and became law. Obviously, it is very difficult to obtain sufficient signatures. Even Members who favor a bill that is being bottled up often refuse to sign on grounds it is disruptive of day-to-day parliamentary procedures. Others refuse to sign on the grounds that it would put them in a position of being unable to refuse to sign other petitions. Still other Members take their cue from House elders, who realize that if a discharge petition is successfully employed on behalf of a bill before some other committee, it can be employed on behalf of bills within their committees. Discharge petitions are, for such reasons, seldom successful.

The most notable exception occurred in 1938 when the procedure was employed to pry loose a fair labor standards bill from Rules. Interestingly, the resort to a discharge petition was necessary in a House that began its term with an enormous Democratic majority —338 Democrats and 88 Republicans. The petition was filed one day in May 1938. Two hours and twenty-two minutes later, 218 signatures were obtained. President Roosevelt was a prime mover in that breath-taking operation. The procedure has been successfully employed one other time in recent years—in connection with the 1960 pay bill opposed by the Eisenhower Administration. Of course, on other occasions it has served to prod the Rules Committee into action. When Rules was sitting on a civil rights bill in 1959, a discharge petition attracted 209 signatures. In the face of such near success for the petition, Rules met and granted the bill a rule that brought it to the floor the following year. A similar situation occurred in December 1962 and January 1964 during the development of civil rights legislation.

Besides the discharge petition, sometimes cynically used as a political gesture to placate minorities, there is a second technique that can be employed. It is called Calendar Wednesday.

Each Wednesday that the House meets, unless formally waived, the Speaker is required to have the names of the committees called in alphabetical order. As the name of a committee is called, its chairman may call up for floor debate any bill properly reported from his committee. On the surface, this seems an easily available escape for a bill that is stranded in Rules. It requires unanimous consent of the Members or a two-to-one majority to dispense with this procedure.

However, to invoke Calendar Wednesday successfully to extract a blocked bill is a difficult procedure seldom resorted to. Its employment is actively discouraged.

First, any action on a bill brought to the floor in this way must be completed within one legislative day—that is, normally, the twenty-four-hour period from noon Wednesday to noon Thursday. Also, as the calendar call is alphabetical, the names of all committees, as will be seen shortly, are not called each and every Wednesday.

From 1937 to 1961, Rules was dominated by the bipartisan conservative coalition—that is, the voting alliance of southern Democrats and Republicans against northern Democrats. It was usually able to have Calendar Wednesday dispensed with by unanimous consent. When a concerted effort was under way to utilize Calendar Wednesday, the conservatives were always forewarned, since the routine request for unanimous consent to dispense with the next Calendar Wednesday always comes at some point the previous week. Many Members of the coalition hold committee chairmanships by virtue of seniority, and the complete call of all committees on Calendar Wednesday can be stalled for weeks.

For example, the Judiciary Committee is a case in point. Its chairman is a liberal, Representative Emanuel Celler of New York. The committee's jurisdiction includes civil rights legislation. If Judiciary wants to bring a civil rights bill to the floor by the Calendar Wednesday procedure, the southern chairmen of the committees preceding Judiciary in the alphabet can successively take possession of the floor with some noncontroversial bills that ordinarily would have gone to Rules and been favorably reported. This way it would take several months of Wednesdays before Judiciary's name would be called.

When occasionally a bill is called up under this procedure, there is a bag full of parliamentary procedures that may be used to stall action. They amount to a limited version of the filibuster in the Senate.

In the Eighty-first Congress, a fair employment practices bill was brought up on Calendar Wednesday. Opponents objected to the customary abbreviated reading of the Journal of the previous day's proceedings, and insisted that it be read in full. As members vanished from the House, a conservative pointed out that a quorum was not present. This necessitated a lengthy roll call of Members, taking twenty to twenty-five minutes. In short, delaying tactic after delaying tactic was employed. The bill was finally acted on near dawn on Thursday.

Because of such grueling legislative sessions, which generate severe physical weariness and discomfort in many Members, invoking Calendar Wednesday is regarded as a form of masochism, akin to volunteering for the medieval rack.

The complaints about the Rules Committee really are rooted in the coalition that began to take form in 1937 when the Democrats held nearly a four-to-one margin over the Republicans. Until then, despite the revolt against Cannon, the Rules Committee, including the chairman, remained reasonably responsive to the party leadership and to most of the majority party in the House. This is as it should be. After all, men elected to committees and to party leadership in the House are chosen first by a majority vote of their own party colleagues. Normally, the fact of their election presumably hinges upon their holding to the legislative objectives of a majority of their party in the House. To elect on any other basis is chaos.

However, in the late 1930's as the emphasis upon the domestic New Deal ebbed with the worsening international situation, the Rules Committee fell out of step with the Democratic majority leadership. Southern Democrats and orthodox Republicans seized effective control of the committee.

This happened only when the Democrats were the majority party in the House. When the Republicans controlled the House they found a pliant Rules Committee, dominated by conservatives of both parties, to follow their bidding. In such periods, the then twelve-member Rules Committee assumed the role it was designed to play.

House liberals, irritated, then roused by the number of bills stalled or consigned to limbo by the Rules Committee, launched a frontal assault in 1948. The late Representative Herman Eberharter of Pennsylvania led the offensive. His aides included Chet Holifield of California, Andrew Biemiller of Wisconsin, now the chief lobbyist for the AFL-CIO, and John A. Carroll of Colorado, later elected to the Senate. President Truman was sympathetic, and Sam Rayburn, about to become Speaker again after two years of a Republican-controlled House, was encouraging.

The device employed to break the power of Rules was the adoption of a "twenty-one-day rule." Under this procedure, adopted in 1949 by a vote of 275 to 142, the chairman of a legislative committee could call up a bill for consideration on the floor of the House under certain conditions: (1) the bill must be accompanied by a favorable report of a majority of the legislative committee; (2) the Rules Committee must either have ruled adversely on it or refused to bring the bill to the floor within twenty-one days.

The twenty-one-day rule was in effect for only two years. During that period, however, successful action was taken by the House on minimum wage, housing, anti-poll-tax and Alaska-Hawaii statehood legislation. Rayburn himself was not fond of the new rule on the grounds it also permitted unwise legislation, such as the Rankin veterans-pension grab legislation, to get to the floor along with more worthy bills. Because of Rayburn's position, Members who had been favorably disposed toward the device backed off.

In 1951 the Dixiecrat-Republican coalition struck back. The rule was repealed that year at the opening of the Eighty-second Congress with its slender Democratic majority, and occasional efforts subsequently failed to reinstate the twenty-one-day rule.

The Rules Committee deadlock was once again clamped on legislation. Instead of exercising its assigned duty of determining the order of business on the floor, Rules again improperly exercised the power of judgment of the merits of bills already approved by the legislative committee that originally held the jurisdiction over them.

I was named to the Rules Committee in the Eighty-fourth Congress, which began in 1955. The Democrats had regained control of the House after having lost it two years previously. Apparently because of a gentleman's agreement between Rayburn, Speaker during Democratic control, and Martin, Speaker during Republican control, the size of the committee was to remain at twelve seats as long as both men led their parties in the House. Normally, such agreements are never breached, although this one played an important role in events that were to take place in 1959.

When I came on Rules, Howard Smith was in line to become chairman, succeeding Eugene Cox of Georgia who had been chairman of Rules in 1952, when the Democrats had last controlled the House and he had died that year.

In order of seniority on the Democratic side came William M. Colmer of Mississippi, a staunch ally of Smith; Ray J. Madden of Indiana, notably pro-organized labor; and James J. Delaney of New York City. Of the four new Democratic appointees, James W. Trimble of Arkansas was the senior. Next was Homer Thornberry of Texas, who had been elected to the seat formerly held by Lyndon Johnson. I was next, and the junior Democrat was Thomas P. "Tip" O'Neill, Jr., of Massachusetts, close ally of the then majority leader McCormack and the first Democratic speaker of the state's House of Representatives.

Among the Republicans, Leo Allen of Illinois was senior. He was followed by Clarence J. Brown of Ohio, a prominent supporter of the late Senator Taft's attempt to secure his party's presidential nomination; Harris Ellsworth of Oregon, and Henry Latham of New York.

The consequence of this line-up was that the committee members split six to six on most major issues. It was a straight liberal-conservative split, with Smith and Colmer, Democrats, joining the four Republicans to create a deadlock.

A tie vote on a motion to report a bill meant the bill was lost. Since a majority vote was needed, there were ordinarily two ways of wresting a bill from Rules. Rayburn could and did appeal directly to Smith on a bill of paramount importance. Or the Eisenhower Administration could attempt to woo Rules Committee Republicans directly or through Joe Martin. However, resort to one or the other was successful only in an ideal combination of circumstances.

The Democratic liberals on the committee managed to blast loose a civil rights bill, but the conservative six had their way in respect to other legislation. The six refused outright to grant a rule to a bill for aid to chronically depressed areas, and their implied threat not to give rules to other vital bills forced legislative committees to water down measures concerning housing, absentee voting, doctors' draft, and a polio vaccine inoculation program.

The 1956 fall elections caused little change in the political coloration of the House. One vacancy occurred on the Rules Committee when the Republican Ellsworth was defeated for re-election. Hugh Scott, Jr., of Pennsylvania, who had been on the committee during Republican control of the Eighty-third Congress, 1953–1954, and had been a leader in the civil rights struggle, regained his seat over the opposition of conservative Republican party-liners. He was responsive to requests to support liberal legislation; but he was soon to run for the Senate.

At this time several major bills from the previous Congress were jammed in the Rules Committee—omnibus housing, a Tennessee Valley Authority financing bill, and a minerals subsidy bill. It was likely that these and other bills would be hung up in Rules again in this Congress. I suggested to Rayburn that he speak to Smith in an effort to find out which bills, if any, the Rules chairman was prepared to release for floor action.

Before I had an opportunity to talk to Rayburn again, I saw Smith, who said he and Rayburn had worked out an agreement on the backlog of legislation. Smith said that Rayburn would tell me about an important role I would have to play to carry out the agreement. Considering the source of this news, I was less than delighted; when I next talked to Rayburn I was downcast. True, there was an agreement, and I would play a part. Rayburn said Smith agreed to release the minerals bill if I would co-operate with him to prevent the housing and TVA bills from being given a rule.

If I consented, it meant that I would support a bill on which I was at most lukewarm, and would be obliged to oppose two bills I heartily favored—housing, which would be helpful to my Kansas City district, and TVA, which I, having grown up in Alabama, strongly endorsed. Somehow Truman's comment "If you can't stand the heat, get out of the kitchen" seemed appropriate at this point.

The kitchen became very hot before I struggled to a decision. I would go along with the Rayburn-Smith agreement, reasoning that I should make the best of a bad bargain. If I refused, Smith would not hold another meeting of Rules in the short time remaining in the session, and no bills would be released, because it was too close to adjournment to force a meeting. Going along meant getting at least one bill to the floor. But I did not like the situation and knew the agreement could possibly cause me unpleasant political trouble. I had a few uneasy moments during the meeting of the committee at which the minerals bill was given a rule. At one point one of my liberal colleagues began asking for action on the housing bill; the Judge rescued me by adjourning the meeting.

The liberal complexion of the House when the Eighty-sixth Congress convened in January 1959 made the Democratic Study Group aware that the Rules Committee could again thwart the views of the majority party. The Democrats numbered 283 against 154 Republicans. Still, some DSG liberals were feeling bullish enough to believe that the Rules Committee could be reformed without the assistance of Speaker Rayburn.

At the same time, three liberals were publicly trying to persuade Rayburn to break the lock of the Rules Committee in one of three ways: restore the twenty-one-day rule; enlarge the membership of the Committee of Twelve; or change the two-to-one ratio of Democrats to Republicans on the committee. Any one of these, if adopted, would appreciably smooth the path of liberal legislation on its way to the floor, and I was privately attempting to convince Rayburn to adopt one of the three courses. I argued vigorously, but Rayburn seemed not to be listening. After one long discussion he remained noncommittal, and I came away with the impression he intended to do nothing.

I tried to discern his reasons. I surmised he had lost some of his zest for legislative battles and was now moved only by reflex action and a sense of duty. Seven years earlier, 1952, I recalled, I was shocked when he told me as we sat by the fireplace in his home at Bonham, that although he loved the House, he loved Bonham more. Sometimes, he said, he wanted so much to remain near "his people," his pastures, and his field. He simply wanted to quit. He had even sounded me out about my views as to possible successors. When the Republicans took control of the House in 1953, he had indicated he did not want to be minority leader, although he assumed the post. And when Democrats regained control in 1955, he again became Speaker.

Now, in 1959, Rayburn was worried about the course the Democratic majority wanted to take. Rayburn was liberal, but he showed increasing caution, as if afraid that some liberals would want to move off too fast and in too many directions. The presidential veto in the hands of an increasingly conservative Eisenhower would cut down some liberal measures. Rayburn feared that if the eager House liberal rank-and-filers pressed their objectives too warmly, the party's chances would be impaired in the 1960 presidential election.

Still another factor in his reluctance to oppose the conservative Democratic chairmen was his belief that Lyndon Johnson would try for the party's presidential nomination a year hence, even though Johnson was publicly denying any such intention.

All these factors played a part in the decision Rayburn was to make. Having thought them over, I went to Rayburn. We had our first argument on the subject. I emphasized that if he did not at-

tempt to improve the Rules Committee, he was placing his reputation as a legislative leader in the hands of those who were de-
monstrably his opponents. I even said bluntly that Howard Smith
might "gut" Rayburn in the present Congress, not as a personal
matter but as an attack against a Speaker attempting to move along
legislation that Smith as chairman of Rules opposed. Rayburn did
not like what I said, nor did he believe it. And he said so.

I became certain that Rayburn was opposed to two of the three
remedies proposed by the liberals.

First, Rayburn simply did not like the twenty-one-day rule. He
felt it tended to disperse power further into the hands of the committee chairmen, reduced the power of the leadership in its roles
as coordinator and guide, and led to irresponsibility.

Rayburn also felt himself apparently honor-bound to observe
the agreement he had made with Republican minority leader Joe
Martin that as long as each was leader of his respective party the
Rules Committee would remain at twelve members in the ratio of
eight members of the majority party and four of the minority. It
was at about this time that Halleck defeated Martin for the leadership of the House Republicans in a surprise maneuver. However,
the decision to leave the Rules Committee unchanged had already
been made.

I tried once more to persuade Rayburn to help in changing the
Rules Committee, but he snapped, "I've heard all I want, and that's
the end of it."

It turned out that my visit had been preceded by a visit of several
DSG leaders, who had left under the impression that Rayburn
would help to get their legislation to the floor. Rayburn, however,
felt he had only told the delegation he would try.

The upshot of it all was that the Eighty-sixth Congress spent its
life under an even more conservative Rules Committee than the
Eighty-fifth Congress. Hugh Scott had made the Senate race, and
won. His replacement on Rules was a conservative primitive, B.
Carroll Reece of Tennessee. Downtown at the White House, Eisenhower continued his move to the right. The reasons were murky.
Perhaps the liberal composition of the Eighty-sixth Congress un-
settled him. In addition, Arthur Burns, one of his more liberal

economic advisers, had left him in 1956. On a memorable October 25, 1958, Sherman Adams had also resigned.

As more major bills backed up in the inactive Rules Committee, other efforts were under way to find a way out of the roadblock. Smith and his allies on the committee were aided by Republicans who tied up bills on the theory that this would prevent the President's having to use his veto on too many pieces of legislation with voter appeal. By the fall of 1959, the most liberal House in two decades had produced no legislative record of any high accomplishment. With the presidential elections of 1960 in sight, some strategy had to be developed to provide a Democratic presidential candidate with a party record to run on.

In my view, at least several major bills should have been brought to the floor—civil rights, aid to economically depressed areas, federal aid to education, minimum-wage legislation, and a housing bill.

In the late stages of the first session, 1959, Representative Celler, chairman of the Judiciary Committee, filed a discharge petition to release the civil rights bill hung up in Rules. Clarence Mitchell, the most able NAACP lobbyist, urged that this be done, but I was opposed, since I felt the petition was premature and would not gather enough momentum to succeed in 1959. But the petition was filed, and when the second session opened in January 1960, it had nowhere near the number of signatures that could provide any pressure upon Rules.

Nevertheless, a number of us House liberals decided to establish a political issue on civil rights, by forcing the bill to the floor by means of the discharge petition. Then, employing the Calendar Wednesday procedure, we would try to move as many other bills as possible. During this effort, the DSG would supply the manpower to staff such an operation. Rayburn would be kept informed. I would attempt again to enlist his assistance.

At the same time, it was determined to dramatize the obstructionism of the Rules Committee, which had never been made a national political issue. I set out to play my hand as a committee member so that the conservative deadlock would be clearly visible. I also pounded away at Members, whose bills were blocked in Rules, that the hope of freeing them was to reform the committee in the next

Congress, which would convene in January 1961. Furthermore, I felt I should make another intensive effort to convince Rayburn that he must lead the fight to recapture control of the Rules Committee. The behavior of the conservatives on Rules during the Eighty-sixth Congress convinced not only Rayburn but the President-to-be, then Senator John Kennedy, that the Rules Committee must be shaken up. Of course, if Nixon were elected and the Republicans also gained in the House, Rules reform would be postponed for at least two years.

As the DSG effort mounted, the relatively minor civil rights bill became law in 1960. The Rules Committee had released it after the discharge petition, filed by Celler, received nearly enough signatures. Violating the rules of the House, someone leaked the names of the signers. Only a few Republicans were among them; the public pressure generated by such spotlighting caused the Republican minority leadership to wilt. Soon the bill emerged from Rules.

The DSG successfully invoked Calendar Wednesday procedure to bring the aid-to-depressed-areas bill to the floor. The House and the Senate passed it. Eisenhower vetoed it.

The threat to employ Calendar Wednesday on behalf of the federal aid-to-education bill brought it out of Rules. It passed the House. A differing version passed the Senate. Under House rules, conservatives on the Rules Committee were able to prevent the measure from going to a House-Senate conference in order to hammer out a bill mutually acceptable to both bodies. Thus this bill died.

The Housing bill died in Rules. The minimum-wage bill was pried from Rules by making concessions. The House passed a bill much narrower than the Senate version. Rules conservatives permitted the bill to go to conference only by forcing a pledge from the House Members managing the bill that they would refuse to compromise. The Senate understandably would not accept an unchanged House version, so this bill died too.

The performance of the Rules Committee was well noted by Kennedy and Johnson, and it did not go unnoticed by outside groups interested in bills that had been interred in Howard Worth

Smith's efficiently run legislative cemetery. A venture to assure that there would be no further graves was hopefully launched.

In October 1960, I spent several days working in the Los Angeles area with Robert F. Kennedy, who had asked me to be chairman of the congressional liaison committee of the Democratic National Committee. The evening before I left Los Angeles, I discussed the Rules situation in detail. His obvious interest and his questions indicated that he considered the issue of high importance.

Shortly after the election he suggested that the President-elect be consulted on breaking the power of the Rules Committee.

Two days later, the President-elect called. He was well aware of the problem Rules posed for his legislative program. His election chances had been rudely rocked during the rump session of Congress in August 1960, immediately after the nominating conventions of the two political parties. I said that the Rules fight could not be won without the active support of Rayburn. The President-elect said he would soon be conferring in Florida with Rayburn, and asked for suggestions on how to approach the matter of a fight against the Rules Committee. I remarked that if a fight were made, Rayburn would determine strategy. John Kennedy did not reveal what he would do or say to anyone; he asked perceptive questions on Rules reform and the possible fate of his legislative proposals without reform. The President-elect's capabilities had been demonstrated to me many times but never more than in that conversation. When the telephone conversation ended, I thought: "That Jack Kennedy! I think he knows more about the Rules situation than I do."

Every possible major support from organized labor and in the House was solicited. The Speaker, it was clear, would keep his views to himself until he returned to Washington for the opening of Congress on January 3.

Meanwhile, three Democrats, Representatives Chet Holifield of California, John A. Blatnik of Minnesota, and Frank Thompson, Jr., of New Jersey, were working to establish some kind of liaison among allies outside Congress. At the same time supporting organizations were urged not to commit themselves at this stage to any particular strategy.

The opposition was also marshaling its forces, with Howard Smith as field general. He could depend on a number of Southerners. Rules reformers would also be obliged to lure some Southerners into supporting reform. Halleck, the minority leader, had made his position clear, and again Republicans had to be persuaded to desert. Major outside groups supporting Halleck included the National Association of Manufacturers, the United States Chamber of Commerce, and the American Farm Bureau Federation.

Many grand phrases masked the power struggle that was taking place. To one side, the purpose of the proposed change was to "let the House work its will"; to defenders of the committee, the change would upset "orderly procedure." To advocates such as myself the struggle was between those who would allow the flow of legislation to remain in the hands of a tightly knit band of senior conservatives and those who felt the leadership of the majority party should guide legislation.

Or, to rephrase it, who was going to run the House: the Speaker or the chairman of Rules?

The reform group was confident, even though the Democrats had lost 20 House seats in the 1960 fall election. Forces outside the new Congress, which would open with 263 Democrats and 174 Republicans, were coalescing in support of revision after a long overdue realization that Rules was frustrating measures they supported. A Democratic President advocated the very legislative program Rules could be expected to maim or kill.

There was still no agreement on the exact means to be used in breaking the Rules Committee. Some advocated a "purge" of Representative William M. Colmer of Mississippi, who had openly supported a ticket of independent electors against the national ticket of his own party, the Democrats, in 1960.

Replacing Colmer with a Member loyal to his party would give the liberals a seven-to-five edge, instead of a six-six tie on Rules. But this course presented a hazard because the opposition characterized it as having a distinct civil rights bias. The charge was not valid, but it made an unfavorable impression in the South at a time when southern votes were needed to push across a change. One way to offset the civil rights label would be to announce in advance that a southern moderate would replace Colmer. The replacement would, of course, be a proponent of the orthodox southern position on civil rights.

Unfortunately, there was still another hitch to the purge route. The Democratic Representative Adam Clayton Powell of New York had not been censured for supporting Eisenhower against his party's candidate Adlai Stevenson, in the 1956 presidential campaign. Purging Colmer would raise the cry among racists and their fellow travelers that the Democrats had held a white Southerner to a higher standard of party loyalty than it had a Negro.

Other strategists wanted to reinstate the twenty-one-day rule or a change in rules that would accomplish a similar result.

Others advocated a sort of numbers game. They suggested that "if we add one Democrat, making it a thirteen-member committee, we'd have a seven-to-six majority. . . . No, let's change the ratio of party to party from two to one to three to one, then we'd have a seven-to-five majority. . . . Why not keep the ratio at two to one but enlarge the committee from twelve to fifteen. That way we'd get an eight-to-seven majority on most issues. . . ."

Amid all this it was sometimes forgotten that Rayburn held the key cards. He had not yet played them.

On the last day of 1960, a Saturday, Rayburn returned to Washington. A few days earlier I had told John W. Holton, his skilled assistant, that it was important that I see the Speaker immediately upon his return. On the afternoon of his return, Rayburn called me to a meeting in his private office that was neither convivial nor relaxed. Instead of the usual small, informal group, there was the full Democratic leadership—the Speaker; Majority Leader McCormack; the Whip, Carl Albert of Oklahoma; three members of the Texas delegation, and Lewis Deschler, the Parliamentarian.

Rayburn engaged in no preliminary pleasantries. He asked for the views of those present on the Rules Committee. Those who replied said that the disloyal southern Democrats such as Colmer must be purged because moderate Southerners could not long afford to be identified with them.

Rayburn, not surprisingly, demurred. He remembered the Powell episode; and besides, purges did not suit him. Then he disclosed that he favored adding three members to the committee. He didn't ask for our reaction. He told the group, and that was that.

Rayburn said he intended to tell Smith that this was the painless method he preferred to use—but that he intended to alter Rules, even if a purge were necessary.

I, at least, misread his meaning. Or perhaps Rayburn changed his mind, because the Speaker phoned the next day to say Smith had rejected the enlargement proposal.

The Democratic caucus was scheduled for Tuesday, two days hence. Time was important. So when Rayburn told me of Smith's position, I replied, "That means we purge them, right?"

"No," Rayburn said. "I never said that."

During the ensuing argument, Rayburn stuck by his statement. Then he said, "We'll go ahead and add three members."

I said several Members should be cued in immediately—Holifield and James Roosevelt of California, Blatnik and Thompson.

When the conversation was ended, I was still astonished. I was certain I had understood Rayburn during the Saturday meeting. A purge would have been easier to accomplish than adding three members in the face of Smith's opposition. The Democratic party caucus would have followed that course at the outset. Once made, the purge would be regarded as a "party matter." Even Republican minority leader Charlie Halleck, the "gut fighter," would not risk leading his party into a public alliance with the Dixiecrats to save racists such as Colmer in the Democratic party. However, it was quite another matter to add three members. Preliminary steps could be taken in party caucus, but the final fight would involve a vote of both parties in a meeting of the full House. The issue would no longer be sharply etched as one of party discipline. It could be obscured to the point that the general public would wonder what the devil the row was all about anyway. If this were the prevailing attitude, the Republicans could get away with voting for obstructionism under the guise of supporting the established order.

Despite grave misgivings, I saw no point in bucking Rayburn on his choice. Without his support, there would be no change. He had not yet talked to the Democratic Study Group leaders about the Rules situation, but I informed them of Rayburn's position.

They refused to hear it secondhand, and I reluctantly called Rayburn at home. I wasn't certain he would even come to the telephone. When he did, I told him the DSG people wanted to talk to him.

"I don't want to talk to them," Rayburn said in a growl. We discussed it, and finally Rayburn agreed.

The meeting did not look promising. Holifield and Blatnik, as senior liberals, were determined on Rules change. Indeed, Blatnik had indicated that if the Speaker did not lead the fight, he, Blatnik, intended to offer a motion in caucus to strip disloyal party members of their party rights.

As a matter of fact the meeting went smoothly. Rayburn indicated his resolve to gain control of Rules, and after outlining his plans in a vague way, asked that they be kept confidential.

After the meeting, Holifield and Blatnik went directly to a DSG meeting, where they reported that they were satisfied with Rayburn's attitude.

At the party caucus, Rayburn and McCormack were renominated for Speaker and majority leader by acclamation. A crisis had passed. If the DSG leaders had not been satisfied, the caucus could have erupted, antagonized Rayburn, and spoiled a co-ordinated effort to revamp Rules.

Although the DSG leaders seemed satisfied, I was uneasy. I had been through many crises with Rayburn. Until now, I had always had implicit faith in his grasp and command of any situation in the House. On this occasion, I felt that his customary sure touch was lacking, but I kept my reservations to myself.

The House met next day. Rayburn was routinely re-elected Speaker, and rules of the House were adopted, including the continuance of the Rules Committee with twelve members. Because of this we relinquished a little of our leverage. Not all, however, because the members of the committee had not been chosen. Ordinarily, members who sat on Rules in the last Congress would be renominated by their respective parties for membership this session, and their election by the House would be routine. In the past this had usually been swiftly done before vacancies were filled.

Rayburn and McCormack maintained solid control of the Democratic Committee on Committees, and thus had power over the

Rules membership. This created a climate of psychological warfare
in which the threat of a purge was quite real. We did nothing to
discourage such speculation in the newspapers.

On this issue, House Democrats could be sorted into three groupings: liberals favoring a change in Rules; conservatives, mostly
Southerners, who opposed change; and an in-between group that
wanted the issue negotiated and a battle avoided. The latter exerted
heavy pressure upon Rayburn—many of them were personally loyal
to him.

Even the inauguration of the first Democratic President in eight
years, in January 1961, did not lessen the tensions among those to
whom the Rules situation was most important.

I was sure that there would be no purge by Rayburn.

Out of the welter of suggestions, a possible plan developed. As I
envisioned it, another Democratic caucus would be held. The first
order of business would be a resolution supporting the enlargement
of Rules. An effort would be made to bind the Members to the
decision of the caucus. If the resolution passed by a two-to-one margin, the Democrats would be bound to vote for the resolution on
the House floor. The two grounds on which a Member could
refuse to be bound were: (1) if he considered the move unconstitutional, or (2) if he was committed to constituents to hold a
different position.

Members who chose to invoke either of these exceptions had to
inform the caucus.

After the caucus vote, the members-to-be on the Rules Committee would be instructed to report to the House the necessary
resolution as to the size of the Committee on Rules. The Democratic
Committee on Committees would nominate Democrats to seven of
the eight seats on Rules to which the party was entitled. The eighth,
Colmer, would not be nominated. This one seat would be left vacant
until the enlargement resolution was passed in the House. If the
resolution was passed, Colmer would be returned to Rules. Until
then he would be kept as a "hostage."

The major flaw in this plan was that it required the co-operation
of Judge Smith. He would be one of the seven Democrats appointed to Rules. It takes seven of the twelve members on Rules

to constitute a quorum. All four of the Republicans could be logically expected to oppose the change. Unless Smith co-operated, there would be only six Democrats on the twelve-member committee to support the move. That meant no resolution could be put forward successfully. Smith and Rayburn were among the few persons who were aware of this flaw.

As a result, indirect negotiations began between the two men. As more persons sensed that Rayburn would not adopt the purge method, messages shuttled back and forth between Rayburn and Smith. At one point, Smith offered to guarantee grants of rules on five major measures contained in the legislative program of President Kennedy. Rayburn rejected this offer on the sound ground that there were many other bills that needed rules. Besides, in a way Smith's offer not only underscored his own power but also implied a recognition of the committee's unauthorized usurpation of the power to pass upon the substantive merits of legislation. One of the five bills Smith would have guaranteed a rule for was a federal aid-to-public-schools bill. The subsequently enlarged Rules Committee killed it. A somewhat narrower version of the bill reached the floor, where it was soundly thrashed.

At last, Rayburn unveiled his final strategy decision. Supporters of a Rules change were staggered. The Speaker had decided there would, indeed, be a party caucus. The carry-over Rules Committee members, including Colmer, would be nominated—tantamount to election. The Speaker apparently reasoned that Southerners, who otherwise might support enlargement of Rules, would leave him if the caucus decision were made binding. Holding Colmer as a hostage would becloud the issue, he reasoned, in view of the fact that Powell had not been disciplined.

Coupled with this approach by Rayburn, it turned out, was a crucial commitment from Smith. He would announce in caucus that he would call Rules together to report out a resolution to enlarge the committee to fifteen members. Smith, of course, reserved the right to vote against it.

As is the case with his commitments, Smith kept his promise. The resolution was scheduled to come before the House on January 26, 1961.

A campaign began to build a majority comprising diverse groupings. Democrats who were customarily part of the conservative coalition were solicited. Rayburn played a chief role in this effort, with assistance from Carl Vinson of Georgia, the President himself, Vice-President Johnson, the White House staff, the Kennedy campaign apparatus, and an assortment of governors, Democratic party officials, and other officeholders who had a stake in the success of the new Administration. Labor, civil rights and kindred organizations worked to corral Republicans—not just the handful of Republican liberals who would vote for enlargement anyway. Every possible persuasive technique was employed to secure a majority.

Smith and his allies broadcast that the issue was a civil rights one. Actually, Rules had cleared such legislation under strong pressure inside and outside the Congress. Rayburn countered by saying the "balance" in the twelve-member committee would be carried over to the enlarged committee. This was a tactful way of stating that one of the three new members would be Carl Elliott of Alabama, moderate Southerner and an Administration supporter on nearly all issues except civil rights.

Coordination and harmony proved a corollary problem in marshaling a majority. A legislative struggle always has problems of personality and of effective communication. In this struggle there were four distinct groups, none of which had established more than passable relations or communications among one another. They included Rayburn and his men, the Democratic Study Group, President Kennedy and his staff, and a mixed bag of support organizations outside the Congress.

I was reassured that the President was in the struggle to win. He called me three days after the Inauguration, and asked sharp and searching questions. I said that the struggle would be extremely harsh and that victory, to whichever side it came, would be secured by a narrow margin. The President telephoned later that day and was told Rayburn would probably pull it off.

In the next day or two, Robert Kennedy telephoned. He seemed disturbed. He implied that I might be partly responsible for leading the President, his brother, and his Administration to damaging defeat in their first congressional test.

A prominent television reporter sponsored a luncheon for the leaders of the four groups. Robert Kennedy and Stewart Udall, the Secretary of the Interior-designate, attended. It was agreed that co-ordinating efforts be conducted as quietly as possible so as to avoid giving any offense to Members sensitive to what they liked to call "interference of the executive branch."

Each group was to make its own count of supporters among House Members. Each tally would be compared with the others. Members listed as opposing the enlargement of Rules would be likewise cross-checked.

As in the case of the Landrum-Griffin labor bill battle, the pressure to obtain advance information as to the position of Members became so intense that some Members literally hid out. Gradually, however, a favorable tally began to become evident. Rayburn was successfully demanding loyalty from his colleagues in the Texas delegation. Committee chairmen were giving him their support on the basis of personal loyalty. At a presidential press conference, Kennedy tactfully said that the issue was for House Members to decide but that as an "interested citizen" he hoped no small group would tie up important legislation.

Biemiller, the AFL-CIO lobbyist, reported encouraging success in rounding up Republican votes in spite of a decision of the Republican conference to oppose the resolution. Republicans ignoring this policy decision ran the risk of losing prized committee assignments if Halleck chose to discipline them.

As the eve of the final battle neared, Rayburn, engaged in one of the most crucial struggles of his long political career, was unaccustomedly worried and unconfident. He seemed discouraged. I suspected some of his personal friends in the House, who did not really wish publicly to face the issue themselves, were conveying to him pessimistic reports. Others who sincerely supported him still did not think the issue could be won.

One night in the hideaway, Frank Thompson and I argued with a doubter in Rayburn's presence. I think the arguments showed well. The doubter seemed to weaken. Rayburn seemed somewhat encouraged, but not much. The day of decision was postponed from January 26 to January 31. The announcement was interpreted as a sure sign that sufficient votes were lacking. I doubted this.

Nevertheless, the delay was disturbing. I wasn't certain at the time how to explain Rayburn's unwonted insecurity. In hindsight, I think it may have been due to the cancer that caused his death ten months later. My concern was kept hidden, as was Rayburn's vacillation.

On January 28, a Saturday, Rayburn decided to face the issue. The day of decision remained January 31. The recounting continued over the weekend and into the day of the voting. Just before the voting it was figured that there were 216 votes at a minimum for enlargement. Three other Members would vote against the resolution on the first roll call, but had agreed to switch their votes if theirs were required to win. I also suspected, on the basis of past experience, that Rayburn had found more such commitments on his own. As usual, he said nothing about them. The opposition leaders, Halleck and Smith, may have made similar agreements on their side.

When Speaker Rayburn walked into the House at noon of January 31, Members and spectators in the galleries all rose and applauded—a rare demonstration.

The debate lasted an hour. It was unremarkable, even when Rayburn left the Speaker's chair to make a plea from the floor that House Members support the change. I am certain it did not alter a vote. The Speaker and others were merely reciting prepared lines.

The roll call began. A faint stirring went through the spectators in the gallery at the calling of each Member's name. There were few surprises, but the tension and the suspense were thick. Switches in anticipated voting occurred that ultimately canceled each other. The roll call was completed and announced by the Speaker: 217 for enlargement to 212 against.

The Speaker had carried the day by five votes. At least for the two years of the Eighty-seventh Congress, the Rules Committee would be somewhat more sympathetic to the House leadership and the Administration. In the Eighty-eighth Congress that opened on January 9, 1963, under Speaker McCormack, the House voted to maintain the Rules Committee at fifteen Members by a margin of thirty-nine votes.

The triumph of January 31, 1961, was, I told a reporter, "the end of the beginning"—a step toward making the Rules Committee an instrument of the majority party in the House. It represented a step toward confining its responsibility to the area of determining, not the substantive merits of legislation, but rather the conditions under which legislation shall be presented and discussed and voted upon by the entire Membership of the House.

Chapter 11

The Road to Reform

In the sixteen years that I have been a Member of Congress, the House has revealed itself to me as ineffective in its role as a coordinate branch of the federal government, negative in its approach to national tasks, generally unresponsive to any but parochial economic interests. Its procedures, time-consuming and unwieldy, mask anonymous centers of irresponsible power. Its legislation is often a travesty of what the national welfare requires. It does not even fulfill one of its possible functions—that of being "the grand inquest of the nation," in William Pitt's phrase.

Other House Members, who have traveled the same road and shared the same experiences, have similar views. After frustrations, setbacks, and compromises, we have taken heart from time to time at new developments: the large liberal majority in the Eighty-sixth Congress, the emergence of an able, modern-minded man as chairman of an important committee or as a party officer, the defeat of retirement of some of the notorious boodlers, social Darwinists, and incompetents, or the arrival of promising new Members. But, again, expectations were disappointed. It has seemed that at least the House Members must rise in anger and dismay and demand a return to the fair procedure, responsible leadership, and awareness of national tasks that have distinguished the House in the past.

Now we have less hope that Congress will reform itself. The burden is too great for a few enlightened and energetic Members to bear alone. The impetus for the reform of the House will have to come from outside pressures. In spite of proposals within the

House for legislative study commissions and internal remedies, reform will require the active concern of the American people.

There are signs that the American voter is becoming aware of the deficiencies of Congress. After the Eighty-eighth Congress failed to pass civil rights legislation in its first session and had engaged in a fratricidal battle over foreign aid, a poll taken by the public opinion analyst Louis Harris early last year indicated that 65 per cent of the sampling voted "no confidence" in the job the Congress had done to date.

Proposals for reform of the House are wide in range. Some are wildly unrealistic, in that they seem to imply that the Congress should be an assembly of philosopher kings. Others are too narrow in scope and would result only in a tidying up of peripheral problems without accomplishing any real reform.

Those that would deal effectively with some of the problems of the House fall into these categories:

1. Eliminating the bias in the establishment of congressional districts by redrawing their boundaries on the basis of present population.

2. Reforms affecting the individual Member of the House. In this are included proposals to eliminate conflicts of interest and require full disclosure of the Member's financial holdings and income, his influence on executive branch departments and regulatory agencies. These proposals also cover length of the term of office, administrative problems in serving constituents, and campaign financing.

3. Reform of congressional procedures. Specific proposals relate to instituting joint meetings of corresponding House and Senate committees to save time in framing and revising legislation: division of time in floor discussions of conference reports and expediting movement of legislation from committees to the floor.

In the reapportionment of electoral districts, reforms are already under way. In most states rural areas have dominated the state legislatures that determine the boundaries of electoral districts, while two-thirds of the population now live in some two hundred metropolitan areas. The number of House seats that each state has is determined by population, but the boundaries of the districts are laid out by the states. As a result, rural citizens have been over-represented in the House, and urban citizens under-represented. In Florida, for example, 12 per cent of the population elected a majority of state senators and 15 per cent a majority of the state representatives and of the state's delegation in the United States House of Representatives. Now the Supreme Court has provided the impetus for reform. In its decision on *Baker* v. *Carr* in March 1962, the Court decreed that the apportionment of legislative seats is a proper subject for judicial consideration under a construction of Section One of the Fourteenth Amendment. In the ensuing two years twenty states revised their legislative districts. In another decision in June 1964, as we have seen, the Supreme Court decreed that the states must revise their districts so as to provide substantially equal representation on a population in both houses of state legislatures.

It was commonly believed that such action would provide more representatives for the strictly big-city voter; but studies now show that it is the suburban rather than the urban areas that were under-represented and that will now gain more seats as a result of reapportionment. They will gain fifteen to twenty seats, and presumably these will be won by moderate Republicans. It is unlikely that there will be a drastic change in the liberal-conservative line-up in the House.

In the matter of conflicts of interest, it is hard for anyone who has spent years in the House to believe that the problem will be solved without unrelenting public pressure. Members of the House are cautious about criticizing each other, for fear of seeming self-righteous or of provoking reprisals that could entail a loss of influence and consequent harm to one's own constituents.

Congress is extremely harsh in dealing with possible conflicts of interest involving officials of the executive branch. It even anticipates them: Thus Robert S. McNamara was required to divest himself of financial ties to the Ford Motor Company before he could be confirmed as Secretary of Defense. Yet Congress will not place limitations on the moonlighting activities and outside financial holdings of its own Members, dubious as they may be.

The subtleties of the problem are not readily apparent to the public whose interests may be at stake. The basic questions are:

What kinds of outside employment and income are compatible with what kinds of committee assignments?

How far should a Member go in voting on matters in which he has some personal stake?

In the early years of the Congress, Thomas Jefferson gave an answer. In 1801 he wrote by hand a strict rule of conduct for legislators:

> "Where the private interests of a Member are concerned in a bill or question, he is to withdraw. And where such an interest has appeared, his voice has been disallowed, even after a division. In a case so contrary not only to the laws of decency, but to the fundamental principal of the social compact, which denies any man to be a judge in his own cause; it is for the honor of the House that this rule of immemorial observance should be strictly adhered to."

Two decades later, however, this "immemorial observance" of which Jefferson wrote was breached by Senator Daniel Webster of Massachusetts. The Senate had before it a controversial bill to renew the charter of the Biddle Bank in Philadelphia. Webster bluntly wrote to Nicholas Biddle:

> "I believe my retainer has not been renewed or refreshed as usual. If it be wished that my relation to the bank should be continued, it may well be well to send me the usual retainers."

James G. Blaine of Maine, Speaker of the House, soothed any qualms Members might have in this area. In April 1874, he ruled that a Member can vote his private interests if the measure is not for his exclusive benefit. Blaine's precedent remains on the rule books of the House today.

Now, no one insists that a Member disqualify himself from taking an active part in shaping legislation involving major transportation carriers simply because he travels to and from his congressional district by airplane. On the other hand, what if he sits on a committee that deals with such legislation and simultaneously keeps a connection with a law firm that has a major airline as a client?

A Member who owns a cattle ranch or wheat farm need not disqualify himself from shaping commodity legislation. Yet what if this Member serves as a consultant to an economic interest that seeks to shape the bill to its own ends?

Certainly, a Member has perfect freedom to speak on legislation before a business, labor, or trade association. But what is the situation if the speaking fee is so large that it is obviously a campaign contribution in disguise?

It would be laughable to suggest that because a Member heats his house by gas or oil he should not vote on the gas-oil depreciation allowance provision in a tax bill. Yet is it so laughable if the Member is a major stockholder or officer in a gas or petroleum corporation?

Where is the Member to draw the line? Or should it be drawn for him? And, if so, by whom?

Certainly, neither custom nor law provides satisfactory answers to these fringe areas. There is a specific statute, of course, relating to acceptance of compensation for services in connection with proceedings before federal agencies and procurement of government contracts. Two Members of the House were recently convicted for violation of this law. There are also statutes relating to bribery.

In general, however, the situation is accurately described in a report published in 1960 by the Bar Association of the City of New York: the tangled web of legislative conflict of interest is "current, complex and controversial. It is also largely unresolved."

The problem of conflict of interest is further complicated by the relations of Members of the House and their staffs with the policy-making officials of executive departments.

For example, a Member may make an inquiry as to the status of a flood-control project in his district that is being considered by the Army Corps of Engineers. Will public hearings be held in the area of the project site? When? If the project is approved, when will it be programed? When will planning appropriations be requested from Congress? When will construction money be requested? All these are perfectly proper questions.

Supposing, however, such inquiries involve the property of an influential constituent, which is to be condemned to make way for the project. Or supposing an appointment is set up for a construction firm to talk to a representative of the Corps. In such cases, the Member's motives might be called into question. Is he acting on behalf of a private economic interest, and why?

Perhaps legislation is needed that would require all communications between a Member and his staff and officers and employees of an executive department to be made part of the public record on any project on which such queries are made. If so, the record would include the name of the inquirer, the date of inquiry, the matter queried, the nature of the query, and the proceeding, if any, involved.

It is interesting to note the action Congress has taken in passing measures that have become sections 203 and 205 of Title 18 of the United States Code. Section 203 prohibits a Member of Congress or an officer or employee of the federal government from soliciting or receiving compensation for services rendered on behalf of another person before a government department or agency in relation to which the government is a party or has a direct and substantial interest. However, it does not preclude compensation for services rendered on behalf of another in court. Section 205 bars officers and employees of the government, but not members of Congress, from acting as an agent or attorney for anyone before a court, agency, or department in connection with any particular matter in which the United States is a party or has a direct and substantial interest.

Such measures have led an encouraging number of Members of the Senate and the House to demand that Congress set its own house in order. A few years ago Senator Clifford Case of New Jersey noted the diligence of Congress in making executive-branch departments strictly accountable and suggested that the process would be more seemly if Members of Congress were subject to the same requirements of disclosure as the executive branch.

Case, a Republican, has introduced a resolution for establishment of a commission on legislative ethics. Unlike similar proposals, mostly by Democrats, this commission's membership would be selected so as to avoid its being dominated by Members of Congress. At least half the membership of any study commission should be selected from outside Congress. Such a commission should make a detailed study of conflict-of-interest areas, and of relations with the executive branch, including the regulatory agencies such as the Federal Communications Commission and the Interstate Commerce Commission. The study group might submit a final public report of its activities at the end of an eighteen-month period. It might be desirable to make the commission a permanent one with authority to issue progress reports from time to time.

Such a commission should certainly be authorized and given the power to study a number of aspects of legislative problems and procedures. One aspect, which has a bearing on conflict of interest, is the salaries of Members of Congress—raised only twice since 1946. At present (July 1964) each Member of the House and Senate receives an annual salary of $22,500 plus allowances for telephone-telegraph, postage, and travel. The salary becomes $30,000 on January 1, 1965. Most Members have found their salary inadequate to the demands made on it by family, constituents, and campaigns. One Member estimates that it has shrunk to less than $10,000 by the time the unavoidable requirements of officeholding are met—a residence in his district, a home in Washington, requests for contributions to various organizations, and handouts to constituents with hard-luck stories. It remains to be seen what impact the recent increase will have.

Members with another source of income, from inheritance or from their business or profession, do not have this personal financial problem, but their outside holdings raise the conflict-of-interest question. A fairly easy means of resolving this is available. If the other source of income results in a conflict of interest, Members could be required to neutralize their investments by turning them into government bonds. Or the management of their holdings could be placed in the control of someone other than relatives, friends, or business associates for the duration of the Member's service.

What of the man who has an interest in a business or law firm which has no salable value? Here the solution is somewhat more difficult. At the outset Members should realize that if a McNamara

is, in effect, required to forego his extensive associations and financial interest in the Ford Motor Company in order to be confirmed
by the Senate as Secretary of Defense, then certainly similar sacri-
fices should be required of a Member of Congress. It is objected that
such a requirement would prevent many a potentially valuable
public servant from undertaking the hazard of seeking election.
As the disordered laissez-faire world of officeholding now stands,
this is perhaps a valid point. Yet steps, such as a "clean elections"
law, could be taken to eliminate some of the major hazards to the
seeking of public office and the commitments that are frequently
made in order to enlist financial support.

In 1961 President Kennedy established a Commission on Campaign Costs. The President stated that "it is not healthy for the
democratic process—or for the ethical standards in our government
—to keep our national candidates in condition of dependence."

Presumably Kennedy referred to the present system, which,
regardless of the specific device employed, results in candidates
for the Presidency and the House and Senate being dependent upon
interests that through private resources or contacts can produce
large amounts of money. The fund-raising dinner—the cash-and-
calorie circuit—is a frequent device—the $1,000-a-place dinner or
$100-a-person cocktail party for presidential candidates. Organiza-
tions, labor unions and business associations, are called upon to support candidates. A national or state political party may impose
revenue quotas on its constituent units. And generally political
party leaders do not care and do not want to know the source of the
funds.

The presidential commission, with bipartisan accord, recommended tax incentives and other points. Tax incentives would
encourage the voter to make political contributions to the party
of his choice by making gifts of $500 a year or less deductible
from taxable income just as religious contributions are deductible.
The House version of the tax reduction bill in 1964 provided for
such a provision, but the Senate did not approve it.

In addition to such a tax incentive, the federal government could
assist in other ways. One proposal would be for the federal government to match small contributions, say $5 or $10, made by the

rank-and-file voter to approved political organizations. The sums so raised could be used to finance approved expenditures. Conceivably, the federal government could in whole or in part finance political campaigns for the Presidency and the Congress. Radio and television stations, licensed by a federal regulatory agency, would be obliged to provide a specified amount of free program time to candidates of major parties—the amount of time varying with the office being sought. This would eliminate a major expense for candidates. It would tend to redress the balance between the affluent candidate and the relatively inpecunious one. Legislation to place realistic campaign ceilings on campaigns for federal office has been introduced over the years, with little success.

Along with larger salaries for Members, home travel allowances and federal pension benefits should be substantially increased. With this, however, would come a stipulation that a Member could derive no outside income, such as legal fees, during his service in the Congress. Service in Congress should be made a full-time job. In addition every Member of the Senate and House and every employee of the Congress who receives an annual salary of $21,500 or more should file yearly with the Sergeant-at-Arms of the Senate and Clerk of the House a report that should be made public. It should contain a full and complete statement of:

First, the amount and sources of all income and gifts totaling more than $100 received during the preceding calendar year.

Second, the value of each asset held by or entrusted to him or by him and to him jointly with another person, including a spouse.

Third, the amount and source of all contributions during the preceding calendar year received by him or by anyone, including spouse and minor children on his behalf or subject to the direction or control of the Member.

Fourth, annual reports listing all dealings in real estate, securities and commodities by the Member or by any person, including spouse, acting on his behalf.

Fifth, the name of any relative who is also an employee of the federal government.

Perhaps other restrictions should be established. It is impossible to expect that each Member will have that capacity for "total ingratitude" which Fiorello La Guardia said is one of the primary qualifications of an elected official. The conviction of two House Members in early 1963 of misuse of their office and, several months later, the resignation of an officer of the Senate following allegations of a simliar nature are symptomatic of the problem.

An effort was made unsuccessfully to require some accounting and restriction on outside income when the congressional pay-raise bill was brought to the House floor in 1964.

The problem of conflict of interest in Congress has many other facets, and it grows more acute as the area of federal responsibility increases. The Member of Congress who comes to Washington from his East Coast constituency on Tuesday and leaves on Thursday, who has lucrative outside sources of income, relatives on the pay roll, and takes long winter trips to warmer climates cannot fulfill his duties. He is, in effect, a part-time member of Congress. The operation of the federal government is the biggest business in the world, involving about $100 billion a year. It demands able, well-paid, full-time legislators.

Even the most conscientious Member who spends his entire time on his congressional duties is hard pressed to keep up with them. One major demand on him comes from constituents, who properly have a claim to his services but who require an inordinate amount of his time. Some Members have made a career of servicing constituents, building their records for re-election on personal letters sent to every high school senior, mailing government-published baby books to mothers and how-to-do-it pamphlets to farmers and homemakers.

If a business organization wants a copy of the 1913 Clayton Anti-Trust Act, the Member sends it. A high school current-events class writes in for a Member's views on international monetary liquidity. A rural constituent wants the Member to fight the whole post-office department over the location of the nearest mailbox. One Member in 1949 described his duties:

> "A Congressman has become an expanded messenger boy, an employment agency, getter-out of the Navy, Army, Marines, ward heeler, wound healer, troubleshooter, law explainer, bill

finder, issue translator, resolution interpreter, controversy oil pourer, glad hand extender, business promoter, convention goer, civil ills skirmisher, veterans' affairs adjuster, ex-serviceman's champion, watchdog of underdog."

With such a patchwork of assignments, which sometimes take up to 90 per cent of the time of Members and their staffs, there is little time left for the primary function of a legislator—making laws.

Much of this burden could be lifted from Members by establishing the office of Administrative Counsel, as in the Scandinavian countries, Japan, and New Zealand. He is an officer of the Parliament whose responsibility it is to investigate complaints from citizens about the way they are treated by government officials. If cause is found, the Administrative Counsel may recommend remedial action.

Representative Henry S. Reuss of Wisconsin has introduced a bill that would establish such an officer for both the House and the Senate. As proposed by Reuss, the function of the Administrative Counsel would be to assist Members in helping their constituents in those cases which are the usual subjects of congressional-constituent relations—social security, veterans' cases, treatment in military services and discharges from them, claims of discriminatory treatment in government contracts, and civil service matters. Cases relating to the President or to federal courts would not be included in the scope of his work.

An Administrative Counsel might well free House Members for legislative duties, expedite the handling of complaints, and reduce the cost of maintaining Members' offices. As Reuss has pointed out, the Administrative Counsel might also uncover root causes of constituents' difficulties. A defective statute or administrative procedure may be causing thousands of complaints, but since these are diffused among the offices of 435 Members of Congress, the basic reasons for them are obscured.

In addition, House Members could devote more time and effort to purely legislative matters if each one had an administrative assistant, such as Senators are provided with.

Extending the length of a Member's term could also enable him to make a more rational and effective use of his time in office. A four-year term has been suggested, with Members elected in presidential years. The present two-year term was provided in the Constitution in a less complicated age when a Member's duties were not so numerous and varied and when legislation was largely confined to domestic matters. Today, a four-year term would make it possible for freshmen Members to learn their jobs better and make some solid achievements before standing for re-election.

At present a Member can concentrate on legislation only in the first year of his term. The second year brings other tasks to engage him—perhaps an early primary election, mending political fences, a search for campaign financing—legitimate activities but hardly conducive to a stable environment in which to devote oneself to purely legislative concerns. President Eisenhower once suggested a four-year term, but Senators have objected on the grounds that it would enable House Members to run for a Senate seat in off-election years without risking their House Membership.

Certainly the problems of conflict of interest, Members' salaries, and campaign costs are worth careful study by a commission.

As an outgrowth of the investigation into the activities of Robert G. "Bobby" Baker, once Senate Democratic Secretary, the Senate in 1964 approved a Republican resolution that would establish a six-member bipartisan committee of its own Members. It would have authority both to police and to investigate the conduct of Senators. Efforts to compel disclosure of income was rebuffed. No immediate action developed to appoint Members to the committee. This led the *Washington Post* to comment that the "Senate didn't know its own strength when it adopted the Cooper [John Sherman Cooper of Kentucky] resolution. Now it wishes it would just go away." At this point, however, a "caveat" should be entered. It is predictable that the work of such a commission, no matter how respected its members, how able its staff, and how sound and well publicized its recommendations, will result in little in the way of effective reform unless the power structure of the House is significantly altered. We need only remember the fact of the vast effort that resulted in the so-called La Follette–Monroney Legislative Reorganization Act of 1946. This statute appeared to make great changes in the institutional form of the Congress. However, time has brought disappointment. The reduction in the number of standing committees has been offset by the creation of more and more standing subcommittees within each full standing legislative committee. The work of Congress, therefore, remains fragmented and unco-ordinated.

The failure of the La Follette–Monroney reforms stems from a mistaken notion of its supporters that institutional change can be achieved by altering the outward form of the Congress while leaving untouched the substance of the internal "power structure" —that is, the internal organization and those influential seniors who man it. In fact, the legislative study commission authorized under the La Follette–Monroney Act specifically was forbidden to trespass, for example, upon Senate Rule Number 22, one of the chief weapons of the power group permitting the filibuster. Unfortunately, the only tangible consequence of the Reorganization Act of 1946 may be the establishment of a pension system that may have lured a few dispensable Members from their seats.

One matter to which a commission should address itself is a recommendation of the 1946 Act that has not been carried out. That Act provided that each committee should appoint by majority vote not more than four professional staff members without regard to their political affiliation. Sponsors of reorganization expected that staffing would be nonpartisan, but the promise has not been fulfilled. Instead, the chairmen and other senior members of committees too often make appointments on the basis of patronage considerations.

Today, Members of the minority party properly complain that their party does not have an adequate staff on certain committees to develop sound legislative alternatives to the proposals of the majority party Members. Without the staff to frame alternative proposals, the minority cannot make its position clear on bills sponsored by the majority. Surely the discussion of alternatives is an important part of the democratic process, because it informs the public, compels a more careful and penetrating consideration of bills, and in my experience nearly always results in sounder legislation. In recent years two Republican Members, Thomas B. Curtis of Missouri and Fred Schwengel of Iowa, have criticized the existing practice of committee staffing; a proposal was made in 1963 to provide larger staffs for minority members of committees, but it failed.

As for committee procedures, the present system of holding protracted and repetitious hearings needs to be simplified. At present, a Secretary of Defense will testify before a House committee in support of a bill his Department wants. He repeats the performance before the Senate counterpart committee. If financing is involved, he may reappear in the House, this time before the Appropriations Committee, and again in the Senate before its Appropriations Committee. Surely a method could be devised whereby top officials of the executive branch would need to make only one appearance before a joint meeting of the House and Senate Members of both the Authorizing committees and Appropriations committees.

Congress as a whole has not provided itself with staffs of experts to serve as consultants in special areas. It has voted billions of dollars to finance research and development in scientific fields, in programs that are administered by the departments of Defense, Health, Education, and Welfare and the National Aeronautics and Space Administration. Yet it relies for information on guidance on agencies of the executive branch, which often have already determined their own policies on major scientific programs. Senator E. L. Bartlett of Alaska, arguing in behalf of a proposal for a Congressional Office of Science and Technology, said:

"It is disturbing but true at the present time Congress does not understand science and it is also true that science does not understand Congress. Communication between the two must be improved."

In appropriating vast sums of money for new scientific programs, Congress should have the independent, nonpartisan advice of the best experts in every field.

It is apparent that Congress is simply not organized to carry out its responsibilities, nor to meet the expectations of the public.

"When a bill goes from the clerk's desk to a committee room, it crosses a parliamentary bridge of sighs to dim dungeons of silence whence it will never return," President Wilson once observed, and subsequent Presidents have echoed his feeling. In the Eighty-seventh Congress, which met after the inauguration of President

Kennedy, 20,316 measures—bills and resolutions—were introduced; about 12 per cent of them passed both House and Senate. At the time of President Kennedy's assassination, November 22, 1963, his legislative program, then eleven months old, was in wretched shape, most of it stalled in committee where it was deliberately held by the committee barons. In a similar period, the British Prime Minister could have had his entire legislative program passed by the House of Commons. It is doubtful that a chief of government in any country other than the United States can be denied a decision on major legislation by a national legislature.

Some of the Kennedy-Johnson legislative program has been finally acted on; but Congress has still to deal with many urgent problems. Urban areas need more programs for slum clearance and for mass transportation; some legislation has been passed, but it is only a beginning. Rural areas demand greater investment in conservation, and support for agricultural and livestock areas. Congress is divided on farm policy. On medical care for the aged, nothing has been accomplished. Educational facilities and the children and students enrolled in them need federal help, and more must be done to create job opportunities for young people. And the demands on Congress for legislation on domestic and foreign affairs can be expected to increase.

It has been suggested that new rules in both House and Senate could expedite the President's legislative program. Walter Lippmann, the columnist, has proposed that rules be amended to provide that a measure designated by the President as of first importance be voted upon within a specified time.

Another change in rules would give the minority as much time on the floor of the House as the majority when a bill is up for final action. At present the majority Member who brings the bill up controls the time of debate; he may allow the minority equal time, but this is not mandatory. A rule to divide debate time equally was proposed by Republicans at the beginning of the Eighty-eighth Congress, but was voted down.

We may be moving slowly toward a formal congressional inquiry into the working of Congress. The expectations of the 1946 Reorganization Act is but an unfulfilled hope. In 1961 two House

Members, Chet Holifield of California and Thomas Curtis of Missouri, assembled a joint memorandum on a proposed study of congressional procedures. It finally led to the establishment of several studies undertaken by groups outside the Congress. Their value remains to be seen.

Electoral reform and reforms eliminating conflicts of interest and relieving Members of nonlegislative duties are obviously needed, and study commissions and formal inquiries into the procedures of the House can help to point the way. But it is idle to suppose that any fundamental reforms can be accomplished without a drastic revision in the power structure of the House. What is the power structure of the House? It can be discerned by studying how the House functioned on the 1959 labor bill and on recent civil rights legislation. How can this power structure be altered? A study of the manner in which it evolved historically provides clues.

When Joseph Cannon, Speaker of the House, was stripped of many of his powers in 1911, he said: "The Speaker does now believe, and has always believed, that this is a government through parties, and that parties can act only through majorities."

For twenty-eight out of the past thirty-two years, the House has been controlled by Democrats. During this period it has been more conservative than any President, even a Republican one, and more conservative than the Senate.

The entire function of the House is determined by the effective action of a majority. Yet the majority of House Democrats has not had effective control of the House. Even the Democrats' own party whip system is symptomatic of the unrepresentative nature of the House. Party whips—the Members responsible for organizing voting of party Members on the House floor—are selected from eighteen geographical areas of the country and are supposed to represent fairly the broad interests of the voters of these zones. But the zones are not based at present on any formula of equal representation by state, region, or population. Some zones consist of several states, others of only one state. If we examine the populations of these zones, we find that each of the whip zones in the South has an average of 7.7 million inhabitants, while each zone in the West has an average of 13.3 million. House Democrats who clamor for equal representation in electoral districts tolerate a whip system that does not represent populations equitably.

Basic flaws in party organization are reflected in the present power structure of the House. They are entirely the responsibility of House Democrats, and the Democrats alone have the means at hand to correct them.

The Republican Members of the House are preponderantly conservative. In a responsible and representative way, House Republican leaders make certain that their party's seats on the powerful committees are filled by Members who reflect their conservative views. There are no Republican liberals on the three most powerful committees, Appropriations, Rules, and Ways and Means. The John Lindsays of the party are given lesser committee assignments.

The Democratic Members of the House are, for the most part, moderate to progressive in their outlook. Nevertheless this majority of Democrats accepts without argument the myth of the inviolability of seniority, permitting conservative Democrats, a numerical minority, to retain many of the most powerful committee positions. Thus the majority of House Democrats permits the power that rightfully belongs to them to be wielded by a minority of conservatives whose only affiliation with the Democratic party is the party label they use at election time. This minority wing subverts the objectives and defies the spirit of the Democratic party as a whole.

It is, of course, gratifying to the Republicans to see the Democrats put conservative foxes in charge of liberal chicken coops, appointing to high committee posts members who reflect Republican rather than Democratic views on great national issues.

The history of the House and the development of its present power structure suggests ways of accomplishing some necessary reforms. Few liberal Democrats seem aware that the cast-iron seniority system is a comparatively new development; until 1911 the Speaker had the power to appoint chairmen and members of all the committees. Liberal Democrats also overlook the fact that the power of their appointive Committee on Committees (the Democratic Members of Ways and Means) to fill committee vacancies is a power delegated by the House Democratic caucus.

The place to reform the procedures of the House is not in study commissions or on the floor of the House, but in the House Democratic caucus. It is here that methods could be adopted by a majority of House Democrats to assure an assignment of committee seats that will reflect the liberal views of the majority. At the same time the power of the party's titular leader could be increased. Three important goals for the Democrats are to enhance the authority of the Speaker; make sure that Democratic membership on legislative committees is representative; and to increase the individual responsibility of each Democrat toward his leaders.

The House has functioned effectively, aside from times of national emergency, only when there was general agreement on policy objectives and on the avenues to achieve them. And this state of affairs has come about when two conditions existed:

A. When the majority party functioned through its caucus, as in the time of Clay and in the time of Speaker Champ Clark and Oscar W. Underwood, his majority leader, from 1913 to 1916.

B. When the Speakership was held by strong and aggressive men such as Reed and Cannon.

To suggest a return to either is surely to bring down on one's head the cry of "King Caucus" or "Czar Speaker." There is no reason, however, why the two approaches cannot be combined in a fashion that eliminates the objections against either.

It is true that the power of the Speakership prior to 1911 was an autocratic and coercive one that few Members would defy if they wished to hold on to their committee seats or their privileges. But a modification of this former grant of power could be put into effect today. To bring this about, each Democratic Member would have to bear an increased accountability and responsibility in establishing the leadership of his party and making it effective. No Member should be able to evade responsibility for the failure of party objectives by blaming seniority or the committee system.

The titular Democratic leader of the House would become the actual operating head of the party's legislative apparatus. His power would be observable and he would be held accountable not only to his party colleagues but also to the voting public.

Under present practice, the Democratic caucus selects its leadership at the beginning of each new Congress—every two years. When the Democrats are the majority party in the House, their candidate for Speaker by rule of numbers subsequently becomes the Speaker at a *pro forma*, party-line election in which House Members as a body take part. The caucus selection of a majority leader is, of course, not subject to a general election by the House. If the Democrats are the minority party in the House, their candidate for Speaker by the same rule of numbers becomes minority leader. Democratic members of the Committee on Ways and Means are, under the seniority system, automatically renominated for seats on that committee. Vacancies on that committee are filled by a majority vote of the caucus. The Democratic Members, who also sit as their party's committee on committees, select other House Democrats as members of other standing committees. These recommendations are submitted to the whole House for ratification, which, again, is a *pro forma* act. So, while in theory the House elects the Speaker and committee members, the party selections are, in practice, final. This could change, as will be seen later.

As a result, there are certain procedures that, if adopted, would make a significant change in the power structure as it pertains to the Democratic party. The change in the direction of becoming a representative institution itself would likewise significantly alter the House because since 1933 the Democrats have controlled the House, as we have seen, except for two widely spaced two-year periods, 1947–1948 and 1953–1954.

The procedures:

1. The election of the leadership shall continue to be the first order of business in the caucus.

2. Upon election as nominee for Speaker or minority leader, as the case may be, the nominee shall have the exclusive power to nominate in the caucus the following:

a. All the Democratic members of the Committee on Ways and Means and its chairman or ranking minority member, as the case may be.

b. All the Democratic members of the Committee on Rules and its chairman, or, again, ranking minority member, as the case may be.

3. After these nominations are made, the caucus will confirm or reject, by majority vote, any or all of the nominees. However, no other nominations may be in order from the floor. In the event one or more of the nominees is rejected, the top leader—whether he is nominated as Speaker or minority leader—will submit additional nominations as necessary.

4. Upon the election of the Democratic members of the Committee on Ways and Means, and the chairman, or minority leader, the caucus will direct that group to meet and to nominate at a later caucus the Democratic membership of all other standing committees.

5. When these nominees are submitted to the later caucus, they are to be confirmed or rejected by majority vote. Other nominations will not be in order from the floor. In the event of one or more rejections, further nominations will be made then or at a later date by the Committee on Committees.

6. At the conclusion of this process the top leader (nominee for Speaker or minority leader) is to nominate the chairman of each of the standing committees. Again, if one or more nominees is rejected, the top party leader will continue to make nominations until all chairmanships are filled.

The House rule that provides for the election of standing committees by the House is meaningless, and should be repealed. It should be replaced by a rule that gives to each party in its caucus (Democrats) or party conference (Republicans) the final power to select members of seats on standing committees. Such a rule would merely conform to present practice. The rule should, however, explicitly state that independents or members of a third party would be given their assignments by the majority party. This would conform to past practice.

This simple organizational procedure would accomplish a number of necessary changes in the power structure of the House. It would increase the power of the party leader. His exclusive power to nominate members of two key committees—Ways and Means and Rules—as well as to nominate the top party member on each committee (as chairman or ranking minority member) would constitute a potent threat to defiant Members. The party leader would become the true leader of a legislative team that would produce a coherent and co-ordinated legislative program. His ability to veto or to replace a man completely out of step with his party viewpoint would nevertheless be subject to ratification by the majority of the Members of his party. It would place final legislative responsibility where it belongs—on the majority of the Democratic party—and thus would make each Member of the party both more accountable and more responsible.

It would modify, but not eliminate, the seniority rule. Seniority, no doubt, would remain as the method of selecting the great majority of committee members. This was the case even during the rule of Speaker Cannon. However, the implied threat of party discipline, as contained in this realignment, would give pause to the Member who would bolt his party's program.

Nor would it be possible for the leader of the party to pass the buck to the seniority system when declared party objectives failed or were consistently shelved. For years, the leadership of both parties publicly supported home rule for the District of Columbia, yet the measure to provide it died every year in the House District Committee, and the titular party leaders could not be held accountable.

On the other hand, the reform would not cause a recurrence of tyranny over a minority of a party, either by the party leader or by the majority of its Members. There would be neither Czar Speaker nor King Caucus. The leader's power would be checked by the right of majority in caucus to reject his nominations. The same force would rein the power of nominations of the Committee on Committees. Moreover, no caucus majority could run wild in time of great political passion because no nominations could be made from the caucus floor. Power of nominations would be vested in the party leader and the Committee on Committees.

The total effect of these alterations would be to relax the bindings of seniority that distort the Democratic party in the House. The possibility of change in a Member's committee or his status on his committees should prove a deterrent to obstructionism.

The proposed changes do not interfere with the undeniable right of a Member to vote his conscience. The present rules of the Democratic caucus provide that a majority vote of the caucus binds all members of the caucus on the election in the House for Speaker, other House offices, and committee position. However, a two-thirds vote is required to bind Members on issues, and even then a Member may announce to the caucus that he refuses to be bound because he believes the position of the majority to be contrary to the Constitution of the United States or he has committed himself to his constituents on the opposite side of the issue. No change in this rule is suggested. The one purpose of the changes is to make the committee system of the House more representative of the majority views of the two parties. This should, as a consequence, increase the party's leadership and the individual Member's responsibility for legislative action and his accountability to the country and to his constituency.

There is no design to achieve the kind of party discipline over Members on individual votes that has prevailed at certain times in the British House of Commons. The United States is too large and diverse, and our political parties too inclusive, to justify a demand for such adherence.

However, there is every reason to justify the right of the majority of the majority to have its major proposals voted on by the whole House without undue delay, much less without deliberate dilatory tactics that prevent a vote on a major issue from ever occurring.

Inevitably, the beneficiaries of the present condition of the House will skillfully seek to thwart any such reform. First this attempt will predictably be made within the Democratic party in the House itself. When the reform is adopted in the Democratic caucus, the House Republican leadership will be faced with a difficult choice. It must decide whether to accept the right of the Democrats to seat Members on the committees who are representative of the majority view, essentially a liberal one. If the Republican leadership decides to interfere in this process, it can do so by bringing into play its ancient coalition with Democratic conservatives. This would be done when the vote on the Democratic Committee on Committees assignments comes to the floor of the House. A conservative effort would probably center on overriding assignment of a Member or Members to a key committee that might alter the balance of power.

Although these committee elections in the past have been *pro forma*, there is, in fact, nothing to prevent a crossing of party lines. And when a major committee's composition is at stake, as in the case of the Rules Committee in 1961, the vote—217 to 212 on that occasion—is often close. The hazard in bringing the coalition into play is that the undertaking would reveal to the country, as perhaps never before, the existence of the coalition and the potential obstructionist nature of the Republican party.

In any case, the differences between the two parties would emerge sharply. The electorate would at last see a real majority party point of view. The active competition between two national parties through which democracy works best in America might return again.

This has a special relevance for the Democrats of the House because we are the only truly national party at present, and our party councils must provide a forum in which Democrats from all parts of the country may participate.

The power structure of the House has been altered on other occasions. Liberals have successfully challenged the party's leadership. A recent occasion was an election to a vacancy on Ways and Means. Liberals assembled enough votes to elect the more progressive W. Pat Jennings of Virginia over Phil M. Landrum of Georgia, even though the Speaker and other Democratic leaders supported Landrum. Such facts dispute contentions that the proposed reform cannot be accomplished. With will and determination, liberal Democrats can effect changes that would be in the interest of a Democratic President, the Democratic leadership in Congress, the party, and in the interest of the American people.

It will not come to pass, however, until the Democrats in the House have a better understanding of the history of the House and of the way in which they are at present manipulated by the conservative coalition. Even then it may require prodding from representatives of powerful interest groups, the liberal press, and political scientists who can inform the American people about the wretched condition of their national legislature. Once this vast educational process is launched, I am confident that a Democratic President and the Democratic leadership of the House will join the majority of the rank-and-file Democratic Members to bring about the reform.

A firm beginning was made when the following provision was included in the Democratic Platform, adopted at the August 1964 national convention:

"The Congress of the United States should revise its rules and procedures to assure majority rule after reasonable debate and to guarantee that major legislative proposals of the President can be brought to a vote after reasonable consideration in committee."

The 1964 Republican platform, adopted at San Francisco in July, contained no such plank.

The failure of the House is the failure of the Democratic party of which I am a member. Its responsibility cannot be evaded much longer without reducing the national assembly to impotence, which would mean a vital failure in the democratic process itself.

Index

Index

ADA; *see* Americans for Democratic Action (ADA)
Adams, John, 23
Adams, John Quincy, 32
Adams, Sherman, 114, 208
AFL-CIO, 131, 132, 133, 156, 162-67
Air Force Association, 134
Albert, Carl, 74, 75, 212
Allen, C. Edmonds, 152; quoted, 153
Allen, Leo, 83, 203
AMA; *see* American Medical Association (AMA)
American Association of University Women, 136
American Bar Association, 127
American Commonwealth, The, 23
American Council on Education, 134
American Farm Bureau, 123, 133, 134, 137, 168, 211
American Legion, 133
American Medical Association (AMA), 131, 133, 135, 143-44
American Political Science Review, 119
American Presidency, The (Laski), 29
American Retail Federation, 168
Americans for Democratic Action (ADA), 136
Ames, Fisher, 22
Andersen, H. Carl, 70
Andolsek, L. J., 113
Anti-Federalists, 23

Area Redevelopment Administration, 131
Aspinall, Wayne N., 103, 107
Association for Higher Education, 134
Association of the Army, 134
Associated Press, 148
Atomic Energy Act, 119

Bagdikian, Ben, quoted, 153
Bailey, Stephen K., 22
Baker, Robert G., 114, 232
Baker v. *Carr,* 26, 223
Bankhead, William B., 73
Barden, Graham, 57, 96-97, 163
Barth, Alan, quoted, 152
Bartlett, E. L., 234
Bayard, James A., quoted, 129-30
Benson, Ezra Taft, 47
Biddle, Nicholas, quoted, 224
Biemiller, Andrew, 165, 167, 187, 218
Bill of Rights, 24
Bingham, Jonathan B., 101
Birkhead, Kenneth, 187
Blaine, James G., 224
Blatnik, John A., 58, 101, 113, 210, 213, 214
Bloom, Sol, 102
Boggs, Hale, 75
Bonner, Herbert C., 96
Boorstin, Daniel J., 149
Brademas, John, 53, 171

Brooks, Jack, 172
Brooks, Overton, 87-88
Brown, Clarence, 58, 59, 81, 82, 83, 192, 194, 203
Brown v. *Tennessee*, 26
Brownell, Herbert, 178
Bryce, Lord, 23, 38; quoted, 25, 28, 129
Buckley, Charles A., 101, 107
Burke, Edmund, quoted, 25, 46
Burke, Frank, 53
Burleson, Omar, 104
Burns, Arthur, 207
Business and Professional Women's Association, 136
Byrd, Harry Flood, 79, 82
Byrd, Robert, 106, 193
Byrnes, Joseph W., 73

Calendar Wednesday, 34
Campbell, Charles, 39
Cannon, Clarence, 53, 66, 70-71, 90-92, 93, 174-75
Cannon, Joseph, 33, 35, 36, 76, 77, 196, 197; quoted, 231
Case, Clifford, 226
Celler, Emanuel, 99-101, 185, 191, 192, 193, 208
Challenge (magazine), 142
China, Communist, 11
Chipperfield, Robert, 102
Churchill, Winston S., 144
Civil Rights, 175; Democrats and, 175; 1956, 175-81; 1957, 182-90; 1964, 190-94; Supreme Court and, 175
Clark, Champ, 35, 37, 67, 91
Clark, Joseph S., 11
Clay, Henry, 27, 32, 35, 117
Cohen, Ben, 120
Cohn, David L., 64-65
Cohn, Roy, 114
Colmer, William M., 82-83, 194, 203, 204, 211, 215, 216
Columbia Journalism *Review*, 153

Commentary (magazine), 154
Communism, 13
Congress Makes a Law (Bailey), 22
Congress, United States, 11-14; committees and, 30-32; executive branch and, 27-30; House of Representatives in (*see* House of Representatives, United States); Senate in (*see* Senate, United States)
Congressional Quarterly, 138, 199
Conservatives, 58-61
Constitution, United States, 21; Bill of Rights and (*see* Bill of Rights); House of Representatives and, 21, 23, 25, 26
Cooley, Harold, 96, 107
Coolidge, Calvin, quoted, 118
Cooper, John Sherman, 232
Corcoran, Thomas, 120
Cox, Archibald, 169
Cox, Eugene, 203
Crisp, Charles F., 197
Curley, James Michael, 74
Curtis, Thomas B., 58, 233, 236

Daly, Charles O., 120
Dawson, William L., 98
Delaney, James J., 203
Democratic party, 11; Committee on Committees, 21, 213; committees and, 37, 40
Democratic Study Group (DSG), 54-58, 93; Committee on Civil Rights, 193; House Committee on Rules and, 205, 208-209
Deschler, Lewis, 110, 111-13, 212
Dewey, Thomas, 59
Diggs, Charles C., Jr., 106, 178
Dirksen, Everett McKinley, 126, 193
Douglas, Paul H., 182, 185, 186, 187
Dowling, Noel T., 129
DSG; *see* Democratic Study Group (DSG)

Eastland, James O., 186
Economist, 154
Editor & Publisher, 149
Eisenhower, Dwight D., 89, 118, 119,
    122, 167, 168, 171, 182, 206, 232;
    quoted, 188-89
Eisenhower Administration, 28, 160,
    161, 167, 176
Eliot, T. S., quoted, 43
Elliott, Carl, 47, 50, 164, 166, 168, 171,
    173, 217
Elliott bill, 166, 167, 168, 169, 170, 172

Fair Employment Practices Com-
    mittee (FEPC), 191, 192
Fallon, George H., 101
Farmers Union, 123
Federal Corrupt Practices Act, 138
*Federal Government and Education,
    The* (Green), 31
Federal Regulation of Lobbying Act,
    133
Federalist, The, 27; quoted, 128
Federalists, 23, 27
Fenno, Richard F., Jr., 109
FEPC; *see* Fair Employment Prac-
    tices Committee (FEPC)
Foreman, Ed, 42
France, 11; Chamber of Deputies, 22
Freeman, Orville L., 123, 187
Fulbright, J. William, quoted, 152,
    153
Full Employment Act (1946), 119

Galloway, George, 28
Garner, John Nance, 73
Gary, Vaughan, 71
George, Walter, 28
Georgia, 38
Gerry, Elbridge, 24
Goldfine, Bernard, 114
Goldwater, Barry M., 126, 151
Gordon, Thomas, 102
Great Britain, 11
Greeley, Horace, 64

Green, Edith, 31, 47, 83, 106, 164, 166

Halleck, Charles A., 80, 83, 85, 87,
    151, 166, 192, 207, 213, 219
Hamilton, Alexander, 22, 27, 117;
    quoted, 128
Harding, Ralph, 47
Harris, Ellsworth, 204
Harris, Louis, 222
Harris, Richard, 108, 132
Harrison, George, 164, 165
Hayden, Carl, 74
Hayes, Al, 164, 165
Herring, Pendleton, quoted, 119
Hoar, Sherman, quoted, 117-18
Hoffa, James, 98
Holifield, Chet, 210, 213, 214, 236
Holton, John W., 212
Hopkins, Harry, 53
House Committee on Un-American
    Activities (HUAC), 99
House of Representatives, United
    States, 21; calendars in, 33-34;
    Committee on Aeronautics and
    Space, 31; Committee on Agri-
    culture, 31; Committee on Ap-
    propriations, 31, 33, 35; Com-
    mittee on District of Columbia,
    33, 38; Committee on Education
    and Labor, 31, 157, 158, 160, 163,
    173; Committee on Rules, 34, 35,
    36, 39, 195-220; Committee on
    Ways and Means, 33, 35, 37, 40;
    committees and, 21-22, 24, 30-32,
    37-40; Constitution and, 21, 23,
    25, 26; electoral basis of, 23-26;
    executive branch and, 27-30, 32-
    33; First Congress and, 23-24;
    leaders of, 62-78, 79-115; members
    of, 20-22, 24, 42-61; powers of,
    26-27; procedures of, 17-19, 21,
    22, 26; reforms for, 221-44; sen-
    iority system in, 21, 24, 38-40;
    speaker of, 17-18, 21, 30, 32, 34-
    37, 39; structure of, 23-26

Hubbard, Elbert, 67
Humphrey, Hubert H., Jr., 182

Ickes, Harold, 53
International News Service (INS), 152
Irwin, Leo H., 115

Jefferson, Thomas, 23, 81, 117; quoted, 224
Jefferson Administration, 27
Jenner, William, 127
Jennings, W. Pat, 76, 243
John Birch Society, 47
Johnson, Andrew, 33
Johnson, Lyndon B., 29, 93, 113; civil rights and, 177, 179, 182-83, 185, 188, 189-90, 194; Committee on Rules and, 209, 219; Landrum-Griffin labor bill and, 171, 172-73; quoted, 88
Johnson Administration (L.B.J.), 29
Johnson, Samuel, quoted, 174
Judd, Walter, 102

Kastenmeier, Robert, 53
Katzenbach, Nick, 192
Kefauver-Harris Drug Act of 1962, 132
Keith, Hastings, 61
Kennedy, John F., 29, 61, 90, 92, 118, 119, 135, 235; civil rights and, 99-101, 190, 191, 192; Committee on Rules and, 71, 209, 210, 216, 217; Landrum-Griffin labor bill and, 156, 161, 167, 173; quoted, 116, 228
Kennedy Administration, 29
Kennedy, Robert F., 156, 167, 192, 210, 217, 218
Kennedy-Ives bill, 157, 158, 161
"King Caucus," 32
Kirwan, Michael J., 92

Knowland, William, 185, 188, 189-90

La Follette, Robert M., 137
La Follette-Monroney Legislative Reorganization Act (1946), 30-31, 232-33
La Guardia, Fiorello, 230
Landrum, Phil M., 75-76, 163, 167, 243
Landrum-Griffin labor bill, 167-73
Laski, Harold J., quoted, 29-30
Latham, Henry, 204
League of Women Voters, 136
Legislative Process in Congress, The (Galloway), 28
Liberals, 51-58
Libonati, Roland V., quoted, 101
Liebling, A. J., quoted, 149
Lincoln, Abraham, 32-33
Lincoln Administration, 32-33
Lindsay, John V., 50, 100
Lippmann, Walter, 154, 235
Lisagor, Peter, quoted, 151-52
Livermore, Samuel, 24
Lobbies, 131-44
Lodge, Henry Cabot, 28
London Sunday Observer, 154
Long, Clarence D., quoted, 142
Longworth, Nicholas, 111

McCaffrey, Joseph F., 39
McCarthy, Eugene, 54, 55, 57
McCarthy, Joseph, 47, 114, 147
McClellan, John L., 124, 151, 156, 161, 167
McClellan Committee, 156-57, 159, 161, 164
McCormack, John W., 21, 55, 72-76, 172, 192, 195, 197, 212, 214, 219
McCormack, John W. (Mrs.), 72
McCulloch, William M., 100, 191, 192
McDevitt, James, 165
McGill, Ralph, 148
McGovern, George, 151
McLeod, William N., Jr., 105-106
McMillan, John L., 105, 106

McNamara, Robert S., 93, 124, 223
Madden, Ray J., 194, 203
Madison, James, 22, 63; quoted, 27
Mahon, George Herman, 88, 92-93, 107
Manchester Guardian (newspaper), 154
Mansfield, Mike, 126
Marsh, Benjamin, 137
Martin, Joseph W., Jr., 70, 189, 204, 207; quoted, 181
Mathias, Charles McC., Jr., 50, 100
Meany, George, 158, 165-66
Member of the House (Miller), 146
Metcalf, Lee, 54, 57, 97, 159, 160, 164, 167, 168, 172
Miller, Clem, quoted, 146
Miller, George P., 107
Miller, William E., 180-81
Mills, Wilbur D., 94-95, 108
Mitchell, Clarence, 176, 208
Mitchell, Erwin, 168
Mitchell, James, 160
Morgan, Thomas E., 102, 103
Morse, Bradford, 50
Muhlenberg, Frederick A. C., 23, 63
Murray, Tom, 104, 107
Murrow, Edward R., 132

NAACP; *see* National Association for the Advancement of Colored People (NAACP)
NAM; *see* National Association of Manufacturers (NAM)
National Aeronautics and Space Administration, 234
National Association for the Advancement of Colored People (NAACP), 137, 175, 176, 177
National Association of Manufacturers (NAM), 137, 168, 211
National Committee for Insurance Taxation, 133
National Council of Churches, 136
National Defense Education Act, 136

National Education Association (NEA), 134
National Rivers and Harbors Congress, 133, 134
Navy League, 134
NEA; *see* National Education Association (NEA)
Neilan, Edwin P., 131
Nelson, John M., 197
New Yorker, The (magazine), 154
Nixon, Richard M., 185, 188
Norris, George, 36, 53

O'Brien, Lawrence F., 90, 120
O'Brien, Thomas J., 42
O'Connor, John, 28, 73
O'Hara, James, 47, 164, 166, 168
O'Neil, Thomas J., Jr., 203

Page, Walter Hines, quoted, 17
Passman, Otto, 71, 93
Patman, Wright, 94, 107, 172
Pearson, Drew, 56, 132
Peel, Robert, quoted, 145
Phillips, William, 56
Pitt, William, quoted, 221
Pope, Alexander, quoted, 156
Powell, Adam Clayton, 57, 83, 96-97, 108, 178, 212, 216
press, the, 145-55
Provisions of Federal Law Held Unconstitutional by the Supreme Court, 128

Railway Labor Act, 119
Rauh, Joseph L., Jr., 186, 187
Rayburn, Sam, 12, 64-72, 75; civil rights and, 179, 180, 181, 183, 184, 189-90; Committee on Rules, 203, 204, 206-210, 212-13, 215-19; Landrum-Griffin labor bill and, 158, 160, 162, 165-67, 169, 170-72; news and, 153, 154; party leadership and, 55, 56; quoted, 48, 85-86, 89-90, 94, 97, 111, 112, 117, 157, 213, 214

Real Voice, The (Harris), 132
Reciprocal Trade Act, 141
Reece, B. Carroll, 207
Reed, Thomas Brackett, 34-35, 36, 64, 196
reform, 221; committee procedures and, 234; conflict of interests and, 222, 223-30; congressional procedure and, 230-44; electoral district reapportionment and, 222-23; power structure and, 236-40
Republican party, 11; Committee on committees, 21, 39-40
Reuss, Henry S., 231
Reuther, Walter, 164, 165, 187
Rhodes, George, 56
Rivers, L. Mendel, 108, 127
Rogers, William, 188
Roosevelt, Franklin Delano, 28, 53, 118, 119, 128, 199
Roosevelt Administration (F.D.R.), 28, 128
Roosevelt, James, 170, 172, 213
Russell, Richard B., 87, 124, 185
Russia; *see* Union of Soviet Socialist Republics (USSR)

Sabath, Adolph, 83
St. George, Katherine, 127
Saxon, James J., 94
Schine, David, 114
Schwartz, Bernard, 114
Schwengel, Fred, 51, 233; quoted, 101
Science (magazine), 154
Scott, Hugh, Jr., 178, 189, 204, 207
Senate, United States, 11-14; Committee on Foreign Relations, 152; Committee on Government Operations, 156 (*see* also McClellan Committee); Committee on Labor and Public Welfare, 156-57; election of, 25
Senate Establishment, The, 11
Shelley, John F., 167
Shelley bill, 169

Sherman, John, 117
Sickles, Carleton R., 106
Smith, Frank, 120-21
Smith, Howard W., 66, 71, 79-87, 105-107; civil rights and, 184, 189, 192, 194; Committee on Rules and, 197, 198, 203, 205, 207, 209-212, 215-17, 219
Snell, B. H., quoted, 118
Southern Manifesto, 54
Soviet Union; *see* Union of Soviet Socialist Republics (USSR)
Spence, Brent, 93
Stam, Colin F., 115
Stein, Gertrude, 41
Stevens, Thaddeus, 33
Stevenson, Adlai E., 182
Strackbein, O. E., 141
Submerged Lands Act (1953), 127
Supreme Court, United States, 25

Taft, Robert, 59
Taft, William Howard, 126
Taft-Hartley Act, 119, 159, 161
Teague, Olin E., 103-104
Teamsters Union, 144, 156, 162, 163
Teller, Edward, 141
Texas, 38
Thomas, Al, 172
Thompson, Clark, 172
Thompson, Frank, Jr., 47, 57, 97, 159, 160, 164, 166-68, 172, 210, 218
Thornberry, Homer, 195, 203
Thurmond, Strom, 74, 189, 193
Time (magazine), 159
Trimble, James W., 203
Trollope, Anthony, quoted, 51
Trujillo, Rafael, 152
Truman, Harry S, 132, 176; quoted, 205
Truman Administration, 28
Tuck, William M., 126

Udall, Stewart L., 47, 57, 97, 159, 160, 164, 166, 167, 172, 218

Underwood, Oscar, 37
Union of Soviet Socialist Republics (USSR), 11
United Mine Workers, 132, 162
United Press, 148, 152
United Press International (UPI), 152; Special Services Bureau, 152-53
United States of America, 11; Congress of (see Congress, United States); Constitution of (see Constitution, United States); Department of Agriculture, 31; Department of Commerce, 139; Department of Defense, 141; Department of Health, Education and Welfare, 139; Department of Justice, 178, 186; Department of State, 139; executive branch of, 116-25, 128-29; House of Representatives of (see House of Representatives, United States); judicial branch of, 125-30; legislative branch of, 116-30; Senate of (see Senate, United States); Supreme Court of (see Supreme Court, United States)
United States Chamber of Commerce, 131, 168, 211
UPI; see United Press International (UPI)
USSR; see Union of Soviet Socialist Republics (USSR)

Vinson, Carl, 75, 81, 87-90, 107, 217

Voorhis, Jerry, quoted, 139
Vorys, John, 102

Wall Street Journal (newspaper), 154
Walter, Francis, 51, 99-100
WANT; see Widgetmakers Association for a National Tariff (WANT)
Washington, George, 22, 117; quoted, 23, 27
Washington Post (newspaper), 197-98, 232
Wayward Pressman, The (Liebling), 149
Weaver, Robert C., 81
Webster, Daniel, quoted, 224
Welfare and Pension Plans Disclosure Act, 158
Whitten, Jamie L., 120-21
Widgetmakers Association for a National Tariff (WANT), 131
Wilde, Oscar, 45
Wilkins, Roy, 187
Wilson, Henry Hall, 120
Wilson, Woodrow, 67; quoted, 118, 234
Wolcott, Jesse, 59, 94
Woodward, C. Vann, 13

Yarmolinsky, Adam, 122
Young, John, 195